ADVERTISING IN BRITAIN

A History

ADVERTISING IN BRITAIN

A History

T. R. NEVETT

The History of Advertising Trust

HEINEMANN : LONDON

Published on behalf of
The History of Advertising Trust

William Heinemann Ltd
10 Upper Grosvenor Street, London W1X 9PA
LONDON MELBOURNE TORONTO
JOHANNESBURG AUCKLAND

First published 1982
SBN 434 49642 1

Printed in Great Britain
by Fletcher & Son Ltd, Norwich

Contents

List of Plates

Between pages 158 and 159

Between pages 186 and 187

Preface

IN THE ARRANGEMENT of this book I have tried to keep in mind the requirements of both the general and the specialist reader. While footnotes are necessary for the specialist, I have limited them to facts or quotations of particular importance, and have grouped them together at the end of the volume. Legal cases mentioned in the text are listed separately with the relevant report references, and the bibliography gives the main sources on which I have drawn.

I should like to express my indebtedness to the following institutions and persons, without whose help the writing of this book would have been impossible:

The Advertising Association – especially Beth Rosenbaum and Philip Spink.
Charles Barker – A. B. H. and James Derriman.
The British Library.
The British Library of Political and Economic Science at the London School of Economics.
The College for the Distributive Trades library staff.
The Greater London Council Historical Library.
Hertfordshire Record Office.
The Institute of Practitioners in Advertising, and Norma Fryer.
The Incorporated Society of British Advertisers – especially Ann Harris and Reg Best.
The John Johnson Collection.
The Kunsthalle, Hamburg.
The London College of Printing library staff.
Lincoln's Inn.
London University, Institute of Historical Research.
London University Library.
Maidstone Reference Library.
Angela Massie.
Museum für Kunst und Gewerbe, Hamburg.

Nestlés.
The Newspaper Society.
Post Office Records.
The Public Record Office.
The Proprietary Association of Great Britain.
The Royal Institution.
The Royal Society of Arts.
Schweppes, and Mr K. Simmonds.
St Bride's Printing Library.
The Times, and Gordon Phillips.
Trinity College, Cambridge.
University College, London.
The Victoria and Albert Museum.
Westminster Council Library service.
White's Recruitment, and Mr Tony Clark.

Timothy Bell, Ron Baddeley, L. B. Curzon, David Dunbar, Derek Mackay and Philip Rawlings lent me items from their private collections, and Mr Curzon and Dr Richard Lawson were kind enough to read through certain of the legal sections. In addition, I have talked over events in advertising's more recent past with a number of people whose memories and individual experiences have been of considerable interest and help. In particular I would like to thank Hubert Oughton O.B.E., Ray Cowen and Bob Riddell.

I should like to express my gratitude to the History of Advertising Trust for allowing me to fulfil a long-cherished ambition in writing this book; to the Inner London Education Authority, the Principal of the College for the Distributive Trades, and the Head of the Department of Marketing and Advertising Studies there for allowing me the time in which to produce the thesis on which part of this book is based; to Professor F. M. L. Thompson for his kindness and guidance during the period of thesis-writing; and to Professors Theo Barker and Harold Perkin for their perceptive comments.

Those who so kindly gave their help are in no way responsible for any errors of fact or judgement, which are mine alone.

Lastly, I owe a monumental debt to my wife and family, who suffered in relative silence so that I could write.

T. R. Nevett
September
1979

Due to circumstances beyond the control of all concerned, publication of the book has been considerably delayed. The final chapter has therefore been updated to April 1981.

T. R. N.

Foreword

OLD ADVERTISING MATERIAL has a great fascination for many people; press advertisements, posters, packaging, tram tickets, and trade cards are lovingly collected, analysed, exhibited and written about.

But how much is known about *why* these old advertisements were written or designed that way, *how* they were planned and produced, *what* they were intended to do, what *results* they had? How much is known about how advertisers organized their activities, and how the huge variety of suppliers and services to advertising came about? What was the economic and social role, and effect, of all these activities?

There is so much to find out, so much to learn about the history of the business of advertising, and how it fits into the development of marketing generally. It will be difficult to do so, unless action is taken now. Already many old records are lost, destroyed, or dispersed. And not just ancient history: the last thirty years have been full of change too. The early development of commercial television, for instance, has largely been forgotten. The origins of modern commercial radio are more recent, but risk going unrecorded.

In 1976 a band of dedicated enthusiasts, all earning their living from contemporary advertising or marketing activities, started to give form to their idea for an organization that would research, preserve, and make available to today's and tomorrow's advertising and marketing men and women the knowledge of yesterday's successes and failures. They had to be dedicated because the communications business is very much of today and tomorrow, with little time or inclination to look back at what grandpa did or did not do. They were responsible for getting initial support from a small group of advertisers, media owners and advertising agencies*; a list of these generous founding sponsors is appended to this introduction.

As a result, the History of Advertising Trust was registered as an educational foundation in 1976; in 1977 it was granted charitable status. In the same year, the recently retired Director General of the Advertising Association, J. S. Williams, O.B.E., accepted an invitation to become Chairman of the Trust. In 1978, the late Lord Barnetson became President until his untimely death early in 1981. I was pleased to accept the Chairman's and Governors' invitation to become President in his stead.

The Trust now has more substantial backing from all sides of the industry and is moving towards its most important objective of setting up an Archive, Library, and Study Centre where students, journalists, researchers, and practitioners can obtain the information they need to learn about the successes and mistakes of the past.

It's a fascinating subject, every bit as interesting as the old advertisements or commercials themselves. But it's not *just* interesting in an abstract sort of way; nor is it remote from everyday business problems of today.

A better understanding of the development of business techniques and practices, and of the field of advertising and marketing within that context, benefits everyone involved in these activities. For instance:

- We can consider "today's" problems or arguments in the light of past discussions – because they've all been considered before – learn from them, and avoid reinventing the same answers all over again.
- We can discuss today's criticisms, direct descendants of all the criticisms of the last 250 years, with a better perspective on past achievements.
- We can assess with pride the contributions of marketing and advertising to the development of the economy and of business techniques and practices.
- We can give our students, the future managers and executives of business, a better understanding of how the ideas we use today have been developed.
- We can discover ideas that have been tried before, and discarded or passed over, and learn from them.
- We can illustrate achievements through advertisements and their effects on the economy, and on society.
- We can, at the least, explode some of the myths and legends about the advertising and marketing business – still, sadly, perpetuated in many existing writings – and set the record straight.

The History of Advertising Trust's main aim is to encourage and sponsor serious, objective and factual study of the growth and development of advertising and marketing. The present book is a major step towards this objective. The Trust commissioned Doctor Terry Nevett to write the first definitive history of advertising from a business point of view.

*Especially in the context of this book the Trust records its thanks to Saatchi & Saatchi Garland-Compton Ltd for guaranteeing the cost of production of part of the edition.

The Trust welcomes this very significant book, believing that, for the increasing number of students, researchers and others who are becoming interested in the subject, it provides: – the first objective source of information and guidance; – a valuable basis, and a spur, to start the detailed exploration of many of the aspects which could only be touched on here.

Gordon C. Brunton
President
The History of Advertising Trust

FOUNDING SPONSORS

Ted Bates
McCann-Erickson Advertising
Ogilvy Benson & Mather
J Walter Thompson Company
Anglia Television
Ulster Television
Beecham Foods
Cadbury Schweppes
Carreras Rothman
Reed International
Rowntree Mackintosh
Smiths Food Group
Unilever

Introduction

THE WRITING OF a history of advertising, as distinct from a book about old advertisements, poses distinct problems. Firstly, since the story continues up to the present day, the writer is dealing with a period and with events which he has experienced at first hand, so that his judgements are likely to be influenced by personal feelings. How far objectivity has been preserved in the present work must be left to the reader to decide.

Secondly, in order to show how advertising evolved, a start has to be made some thousands of years ago, where the main difficulty is the fragmentary nature of the evidence. When the story reaches the present day, however, there is such a tremendous mass of information that the problem becomes one of compression and selection. While this in itself affects the form and balance of the book, it is not enough simply to allot space according to the volume of evidence available. The writer has to make his own judgement as to the relative importance of the events which were taking place, and deal more fully with those he believes to be of greatest consequence in the context of history. The bias of this book is accordingly towards the nineteenth century, which began with the advertising business taking on a separate existence, and ended with it generally in the form in which we know it today.

As far as is possible with the evidence available, this account concentrates on certain key aspects of the development of advertising. It looks at what kinds of businesses were using advertising, and the amounts of money being spent; what kinds of communications media were carrying advertising messages; the emergence of a separate advertising industry, notably in the shape of the advertising agents; the nature and extent of criticism directed against advertising; and the extent to which advertising was controlled, either by law or by constraints from within the industry itself. What emerges, in the writer's view, is that advertising grew naturally out of the social, economic and commercial developments which took place at an earlier stage in our history. Whatever one's feelings about advertising, it has filled a distinct need. And so long as we continue to live in a society in which sales promotion and the regulation of demand are necessary parts of commercial practice, it seems that advertising will remain with us.

The Beginnings

THE FIRST EVIDENCE of the use of advertising is to be found far beyond the shores of Britain. Since this book is concerned essentially with advertising in a commercial context, we shall not indulge in speculation as to whether prehistoric cave paintings, Babylonian inscriptions, the Ten Commandments or the writing on the wall at Belshazzar's Feast constitute advertisements. We shall begin instead with the ancient Greeks, who provide the first clear evidence of the use of advertising for commercial purposes.

The crier, whose main occupation appears to have been the proclaiming of new laws, was also available for hire by traders wishing to publicise their wares. One who availed himself of this service was Aesclyptöe, an Athenian vendor of cosmetics, whose sales message shows how little basic appeals have changed over the centuries:

> For eyes that are shining, for cheeks like the dawn,
> For beauty that lasts after girlhood has gone,
> For prices in reason the woman who knows
> Will buy her cosmetics of Aesclyptöe.[1]

Public announcements relating to such matters as events at the games were made by means of the *axones*, rectangular columns of panels which were rotated by an internal mechanism, and which carried details of the contests and the athletes. Signs were also in use, Aristotle mentioning '. . . the things drawn above the shops, which though small, appear to have breadth and depth'. Another form of sign was used by the oldest profession, prostitutes in one instance having nails set in the soles of their sandals so that they printed the message 'follow me' in the dust.

By Roman times, advertising was clearly in widespread use. There are a number of literary allusions, Cicero for example mentioning in *De Oratore* 'the cock painted on the signboard of Marius the Cimburian', and Horace in his *Ars Poetica* describing how booksellers displayed notices of manuscripts they had for sale. The most direct evidence, however, comes from the ruins of Pompeii, preserved under a blanket of volcanic ash following the eruption of Vesuvius in AD 79. Here can be found numerous examples not only of signs – the goat for a dairy, the mill for a baker, the boy being birched for a school, and so on – but also of actual advertisements written or inscribed on the walls.

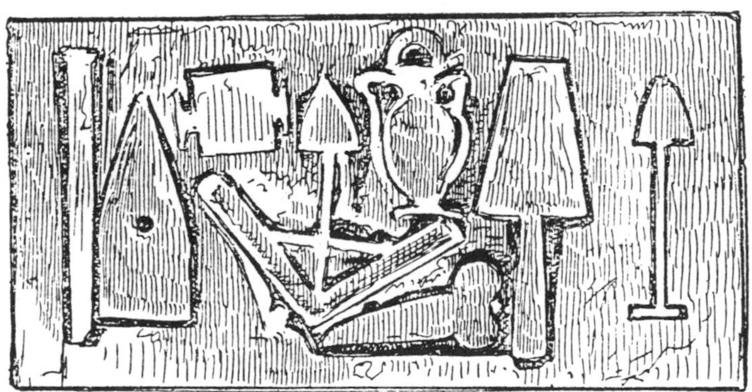

Tradesmen's signs from Pompeii

Some of these advertisements are little more than messages scratched into the plaster with a sharp implement such as a nail, and were presumably the work of amateur publicists. In other cases, however, the task was taken very seriously, announcements being painted in red or black letters up to twelve inches high, obviously intended to be seen from a considerable distance. Work of this kind was undertaken by the *scriptores*, professional sign-writers, and their assistants, the *adstantes* who steadied the ladder, and the *lanternari* who held the torch. We can only wonder at the circumstances which caused the writer of an election advertisement to end with the plaintive appeal *Lanternari, tene scalam* ('*Lanternari*, hold the ladder').

The places selected for such displays seem to be those where people would naturally tend to congregate – on street corners, for example, and particularly under the portico of the baths. The advertisements themselves cover a wide range of subjects. Rewards are offered for articles lost or stolen, traders or inn-keepers solicit customers, friends of political candidates recommend them as being worthy of office, and forthcoming events are announced for the amphitheatre – among them gladiatorial combats, fights with wild animals and athletics. Shop signs and mural advertising, reinforced by lusty shouting, would normally have been sufficient to enable the tradesman to attract customers. With trade flourishing, however, and merchants travelling even beyond the frontiers of the Empire, circumstances sometimes arose in which it was necessary to dispose of bulk shipments, or of expensive goods which had a limited appeal. In such cases, use could be made of the *coactor*, who seems to have acted as a broker, and the *praeco*, an official crier who would proclaim what was for sale.

In the centuries which followed the barbarian invasions, evidence is scant as to the pattern of everyday life. It is clear, however, that there was widespread destruction of towns, and though there was some continuity of urban life and institutions between attacks, there was at least drastic disruption, and in some cases towns were abandoned completely. The conditions which had produced the need to advertise had disappeared.

For the revival of commerce, and of circumstances which would again demand the use of advertising, we must look for signs of the renewed growth of towns. In England, Alfred the Great and Edward the Elder set up fortified burghs to protect areas of the country against Viking attacks. Concentrations of people needed food, and though these settlements often possessed arable fields and grazing, they were probably not self-sufficient, so that produce would have to be brought in from the surrounding countryside. At the same time, the towns needed manufactured goods and services, which were provided by specialised traders and craftsmen. They in turn would be attracted to the town because it offered a convenient concentration of consumers, and protection from attack. We know from the so-called Winton Domesday that by the reign of Edward the Confessor, tradesmen in Winchester were conducting their businesses from stalls or shops, and that some at least were able to live in relative prosperity, the list of householders including among others a goldsmith, a shoemaker, a hosier, a turner and a soap-maker.

The Norman Conquest brought a temporary setback to town life, with houses destroyed to make way for castles, and taxes falling more heavily on the remaining inhabitants. Soon, however, England was to feel the benefits of the general economic growth taking place throughout Europe, and this in turn gave a new impetus to urban development.

In the towns there was now a trend towards larger-scale specialised production, supplying not only the inhabitants of the town itself, but also the surrounding countryside and outlying villages. The larger the town, the greater the degree of specialisation, and the greater the volume of goods produced. This meant a need for the services of merchants who would dispose of surplus production, especially at the great international fairs. The merchants in their turn made use of couriers, who would ride ahead to inform potential buyers about consignments which were on the road – perhaps the origin of today's trade advertising, which is carried in publications directed to wholesalers and retailers.

Within the larger towns, the growing variety of articles offered for sale, together with the sheer size of the population, meant that the inhabitants could no longer have complete knowledge of what was available and from whom. Again, therefore, there was a need for advertising, and by the twelfth and thirteenth centuries there are a number of instances of its use. The crier, still known by his Latin title of *praeco*, seems to have been widely employed in France, being mentioned in a charter granted by Louis VII (1141), in statutes issued by Philip Augustus (1258), and by the scholar John Garland (*c.*1180–*c.*1252) in connection with the advertising of wine by taverns. By the end of the twelfth century, Paris had sufficient criers to warrant the appointment of two masters of criers, one for the left bank and one for the right. Although the earliest known mention of a crier in England is in 1299, there is every reason to suppose that they existed much earlier than this, in view of the close political and trading links between England and France at the time.

A feature of the medieval town was its shop-signs. Narrow streets with houses as yet unnumbered would have made some kind of indication essential to enable the intending purchaser to locate the tradesman he wanted. The upper storey of the house would have provided a suitable place for fixing, so as to attract attention and to be seen above the heads of the crowd. The sign took on a variety of forms, which have been classified as follows by Marcel Galliot:

- religious symbols, such as images of saints
- objects characteristic of a trade
- geographical references denoting the origin of the trader or his goods
- symbols designed to lend prestige, such as the arms of some royal or noble family
- literary allusions
- indications of skill
- visual puns, especially on the name of the proprietor (the so-called *rebus*). In England, this might take the form, for example, of two cocks for Cox.

Already, it will be noted, tradesmen were trying to attract attention, and often to introduce an element of promotion or of reassurance. They have taken a further small step along the road towards modern advertising. Yet the basic techniques of making known – the use of criers and signboards – were still the same as those used by the Romans. The medieval advertiser probably also wrote his announcements on walls, like his Roman counterpart, or on parchment which could be displayed in a public place.

The first really modern innovation in method came with the spread of printing in the second half of the fifteenth century. This opened up a range of new possibilities, since notices could now be produced more quickly and cheaply, and in larger quantities than if written by hand. They could not only be displayed, but also given out for the recipient to take away, read at his leisure, and keep for reference. There was still, however, considerable illiteracy, particularly among the poorer classes, which limited the potential of this new invention for the time being. Not surprisingly, it seems to have been printers who were the first to use printed announcements as a means of publicity. The earliest surviving example in Britain was produced by Caxton about 1477, and advertised *The Pyes of Salisbury*, a set of rules for the clergy for dealing with the concurrence of offices during the Easter festival. Although it measures only about 5¼″ × 3″, we know that it was meant to be displayed like a poster, rather than handed out, from the phrase *supplico stet cedula*, freely translated in an eighteenth-century annotation to the copy in the John Rylands Library as 'Pray do not pull down this advertisement.' The words seem to indicate that passers-by would normally expect to help themselves to an item of this kind. It has also been suggested that as the words are in Latin while the rest of the bill is in English, they probably constitute a phrase in common use, which again points to the use of bills as well-established practice.

The printed individual advertisement represents one line of evolution in the history of advertising which was to lead eventually to the modern poster. In Elizabethan and Jacobean England, it took the form of the broadside or broadsheet, surviving examples of which are mainly invitations to view freaks whose physical deformities are catalogued in painstaking detail to stimulate the morbid curiosity of the reader. But there are also examples of a more commercial nature relating to new inventions, or lotteries to help finance the colonisation of Virginia. Printing seems to have supplanted the handwritten notice only gradually, however, since in 1539 Francis I of France issued a proclamation laying down that royal edicts should be made known by writing them in large letters on pieces of parchment which could be displayed on boards.

The invention of printing also made possible a second line of advertising evolution linked to the development of the newspaper. The original forerunners of today's national papers were probably the manuscript newsletters circulated in the Middle Ages by banking houses such as the Fuggers of Augsburg. By the mid-sixteenth century, the Venetian government was issuing *fogli d'avvisi* for reading aloud, the charge for listening to which was one *gazeta* (about 3 farthings), which is said to have been the origin of the general term 'gazette' for newssheets. The earliest known example in England is an account of the battle of Flodden Field issued by Richard Fawkes in 1513, though it was not until later in the same century that they were to appear in appreciable numbers.

It is difficult, living as we do in an age of daily newspapers and television, to imagine the time when knowledge of current events depended on official proclamations and word of mouth; and we can only guess at the tremendous impact which must have been achieved by these early publications. They were produced irregularly as some newsworthy occurrence arose, and were often wildly inaccurate in terms of the information they carried, even inventing happenings likely to catch the public imagination so as to ensure a ready sale. As yet, it should be noted, they did not carry advertisements.

The first decade of the seventeenth century saw an element of continuity come into news publishing. In Germany and the Netherlands, papers which became known as *corantos*, literally 'currents' (of news) began to appear with relative regularity. By the early 1620s, the idea had been adopted in London, with consecutively-numbered publications beginning to appear in the form of quarto pamphlets referred to variously as *corantos*, relations, mercuries or news-books. The circulation of the English *corantos* was minute compared with the newspapers of today, probably reaching a maximum of between 400 and 500 per issue, and selling at twopence – a considerable sum at that time. Judging, however, from the amount of heated discussion they generated, it would appear that they had a high number of readers per copy, and that those readers were people of importance. Bearing this in mind, the appearance of the first newspaper advertisement ought to have resulted from someone seeing the potential offered for reaching an influential public. Instead, the earliest known example was inserted by the printer of a paper, apparently almost as an afterthought, and is of little significance. It appeared in the *Weekly Relations of Newes* dated 23 August 1622:

> If any Gentleman or other accustomed to buy the Weekly Relations of Newes, be desirous to continue the same, let them know that the Writer or Transcriber rather of this Newes hath published two former Newes, the one dated the second and the other the thirteenth of August, all of which doe carrie a like title, with the Armes of the King of Bohemia on the other side of the title page, and have dependance one upon another: which manner of writing and printing he doth propose to continue weekly by God's assistance, from the best and most certain intelligence.
>
> Farewell; this twenty third of August 1622.

From such humble beginnings as a printer trying to dispose of his back numbers has modern press advertising developed!

The same publication carried another announcment in September 1624:

> In the last printed Newes of September 11, I told you there could be no perfect description of the siege of Breda, by reason the enemy had not fully set himselfe downe before it, nor made any workes to purpose against it: since this, is come over a perfect description of the same, the substance whereof is formerly set down in this Relation. I doe purpose likewise to cut the Map, wherein you may with the eye behold the siege, in a manner as lively as if you were an eye witnesse: you may not expect this Map this six dayes.

It is impossible to chart accurately the growth of advertising in *corantos* and newsbooks during the next troubled years, not least because so few of them have survived – according to one estimate only about 0.13 per cent.[2] There seems, however, to have been a steady expansion both in terms of volume and of the range of products advertised. The earliest announcements related to books, property and patent medicines, with medical quacks provoking the following attack on newsbooks from Fleetwood Sheppard, poet and future favourite of Charles II, in 1652:

> They have now found out another quaint device in their trading. There is never a mountebank who either by professing of chymistry or other such art drains money from the people of the nation but these arch-cheats have a share in the booty and besides filling up his paper, which he knew not how to do otherwise, he must have a feeling to authorize the charlatan, forsooth, by putting him into the news book.[3]

Advertising of all types continued to expand, so that it quickly became an established practice with which the public was well acquainted. Were this not the case, it would not so quickly have become the butt of satirists, such as the writer in the ribald *Mercurius Fumigosus* of the Commonwealth period who penned the following 'advertisment':

> If any Man or Woman . . . can tell any Tale or Tidings of a Maidenhead of Two and Twenty years of age, lately lost at Placato between the Hamms of Bedfordshior, let them bring word to the figure of the Dildoe of Fucklesbury, or to the Divel over against Roague's Lane, not farr from Pintle Barr (5 September 1655).

Such indeed was the success of press advertising that in 1657 permission was given for the first publication devoted entirely to advertisements. Entitled *The Publick Advertiser*, it was a quarto newsbook selling for one penny, and proclaimed itself as:

> Communicating unto the whole Nation the several occasions of all persons that are in any way concerned in the matter of Buying or Selling, or in any kind of Imployment or Dealings whatsoever. For the better Accommodation and Ease of the people and Universal benefit of the Commonwealth in point of Publick Intercourse.

Besides carrying the usual announcements about ships, property for sale, patent medicines and various trades and services, the first issue also includes the following under the heading of 'Physitians':

> In Bartholomew Lane on the back side of the Old Exchange, the drink called Coffee (which is a very wholsom and physical drink, having many excellent vertues, closes the Orifice of the Stomack, fortifies the heat within, helpeth Digestion, quickneth the Spirits, maketh the heart lighten, is good against Eye-sores, Coughs, or Colds, Rhumes, Consumption, Head-ach, Dropsie, Gout, Scurvy, Kings Evil, and many others) is to be sold both in the morning and at three o'clock in the afternoon.

Outrageous hyperbole has ever been part of the history of advertising.

The restoration saw an increasingly firm control of the press. The Printing Act of 1662 limited printing to the master printers, the two universities and the

Archbishop of York. The number of master printers was to be reduced from 59 to 20, and the number of apprentices and presses strictly controlled. The following year, Sir Roger L'Estrange was appointed Surveyor of the Press to enforce the Act, and was granted a patent for the exclusive right of publishing 'all narratives or relacons not exceeding two sheets of paper and all advertisements, mercuries, diurnals and books of public intelligence'. A public taste for news was not suppressed this easily, however, and the result was a proliferation of unofficial newsletters, many probably emanating from the growing number of coffee-houses. The freedom to print and publish newspapers, one of the most cherished of our liberties and an essential factor in the growth of advertising in this country, dates from 1695. In that year, the Printing Act lapsed, and the government of the day found itself unable to secure sufficient agreement in Parliament as to what form a new measure should take. Four bills were introduced, each in turn being rejected. Eventually the government abandoned its efforts and the freedom of the press had been won by default.

There had been considerable changes since the first appearance of printing. The old pattern of trade, in which each region was largely self-sufficient, had begun to break down in the later Middle Ages, and this trend was to continue as various areas of the country began to specialise in the production of different articles and commodities. Inevitably, tradesmen began to find that their customers no longer constituted a group isolated from outside influences, and thus from outside competition. The cappers of Chester, for instance, were complaining as early as 1520 that cheap caps were being brought in from London and other places.

At the same time, the population was increasing. At the beginning of the sixteenth century, it has been estimated at between two and three million. The overall picture for trade, therefore, was one of an upward trend in demand. Yet what is equally important is the distribution of that growth. This shows a heavy concentration in the southeast of the country, and particularly along the Thames valley, where some one-fifth of the country's population lived by 1700. Dominating the area was London, which grew from an estimated 75,000 people in 1500 to some 200,000 by 1600 and probably more than 500,000 a century later. The capital and its environs thus provided at the time a vast manufacturing and trading complex, a concentration of wealth probably unrivalled in Europe, and a massive aggregation of consumers into a single compact but expanding market for goods and services. Sheer size, however, brought its own problems. The pattern of life in London had become so complex, and the numbers of people so large, that there was often no effective way of bringing information to the notice of those to whom it might be relevant. No longer could a master in need of a servant rely on word-of-mouth communication as he might in a small town. Nor could a man with something to sell be sure that potential buyers would come to hear of it. There arose a situation, therefore, in which there was a need for some means by which a member of the community could communicate with other members having a similar interest.

The *corantos* and newsbooks provided political and commercial information which the capital needed, and so had an entrée to many important offices and households. The advertisements they carried were therefore able to put buyers, sellers and investors in touch on an unprecedented scale. The initial novelty of advertisements, allied to the fact that readers of newsbooks were generally drawn from the more affluent members of society and therefore able to afford what was being advertised, must have helped to make advertising particularly rewarding and effective, thus contributing further to the rapid increase in its use.

During the last quarter of the seventeenth century, while the Printing Act was still in force, a more specialised type of publication made its appearance, concerning itself almost exclusively with trade or business, so appearing unobjectionable to the official eye. Probably the most famous example is John Houghton's *Collection for the Improvement of Husbandry and Trade.* Beginning in 1692, after Houghton had failed with a similar publication ten years earlier, it soon began to attract a considerable volume of advertising. Initially this consisted of notices for books, but gradually its scope widened to include for instance blacking, ink, coffins and situations vacant. The early advertisements invited the reader to apply to Houghton himself for particulars, but soon addresses also began to be included if desired by the advertiser. The products concerned were often endorsed by Houghton, who wrote for example of a gardener selling trees and shrubs: 'I have made him promise with all solemnity that whatever he sends shall be purely good, and I verily believe he may be depended on.' On another occasion, he seems to have anticipated the attitude of many people working in advertising today, when he included the following caution above a group of advertisements for patent medicines: 'Pray, mind the preface to this half sheet. Like lawyers, I take all causes. I may fairly. Who likes not may stop here.'

Houghton seems undoubtedly to have appreciated the potential offered to the publisher by advertising, and to have sensed that when interestingly presented, it was likely to produce a better response from readers. It would be a mistake, however, to exaggerate his importance. Houghton was scarcely an innovator, and was not unique. He typified the growing facility in handling advertising rather than initiating it. To confer on him the title 'Father of English Advertising', as has been done in the past, hardly seems justifiable.

Considerable attention has been paid to newspaper advertising in this period because of the predominance it was to achieve in later centuries. It must be emphasised, however, that during the seventeenth century the press – such as it was – scarcely constituted the major medium, and that outside London its effect was minimal. Shopkeepers would have relied on their signs, much as their predecessors had done. In London, they were granted a charter by Charles II on his accession giving them the right of display. Although many signs were destroyed in the Great Fire of London in 1666, they continued to be used, with signs growing ever larger until it was complained that they shut out air and light from the streets, and that many were so insecurely fixed that they constituted a danger to people beneath. Apart from its value in denoting a particular trade and indicating an address, the sign was also sometimes used on a promotional device called the 'trade token'. This resembled a half-penny or farthing made either of metal or leather, and was usually stamped with the tradesman's emblem.

Another form of advertising seemingly in common use was the printed poster. In *A Journal of the Plague Year*, Defoe paints a grizzly picture of the way this medium was employed by medicine vendors and quack doctors:

> ... it is incredible, and scarce to be imagin'd, how the Posts of Houses, and Corners of Streets were plaster'd over with Doctors Bills, and Papers of ignorant Fellows; quacking and tampering in Physick, and inviting the People to come to them for Remedies; which was generally set off, with such flourishes as these, (viz.) INFALLIBLE preventive Pills against the Plague. NEVER FAILING Preservatives against the Infection. SOVERAIGN Cordials against the Corruption of the Air. EXACT Regulations for the Conduct of the Body, in Case of an Infection: Antipestilential Pills. INCOMPARABLE Drink against the Plague, never found out before. An UNIVERSAL Remedy for the Plague. The ONLY-TRUE Plague-Water. The ROYAL-ANTIDOTE against Kinds of Infection; and such a Number more that I cannot reckon up; and if I could, would fill a Book of themselves to set them down.
>
> Others set up Bills, to summons People to their Lodgings for Directions and Advice in the Case of Infection: These had spacious Titles also, such as these.
>
> An eminent High-Dutch Physician, newly come over from Holland, where he resided during all the Time of the great Plague, last year, in Amsterdam; and cured multitudes of People, that actually had the Plague upon them.
>
> An Italian Gentlewoman just arrived from Naples, having a choice Secret to prevent Infection, which she found out by her great Experience, and did wonderful Cures with it in the last Plague there; wherein there died 20000 in one Day. An antient Gentlewoman having practised with great Success, in the late Plague in the City, Anno 1636, gives her advice only to the Female Sex. To be spoke with &c.
>
> An experienc'd Physician, who long studied the Doctrine of Antidotes against all Sorts of Poison and Infection, has after 40 Years Practice, arrived to such Skill, as may, with God's Blessing, direct Persons how to prevent their being touch'd by any Contagious Distemper whatsoever. He directs the Poor gratis.
>
> I take notice of these by way of Specimen: I could give you two or three Dozen of the like, and yet have abundance left behind.[4]

A contemporary engraving shows a billposter at work, with a device for placing his bill high on the wall and out of normal reach, suggesting that the trade was already well developed. Beyond this, however, little is known.

Certain astute business minds sought an answer to the problem of publicity in the setting up of some form of public register, in which sellers could enter details of what they had for disposal, and which would be inspected by potential buyers. The idea seems to have been mentioned originally in Montaigne's Essay *Of a Defect in our Policies* (1595), where he attributed it to his father. It first appeared in England in 1611, when Sir Arthur Gorges and Sir Walter Cope obtained Letters Patent for the opening of an office to be called *The Publicke Register for Generall Commerce*. The wording shows how closely the need had been indentified:

> Whereas all Trade and Commerce whatsoever amongst our wellbeloved Subjects, doth chiefly consist either in *Buying and Selling* or in *Borrowing and Lending*. And that a great defect is daily found in the Policie of our State for want of some good, trusty and ready measure of intelligence and intercourse between our said Subjects in that behalfe. By means whereof many men oftentimes upon occasion of necessity and sudden accidents, are inforced to put awaye and sell landes, leases or other goods and chattels, to great loss and disadvantage for want of good and ready meanes to give generall notice and publique intelligence of their intentions, to many that would (if they knew thereof) as willingly buy as the others would gladly sell . . .[5]

For whatever reason, this attempt seems to have failed, since the patent was relinquished the next year. Another patent along similar lines was granted in 1637 to Captain Robert Innys, though its wording suggests that on this occasion the motives were more humanitarian than commercial. It was for:

> An erection of a voluntary office whither Masters, Mistresses and Servants or any others having lost goods, women for satisfaction whether their absent husbands be living or dead, parents for lost children or any others, for discovering Murthers or Roberies and for all Bargaines and Intelligences may refer if they please and not otherwise, to enter their names, goods and the rest . . .[6]

Innys seems to have based his ideas on those of Theophraste Renaudot, who in 1630 had opened in Paris his *Bureau d'Adresse*, the aim of which was to put workers in touch with employers, thereby (he hoped) combating poverty and so reducing the level of crime. Innys' patent actually mentions 'the like whereof hath been seene in Venice, Constantinople, and are now in use in the City of Paris in France as we are informed'. Presumably his efforts were overtaken by the Civil War, for nothing further is heard of them.

After the Civil War, farsighted businessmen again made various attempts to launch similar enterprises, all of them apparently unsuccessful. By this time, another consideration had to be taken into account – that of economy. An announcement in the paper *Perfect Occurrences* of the opening of an Office of Entries declared that '. . . whatsoever is made known to the publique by expensive way of Bills posted or otherwise may be speedily known for the said 4d only and no more charge.'

With newspapers firmly established, and expanding in terms both of titles published and of copies sold, the future of advertising was to lie elsewhere than with these giant lists. This set the pattern of advertising in the centuries to come, making it essentially an active business forcing itself brashly upon the consumer, rather than waiting passively to be consulted at a time and for a purpose of the consumer's own choosing, as would have been the case under Montaigne's plan. (Even today's computerised registers of cars, jobs, and so on have to advertise themselves to make sure that the public knows of their existence!) Whatever one's feelings about the subsequent development of advertising, the failure of these schemes was unfortunate since they usually included special provisions designed to help the poor and needy, for example with free entries. This very section of the population was least able to afford to advertise in newspapers, particularly when each advertisement was subject to a flat rate of duty.

The Industrial Revolution

THE ADVENT OF the Industrial Revolution marked an important transition in the character of advertising. From being a novelty, something of an oddity, it gradually began to gain acceptance as a commercial weapon, and to be employed – though as yet on a limited basis and rather crudely – as a means of regulating demand.

This became necessary because Britain was moving into an era when concentrated mass-consumption would necessitate mass production. The total market for manufactured goods was expanding. Buoyancy of demand was ensured by a growth of population from about 6 million in 1740 to 8.9 million at the time of the first census in 1801, over 10 million in 1811, and 12 million by 1821. Agrarian improvements taking place at this period as well as producing improved crop yields, also involved methods of cultivation which were less labour-intensive. Hence, at a time when the population was increasing, fewer labourers were needed to undertake traditional tasks on the land – a trend accentuated by the continuing enclosure of common land and open fields. The result was a large-scale relocation and redeployment of these workers into manufacturing industries in the new industrial towns with their more attractive wage rates.

Improvements in transportation were making it easier to reach these urban areas efficiently with bulk consignments. Innovations in road-building, the construction of canals, and later the building of railways, all helped to make easier the movement of raw materials and manufactured goods. The towns, it should be remembered, constituted not only pools of labour for manufacturing industries, but convenient concentrations of consumers. With the average density of population per square mile probably more than doubling between 1721 and 1821, the processes of distribution and selling were made more efficient and cheaper than ever before.

Although a fundamental change was taking place in the geographical distribution of the population, with a pronounced shift in the balance from south to north, the pre-eminent position of London was if anything enhanced. By the beginning of the nineteenth century the capital contained over one million people, and by 1821 this figure had reached 1.27 million. London had become the largest and wealthiest city in the western world, so it is not surprising that the story of advertising is concentrated there, not only throughout the eighteenth century but also for much of the nineteenth.

The growth of advertising during the Industrial Revolution is linked inextricably with the development of newspapers. As it became clear that the Printing Act was not going to be renewed, many new titles appeared. The circulation levels reached by the leading publications early in the century are shown in Table I below. Of particular note is the *Daily Courant*, the first paper to

TABLE I

The Circulation of Newspapers in the Early Eighteenth Century.

	Monday	*Tuesday*	*Wednesday*	*Thursday*	*Friday*	*Saturday*
Daily Courant	800	800	800	800	800	800
London Post	400		400		400	
Post-Man		3,800		3,800		4,000
English Post	400		400		400	
Observator			1,000			1,000
Flying Post		400		400		400
London Gazette	6,000			6,000		
Review		400				400
Post-Boy		3,000		3,000		3,000

Monday	7,600
Tuesday	8,400
Wednesday	2,600
Thursday	14,000
Friday	1,600
Saturday	9,600
	43,800

Source: J. R. Sutherland: 'The Circulation of Newspapers and Literary Periodicals, 1700–30', *The Library*, 4th series, 15 (1934–5).

be published daily in Britain. Table II (p. 17) shows a continuous rise throughout the eighteenth century in the number of titles printed, and accordingly in the total number of copies sold. At the same time there was a growing variety of types of publication available. With such a large potential reading public concentrated on London, publishers were able to specialise in such areas as political news, the literary world, and commercial affairs. From an advertising point of view, this would have helped to make the press more effective, by

TABLE II

Number of Newspaper Titles Published and Combined Circulations 1700–1800.

Year	*Number of titles*	*Circulation (000)*
1700	25	1,500
1710	53	2,000
1720	84	3,500
1730	76	4,600
1740	75	6,000
1750	90	7,314
1760	103	9,464
1770	133	—
1780	159	14,217
1790	208	14,036
1800	258	16,085

Source: Bruttini, Advertising and the Industrial Revolution.

allowing advertisers to select the kind of reader who would be interested in their particular products.

Although press advertising in the early years of the eighteenth century was centred on London, the *Post-Man* and *Post-Boy*, both tri-weekly evening papers printed in the capital, were intended for a country audience. As the century progressed, there was a rapid growth in the importance of the so-called 'country' papers – that is to say, those printed and read outside London. The first was probably the *Warwick Post* in 1701, soon to be followed by others in Bristol and Exeter. Many of the early country papers were doomed to failure. By 1760 there had been over 130 newspapers founded, of which only 35 were still in existence. Gradually, however, papers appeared in more towns, particularly in the midlands and north where the Industrial Revolution was already beginning. At the same time circulations were increasing from perhaps a hundred or so early in the century to between 200 and 400 by the 1720s. In the manufacturing towns of the north, sales could be much larger, with the *Newcastle Journal* claiming a weekly total of nearly 2,000 copies as early as 1739. Such figures were exceptional, however, and many country papers continued to measure their circulations in hundreds rather than thousands until the end of the nineteenth century.

The country newspapers offered obvious advantages to the advertiser wishing to reach a particular town or area. As Table III (p. 18) shows, this is reflected in the increasing amounts of advertisement duty collected from publishers outside London. While advertising in the London press was growing, the growth rate was generally faster in the country papers, especially in the last decade of the century, with London being overtaken in 1797.

The remarkable expansion of the press was achieved in spite of government opposition. Not wishing to re-introduce the Printing Act, the administration attempted to muzzle its journalist critics by means of the Stamp Act of 1712,

TABLE III
Gross Product of the Advertisement Duty, 1715–97.

Year (introduced 1712, at 1s 0d)	*Paid at Head Office (i.e. London papers)*	*Collected by Distributors of Stamps (i.e. Country papers)*
	£	£
1715	931	92
1720	1,319	136
1730	1,882	436
1740	2,969	814
1750	4,951	1,248
1760	11,239	4,567
(2s 0d from 1757)		
1770	15,642	9,505
(2s 6d from 1776)		
1780	20,796	15,748
(3s 0d from 1789)		
1790	36,660	18,230
(3s 6d from 1794)		
1797	36,346	40,409

Source: Bruttini *op. cit.*

which as well as imposing on newspapers a duty of one halfpenny or one penny according to the size of the printed sheet, struck at their revenue by means of a flat-rate tax of one shilling on every advertisement. These measures, introduced at the beginning of a period of relative peace and therefore of little exciting news, brought quick death to many news publishing ventures, and for a time it seemed as though the newspaper boom was at an end. The casualties were soon replaced, however, and although in 1757 the stamp duty was raised to one penny regardless of size and the advertisment tax doubled to two shillings, the expansion of the press was to continue throughout the century.

It is impossible to give an accurate picture of the proportion of the population likely to have been reached by newspapers so that to form any kind of opinion as to their effectiveness for advertising purposes, we must rely on indicators of a fairly general nature. Firstly, part of the population – the very poor and illiterate – can be discounted. There was no point in newspapers or indeed advertisers trying to reach them since, even if they could read, they probably would not have the 2½d or so needed to buy a newspaper, let alone the products advertised in it.

Secondly, in spite of the undoubted existence of poverty and illiteracy, it appears that newspapers were widely read by the labouring classes, particularly in towns. The late Professor Aspinall, a distinguished historian of the press, described the situation in these words:

> At no time were newspapers beyond the reach of town workers. As long ago as the 1730s, Montesquieu, whilst in England, had been struck not only with the number and licentiousness of the London newspapers (the dailies and weeklies together being about twenty) but also with the ease with which their information reached

If it plese ony man spirituel or temporel to bye ony pyes of two and thre comemoraciõs of salisburi vse enpryntid after the forme of this presẽt lettre whiche ben wel and truly correct, late hym come to westmo-nester in to the almonesrye at the reed pale and he shal haue them good chepe ./.

Supplico stet cedula

The oldest surviving print advertisement, produced in 1477 by William Caxton to promote his publication *The Pyes of Salisbury*. (By courtesy of the Bodleian Library)

The introduction of printing made possible long runs of advertising notices, so that by the seventeenth century billposting had become an established trade. This shows a French expert at work.

During the eighteenth century 'tradesmen's cards' were used for a variety of purposes. The illustrations on Allenby's and Bromby's cards are relevant to their subjects; that of R. H. Fanton seems more abstract. (By courtesy of the Trustees of the British Museum)

The introduction of newspaper advertising duty at the end of the eighteenth century gave added impetus to alternative media such as billposting. (By courtesy of the John Johnson Collection)

James White and his wife Margaret, who took over the business when he died, were among the earliest advertising agents. (By courtesy of Mr Tony Clarke)

> working men. The very slaters had newspapers brought to them on the roofs of the houses on which they were working, that they might read them. Nor were newspapers beyond the reach of agricultural labourers, though there were doubtless many villages during the last decade of the nineteenth century which saw a newspaper only at irregular intervals.[1]

Thirdly, the number of people reading newspapers was many times greater than the number of copies sold. Papers were commonly taken in coffee-houses and were available for anyone there to read. The *British Mercury* of 2 August 1712 complained of 'the meanest of Shopkeepers and Handicrafts, spending whole Days in Coffee-houses, to hear News, and talk Politicks, whilst their Wives and Children wanted Bread at Home'. At the end of the century, as will be seen later, formalised systems arose for reselling and passing on newspapers when the government, fearing them to be agents of sedition, tried to put them beyond the reach of the masses by enormous increases in stamp duty.

Lastly, an examination of the advertisements carried by various newspapers shows them catering for a wide range of tastes and income levels. For example, in the early years of the century, while the high-class evening journals carried advertisements for country estates, expensive books and race meetings, announcements in the halfpenny papers are of an altogether different character, relating to such items as soap, tobacco, cheap brandy, and articles lost or stolen. Patent medicines also tend to appear more frequently in the cheaper papers. It has even been suggested that it might be possible to show a correlation between the social class of a newspaper readership and the book and property advertisements; and an inverse correlation with quack medicines.[2] What is ostensibly a publisher's announcement often turns out on closer inspection to be concerned with some quack doctor's treatise on the treatment of venereal disease. In one instance, the purchaser of a particular work was entitled to a free copy of:

> The Treatise of *Unfortunate Women*. Being the PRESENT STATE as is NOW at *this Time* of the COMMON WOMEN *of the Town*, and KEPT WOMEN in *London*, 15 Miles round, Considered. It Being *Always* BAD with them at this SEASON of the Year. With the *Prints*, (from the Life) Finely Engraved, of the more NOTED of *These* Ladies, that their Persons may be *At First Sight* Known. Also, Their NAMES – and *Where* they Live.

As Professor Cranfield comments, 'This advertisement can only be classed as a classic example of cause and effect.'

Taking general indications of readership and advertisement content, it would appear that during the eighteenth century newspapers probably extended their coverage to include all those sections of society of interest to the advertiser. What we cannot attempt to estimate is how often the average reader would see a newspaper, or how many different titles might reach him.

It is clear that, even by the early years of the eighteenth century, considerable thought was being put into the writing and presentation of advertisements.

These early attempts to attract the reader's attention, and to emphasise particular words or points, often tended to be somewhat crude, and seem to have upset contemporaries by their brashness. The approaches being employed drew some scathing comments from Addison writing in the *Tatler* on 14 September 1710:

> The great Art in writing Advertisements, is the finding out of a proper Method to catch the Reader's Eye; without which a good Thing may pass over unobserved, or be lost among the Commissions of Bankrupt. Asterisks and Hands were formerly of great Use for this Purpose. Of late year, the N.B. has been much in Fashion; as also little Cuts and Figures, the invention of which we must ascribe to the Author of Spring Trusses. I must not here omit the blind Italian character, which being scarce legible, always fixes and detains the eye, and gives the curious reader something like the satisfaction of prying into a secret. But the great skill in an advertiser is seen chiefly in the style which he makes use of. He is to mention the *Universal Esteem*, or *General Reputation* of things that were never heard of. If he is a Physician or Astrologer, he must change his *Logicks frequently* . . .

There is a natural tendency to think of eighteenth-century advertising in terms of what appeared in the columns of newspapers, which is understandable since the press provides much of our knowledge. Newspaper advertisements, however, were only concerned with a limited range of products. While some categories of consumer goods appear in the advertising columns, as has been seen, their incidence tends to be fairly low. Common foods are largely absent, as are large brewers, while luxury products, such as tea and chocolate, seldom appear once their initial novelty value has worn off. Retailers, too, are rarely in evidence, preferring to rely on the trade card, and no doubt on the apprentice in the shop doorway touting for business among passers-by.[3] It must also be remembered that newspapers were spread extremely thinly in the first half of the century, when few centres outside London could boast their own. Anyone wishing to advertise in a provincial town at this time must therefore have done so basically in some other medium, using the press for additional support. Later in the century, this situation was to change rapidly as more titles appeared and advertising expenditure in the country papers overtook that in their London counterparts (see Tables II and III above).

The main advertising medium in the eighteenth century was probably billposting, though few examples have survived apart from the occasional official proclamation, or bill for a quack doctor. We can gain some idea of prevailing conditions from an article by Charles Dickens which appeared in the middle of the following century.[4] The author described a meeting with 'The King of the Bill-Stickers' in which they discussed among other things the way the business had developed over the years. According to the 'King', his father had held the appointment of 'Engineer, Beadle and Bill-Sticker to the Parish of St Andrews Holborn' in 1780. The bills to be posted were mainly of an official nature – proclamations and declarations – and demy size (22½″ × 17½″). Apparently because the bills were small and easily handled, the actual posting was done mainly by women. When the State Lottery was introduced, printers began to produce larger bills, and men were employed instead. They had the added virtue of greater mobility, and so-called 'trampers' were despatched with their bills to all parts of the country for periods of up to six or eight months, being paid at a rate of ten shillings per day plus expenses. There is no means of

FOR READY MONEY ONLY.

BUGS

Completely Destroyed

BY M. RIBBINS,

WIDOW of the late JOHN MORIARTY,

Who was Grandson and Successor to George Brydges the first Inventor of the Art; for which His Majesty granted

HIS ROYAL LETTERS PATENT,

No. 276, STRAND,

NEARLY OPPOSITE NORFOLK STREET.

M. R. returns her sincere Thanks to those Ladies and Gentlemen whom she has had the Honor to serve: and informs the Public, that she can give the most respectable Reference to the First Families in Town and Country; and begs leave to inform the Nobility, Gentry, and others, that she continues to destroy those noxious Vermin, in *Bedsteads*, *Rooms*, and *Furniture*, on the same reasonable Terms as she has done for the last Thirty Years, viz. Four-post, Settee, Bereau, Half-tester, and Press Bedsteads, at 10s. 6d. each—Cornished ditto, at 15s.—Raised Testers, at £1. 1s. each—and will undertake to keep them free at 2s. each Bed per Year afterwards.

GENTLEMEN

Of Hotels, Coffee-houses, Boarding-Schools, Captains of Vessels, &c. may be accommodated with the Liquid for destroying Bugs, by addressing a letter, post-paid, with the money inclosed to the above M. Ribbins, 276, Strand; who will send the before-mentioned Liquid to any place required; having been in the habit of sending it to Edinburgh, Bath, and Portsmouth. Price 10s. per gall. or 2s. 6d. per quart.

Beware of Impositions.

N. B. Having discharged a Man lately employed by me in the said Business, request that no person will permit him to do any Work, or receive any Money on my account.

E. Thomas, Printer, Denmark-Court, Exete Change, Strand.

A bill from the second half of the eighteenth century.
(By courtesy of the John Johnson Collection)

verifying the details given by the 'King'. It would seem, however, that he told only part of the story, making no mention of bills such as those for patent medicines, which we know were in use at this time. It may be that this type of work would be considered too disreputable to be handled by a parish official, and was undertaken by the advertisers themselves. (A similar situation was to occur in the nineteenth century, when the lowest-class theatrical companies made their own arrangements for posting bills which would not be handled by reputable contractors.)

Another method of advertising in considerable use during the eighteenth century was the so-called trade card or tradesman's card. These 'cards' bear little resemblance to the business card of today. They were printed on paper, often of a quite flimsy nature, and might range in size from about 1¾″ × 2¾″ to 10″ × 16″. They normally carried a design, which might incorporate the shop sign, though the trend in later examples seems to have been to show some kind of product illustration. Trade cards may well be regarded as forerunners of the illustrated advertisement, since the engravings, often beautifully executed by craftsmen of the calibre of Hogarth, were allowing the advertiser to portray visually what he had for sale. This was not yet possible in newspapers, where illustrations were limited to tiny symbolic woodcuts used to designate the category of an advertisement rather than to tell the reader anything about the advertiser or his goods. The possibility of illustration may well be the chief reason why trade cards were popular, though it is also true that they were enormously versatile, capable of serving – depending on size and design – as billhead, letter-head, message pad, *aide mémoire*, handbill or poster. It may be also that tradesmen advertised in this way in order to avoid paying the advertisement duty.

During the first half of the eighteenth century, advertising was beginning to develop into an effective, if imperfect, means of mass communication. It seems strange, therefore, that until recent years historians have tended to ignore its possible effects on the course of the Industrial Revolution. Some interesting work in this area, carried out by Adriano Bruttini, indicates that advertising may well have been an important influence.[5] For example, it helped in the spread of technical knowledge which was to form an important spring-board for later technological innovation. Announcements appear in the early decades of the century for courses of lectures in such fields as chemistry, mathematics, mechanics, optics, hydrostatics and pneumatics, while an analysis of book advertisements in the *Gentleman's Magazine* shows a general increase in the number of titles relating to mathematics, physics and science. In a similar way, the aspiring businessman of whatever background could also discover from advertisements how to acquire the basic knowledge he needed to operate a business successfully, with courses being offered on writing, arithmetic and accounts, as well as books on various aspects of commerce and economics. Advertising helped inventors and innovators obtain wide publicity for their discoveries, which in turn could mean a quicker return on capital invested – Savery, for instance, was advertising his engines to mine and colliery owners in 1702.

In addition, advertising stimulated the movement of capital, enabling investors to be sought through the columns of newspapers. Though this may well have brought many of them into the clutches of the bubble companies in 1720 (at one point in April the financial advertisements in the *Daily Post* occupied more than half the paper) advertising was also employed to attract finance for reputable concerns, to offer shares in existing businesses, and to help raise cash by the sale of surplus machinery and equipment.

The influence of advertising can also be seen in other areas. Improvements in transport and communications, such as new wagon services and improved coach times, were made known by means of advertisements. Improved standards of hygiene, which helped bring about a decline in the mortality rate, may have been due in some measure to the advertising of soaps and dentifrices. And advertising as a stimulant to consumption must surely have contributed to the general increase in trade.

The Industrial Revolution saw advertising become more widely accepted as a feature of business activity. Industrialisation meant that considerable amounts of capital were being invested in machinery which, in order to show a satisfactory return, had to produce in greater quantities than were possible by hand. This left the manufacturer with the problem of disposing of extra production, which often entailed extending the area of his selling operation to cover the new concentrations of population – something which became increasingly feasible with continuing improvements in transport. As more firms expanded their production, so there would have been increasingly fierce competition for orders from the retailer, who would already have his own sources of supply and could not stock every product offered to him. Most trade at this time was in any case in unbranded merchandise, the differences between which might be so slight as to be indiscernible to the public.

In this situation, manufacturers gradually began to make use of advertising, employing it in two distinct ways. Firstly, it was offered to retailers as an inducement to buy stocks. For example, by the 1780s, William Jones, a London chemist and druggist supplying country apothecaries and booksellers, was offering a free advertisement in a selected local newspaper to any stockist taking a dozen bottles of Tincture of Peruvian Bark.[6] Secondly, manufacturers used advertising to promote knowledge of their own products and to try to establish public confidence in them. It seems to have been the case even at this time that the public were more likely to buy something if they had read about it in a newspaper. This aim would be realised to some extent, of course, by the first use of advertising, especially since linking the product with a well-known local retailer would help to establish its respectability. Advertisements placed directly by the manufacturer, however, probably dwelt to a greater extent on the virtues of the product, though they normally also contained a list of local outlets.

In cases where a manufacturer was the only supplier of a product to a particular retailer, it was sufficient to advertise the fact that the retailer had that product in stock. A sale for the retailer meant a sale for the manufacturer, and there was no need to distinguish the product in any way. At an early stage, however, manufacturers seem to have realised the advantage of designating their products by a particular name. Not only did this put the producer in a stronger position at retail level if a shopkeeper kept more than one variety. It also enabled the manufacturer to communicate directly with the ultimate purchaser, and thus to apply extra pressure on the retailer, by persuading customers to ask for a particular product by name. The practice of branding – which is what we are seeing here – had its origins long before the Industrial Revolution, in product areas where the production process consisted basically of mixing together certain ingredients. Economies of scale in this case could be achieved by the bulk purchase of materials, rather than the use of machines as was to be the case with manufactured articles. There was, nevertheless, an incentive to produce in larger quantity so as not to have money tied up in stocks of materials, and as sales were expanded over a larger area, the benefits of brand identification must have been obvious. Advertising for Holman's Ink Powder, for example, may be found in the 1720s, while other early instances of branding include polishes, blackings and sauces.

A similar rationale applied in the case of patent medicines, which were also basically mixed products, though in their case there were additional factors which made branding a logical development. From the producer's point of view, it was desirable that each unit sold should be packaged separately so that it could carry a notice about the patent, and a warning regarding infringements and imitations. There was also a legal requirement, since duty was payable on patent medicines, and each bottle or box therefore had to carry the government stamp. A product available in its own separate and distinctive packaging was an obvious candidate for advertising, particularly since the medicine area was extremely competitive, with so many products, most of which offered to cure an incredibly wide range of complaints, as well as performing other socially useful tasks such as sharpening knives. Sordid though this form of enterprise unquestionably was, the medicine vendors may well be regarded as the pioneers of modern marketing, branding their products, advertising them widely, and distributing them over large areas of the country. We know from John Houghton's *Collection* (1692), for example, that the *Elixir Magnum Stomachicum* could be bought in most towns, while in 1731 there were wholesale distributors of *Dr Godfrey's Cordial* in London, Bristol, Norwich, Chester, Newcastle on Tyne and Dublin.[7] Where the quack doctors led, others were to follow. The results of the desire to advertise, allied with the increasingly wide range of media, was to be the development of advertising as a business in its own right.

Advertising Takes Shape 1800–1855

THE FIRST HALF of the nineteenth century was the period during which advertising evolved into something akin to its present form. Its progress was restricted by taxes levied on individual advertisements, on paper and on newspapers, the details of which are shown in Table IV below. The growth in expenditure is nevertheless impressive. Businessmen were finding that advertising paid.

TABLE IV

Newspaper Taxation from 1800.

The Newspaper Stamp Duty

From 1797	3½d
1815	4d (effectively 3d net)
1836	1d (½d extra for supplements)
1855	abolished

The Advertisement Duty
(levied at a flat rate on each advertisement)

From 1797	3s 0d
1815	3s 6d
1833	1s 6d
1853	abolished

The Paper Duty
(per lb.)

1803	3d
1836	1½d
1861	abolished

Source: A. P. Wadsworth, *Newspaper Circulations 1800–1954.*

There are of course no contemporary statistics on advertising expenditure as such, but we do have annual returns which give, or enable us to calculate, the number of advertisements appearing each year upon which duty was payable. From these it is possible to work out a rough expenditure pattern.

The advertisement duty and its effect

Table V below shows the amount of duty collected each year from 1800 to 1848 and the number of advertisements on which it was levied. It is based on Inland Revenue returns included in the House of Commons *Accounts and Papers* for 1826–7 and 1848. In the former case, the returns give only the amount of duty, so the number of advertisements has been calculated by dividing the amount payable on each insertion into the sum shown for each year. The later returns show both the duty and the number of advertisements.

TABLE V

Advertisement Duty Collected and the Number of Advertisements, 1800–48.

Year	*Revenue Collected* £	*s*	*d*	*No. of Advertisements*
1800	76,668	14	0	511,258
1801	83,094	3	10	533,961
1802	87,837	3	8	585,581
1803	90,581	3	6	603,874
1804	91,659	10	0	611,063
1805	99,231	11	4	661,543
1806	102,839	12	0	685,597
1807	105,027	1	10	700,180
1808	111,566	1	4	743,773
1809	117,334	16	1	782,232
1810	128,588	7	1	857,255
1811	128,593	0	5	857,286
1812	130,324	4	3	868,828
1813	128,734	19	10	858,233
1814	119,985	12	8	799,904
1815	124,958	13	6	714,051
1816	133,555	14	10	763,176
1817	133,018	17	10	760,108
1818	137,029	5	4	783,024
1819	139,138	12	9	795,078
1820	140,189	10	6	801,083
1821	142,060	19	5	811,777
1822	148,319	8	6	847,539
1823	141,495	17	7	805,547
1824	152,459	16	3½	871,199
1825	163,460	0	6½	934,057

TABLE V—*continued*

Year	*Revenue Collected* £ *s d*	*No. of Advertisements*
1826	153,466 19 2	876,954
1827	153,379 10 0	870,740
1828	155,308 6 0	887,476
1829	153,645 2 0	877,972
1830	157,482 6 6	899,899
1831	156,898 10 6	896,563
1832	155,400 14 0	880,004
1833	(*rate of duty reduced*)	
1834	83,422 17 6	1,112,305
1835	88,440 18 0	1,179,212
1836	98,336 9 6	1,311,153
1837	101,939 17 0	1,359,198
1838	111,899 8 0	1,491,992
1839	115,284 9 0	1,537,126
1840	121,422 7 6	1,618,965
1841	117,554 14 6	1,567,396
1842	114,798 18 0	1,530,642
1843	114,548 14 0	1,527,316
1844	123,178 9 6	1,642,419
1845	145,010 13 0	1,933,476
1846	144,577 6 0	1,927,696
1847	146,875 15 0	1,958,343
1848	142,674 2 0	1,902,322

Source: *House of Commons Accounts and Papers*, 1826–27, XVII: 99; and 1849, XXX: 160 and 506.

In assessing the effect of the duty on the growth of advertising, two reservations must be made about the kind of picture which the returns provide. Firstly, it is important to bear in mind that the duty was levied at a flat rate per insertion. We have therefore a record of the number of advertisements appearing, but our knowledge about their length is limited – apart from personal observation – to an estimate by the editor of the *Scotsman* that 95 per cent of advertisements were 'short'. Secondly, newspapers were only one of several media from which advertisers could choose, and might not necessarily reflect the state of advertising as a whole. What may well have happened in the case of an increase in the rate of duty is that advertisers reacted by switching their expenditure to alternative media. Such is the basis of the complaint made by R. K. D. in his *Letter to Viscount Lord Althorp*:

> . . . As one channel narrows, so other channels become proportionately enlarged. The advertisement duty merely swells the number of placards and circulars, and compels the shopkeeper to have recourse to roundabout and less efficient methods of setting forth the merits and cheapness of his wares, instead of courting the attention of customers in the pages of a public journal.

Advertisers also used the unstamped press – that is to say the papers which were published illegally without paying the stamp duty. It is impossible to make any accurate calculation of the volume of advertising they attracted, but it may perhaps be significant that between 1830 and 1832 when they were most active, the number of advertisements on which duty was paid fell from 899,899 to 880,004, with a corresponding reduction in the duty collected from £157,482 to £155,400. It would seem, therefore, that although the effect of the duty was to restrict the volume of advertising carried by the stamped newspapers, this probably represents a diversion of funds rather than a cutback in spending. Indeed, the money diverted may actually have helped to stimulate the growth of alternative advertising media.

Table VI below represents an estimate of the annual national expenditure on newspaper advertising up to 1848. This has been calculated by taking the number of advertisements, appearing each year and multiplying by the cost, assuming that 95 per cent of all insertions fell into the 'short' category, for which the average charge was 6s 0d per insertion before 1833 and 5s 0d thereafter, with a further 5 per cent allowed for longer advertisements.

It must be emphasised that the figures apply only to stamped newspapers, and that advertisers made considerable use of the unstamped press and of other

TABLE VI

Estimated National Expenditure on Newspaper Advertising, 1800–48.

Year	£	*Year*	£
1800	160,960	1825	294,230
1801	174,500	1826	276,240
1802	184,460	1827	274,280
1803	190,220	1828	279,550
1804	192,480	1829	276,560
1805	208,380	1830	283,470
1806	215,960	1831	282,420
1807	220,560	1832	277,200
1808	234,290	1833	(duty reduced)
1809	246,400	1834	291,980
1810	270,030	1835	309,540
1811	270,040	1836	344,180
1812	273,680	1837	356,790
1813	270,340	1838	391,650
1814	251,970	1839	403,490
1815	224,920	1840	424,980
1816	240,400	1841	411,440
1817	239,430	1842	401,790
1818	246,650	1843	400,920
1819	250,450	1844	431,130
1820	252,340	1845	507,540
1821	255,710	1846	506,000
1822	266,970	1847	514,060
1823	253,750	1848	499,360
1824	274,430		

media such as posters. Thus the total national expenditure across all media was probably at least double the level indicated in Table VI, putting it by mid-century at around £1 million.

The pattern shown by Table VI indicates that advertising was sensitive to economic and fiscal pressure. Volume declined when the rate of duty was raised from 3/- to 3/6d in 1815, and expanded rapidly after the reduction to 1/6d in 1833. It rose with the boom in 1825 and fell again during the depression of the early forties. The significance of these figures must not, however, be over-estimated. While they provide a broad indication of the overall expansion of advertising, the level of spending by individual businesses varied enormously, with many – particularly at the 'better' end – steadfastly refusing to advertise at all.

The heaviest advertiser by mid-century was reputed to be Thomas Holloway, the patent-medicine manufacturer, whose expenditure was quoted by several sources as growing at the following rate:

Year	£
1842	5,000
1845	10,000
1851	20,000
1855	30,000

These figures are probably fairly accurate, since they equate roughly with evidence produced in 1850 in a court case involving Holloway and his brother, in which it was stated in an affidavit with reference to Thomas's medicines that he 'had expended nearly 150,000L in making them known and establishing a connection for the sale thereof'.

The ranks of the medical advertisers also contained other major spenders, though not on the same scale. According to the *Quarterly Review*, both Rowland & Co, famous for their *Kalydor* and macassar oil, and Dr De Jongh, supplier of cod-liver oil, each spent £10,000 annually on advertising, while there are many other names which seem to crop up equally frequently in the columns of newspapers, and whose expenditure must have been at this level.

Auctioneers and booksellers were among the heaviest advertisers in terms of the numbers of advertisements taken. While no details have been discovered concerning any auctioneering firm there are occasional references in contemporary writings to the costs involved in publicising a book. According to the *Edinburgh Review*, 'It is considered hardly worth a publisher's while to publish a cheap or single-volume book, since forty or fifty pounds must be laid out on advertisements to give any publication a chance.' J. Livesey discovered as much when he launched his own journal, *The Moral Reformer:* 'The expence of advertising has been very heavy; this, together with the duty, postages, carriages and incidentals, amount to £45.' Charles Babbage, too, in advertising *On the Economy of Machinery and Manufacturers*, spent £40, finding in the process that newspapers were the most effective medium. Perhaps the heaviest spender in this field, however, was Henry Colborn, publisher of Thomas Hood, Disraeli and Fennimore Cooper, whose advertising budget is said to have reached £9,000 per annum.

Advertising expenditure by retailers varied widely, according to the scale of the business. At one extreme, the large retail businesses were among the country's heaviest advertisers, the *Quarterly Review* in 1855 naming several retailers as being among the leading spenders – Moses & Son (tailors) at £10,000 per annum, Heal & Son at £6,000, and Nicholas (tailors) at £4,500. At the other end of the scale came small retailers who probably spent little, if anything, on advertising. Where their names appear in newspapers, it is usually in connection with a particular manufacturer's products, in which case, as we have seen, the manufacturer may well have carried the cost of the advertisement. Otherwise the small retailer generally confined himself to bills and trade cards. David Alexander, in *Retailing in England during the Industrial Revolution*, quotes two typical cases of bankrupt grocers in the 1840s, one of whom spent £5 per annum on advertising, and the other £2.10s.

The expansion of commerce and industry meant that advertising was required not only to stimulate the sale of manufactured goods, but also to invite applications for shares in newly-floated companies. The Lawson and Barker (later Charles Barker) advertising agency was particularly involved in this kind of advertising, and its records give a unique insight into the costs involved.[1] Rothschilds, for example, spent £449.5s.6d. in 1824, most of that in advertising foreign loans, while between 30 July and 2 October 1833 the sum of £703.12s.0d. was spent by the promoters of the Westminster Bank. It was the railway mania of the forties, however, which saw really heavy advertising by company promoters using Charles Barker's agency. In a number of instances, this was of a highly speculative nature, since between 1847 and 1850 Barker was trying to recover bad debts to the value of £5,205.0s.3d, most of this relating to railway companies. The total value of railway advertising handled by the agency during the years 1845–6 was £9,655.12s.4d. To give some instances of expenditure by individual companies, the Direct London, Holyhead and Port Dynllaen Railway spent £1,255.18s.8d between August and October 1845, the Jamaica Atmospheric Railway spent £797.7s.6d between October 1845 and January 1846, the Irish West Coast Railway spent £1,188.6s.0d in the twelve months ending April 1846, and the Eastern and Northern Counties Junction Railway Company £797.7s.6d. between September and November 1845. The heaviest expenditure among railway companies using Charles Barker, however, seems to have been by the Great Leeds and London Direct Railway Company, which was calculated early in 1846 to owe the agency £3,093.17s.2d.

Barker handled a certain amount of non-commercial advertising, his clients including London University, George Grote, the Seamen's Hospital and the Royal National Institution, with the latter spending as much as £447.18s.3d in 1824 – only £2 less than Rothschilds. The agency also undertook to place advertisements on behalf of certain election candidates, with Sir Edward Knatchbull spending £103.7s.6d. in the East Kent Election in 1832, and Sir William Geary £103.12s.0d. in West Kent in the same year. Even the election of an alderman for Portsoken tempted one of the candidates, Mr Harvey, to spend £29.12s.8d. The reason for such heavy expenditure in the case of parliamentary elections may perhaps be found in a complaint made in parliament by Sir Mathew Ridley, that newspapers charged for election notices at double their normal rates.[2]

It should be remembered that these figures give a general indication of expenditure levels. The published figures are presumably based on hearsay, and therefore of doubtful accuracy, and it is often not clear whether they relate to press advertising alone or include other media such as posters, in which case an advertiser's total promotional spending might be considerably higher.

The commercial uses of advertising

Even during the early years of the nineteenth century, leading advertisers were running campaigns which covered wide areas of the country. Of particular note are such names as Schweppes, Crosse & Blackwell, Elizabeth Lazenby, Lea & Perrins and Day & Martin, as well as a number of insurance companies and patent medicine suppliers. As early as 1793, Jacob Schweppe, who had arrived in London the previous year and had been setting up a factory, wrote of '*ce moment où je suis occupé a faire connaître la chose par la presse*'.[3] Generally such advertisements carried the name not only of the manufacturer or supplier, but also of the local agent or stockist. As we have seen, they were used both to establish a product's name in districts where it had not previously been offered for sale, the inclusion of the name of a reputable local trader being useful in conveying an impression of respectability, and as an incentive to retailers to buy the product.

In an effort to build up a picture of who was advertising and to what extent, the present writer analysed a sample of some 3,500 advertisements taken from selected newspapers at fifteen-year intervals from 1810 to 1855.[4] This showed the most important category to be auctioneers with 16 per cent of the total, followed by retailers (who became considerably more important in the second quarter of the century) with 13.6 per cent, legal and public notices with 11.7 per cent, and situations vacant, property sales and publications having over 7 per cent each. In view of the volume of criticism attracted by the medical advertisers of the period, it is perhaps surprising to find them accounting for only 6.5 per cent.

Looking in more detail at the individual categories, the influence of the auctioneers may have been somewhat greater than the figures in the survey imply. The impression gained by looking through the newspapers is that auctioneers' advertisements tended to be longer than average, often containing detailed particulars of estates they were offering. There is an outstanding example in *Felix Farley's Journal* for 4 July, 1840 in which a single auctioneer's advertisement covers two columns of the paper, and gives details of 58 different lots. Therefore, in terms of a particular newspaper's income, based on the number of lines of advertising rather than on the number of advertisements, auctioneers would have assumed rather greater importance. Some hint of this is contained in the statement by Daniel Stuart, the newspaper proprietor, that 'Auctioneers to this day stipulate to have their advertisements inserted at once, that they may impress the public with the great ideas of their extensive business. They will not have them dribbled out, a few at a time, as the days of sale approach.'[5]

Their influence was not confined to the press alone. They paid the bill-stickers who worked for them more than the rate for general or theatrical posting, and they were able to bring considerable pressure to bear on the printers of their posters and catalogues, as is clear from the complaints made in 1849 by the compiler of a printers' price-list:

> The extraordinary fact of Auctioneers requiring such a commission as 25 and 30 per cent upon the amount of their Printing precludes the possibility of their being charged fair prices.
>
> In charging work from the following lists of Hand Bills, Posters, &c., the Printer will of course add to it whatever commission he will be required to allow. It is quite time the public were made aware that Auctioneers, in addition to their fair Commission for the Sale of Goods, extract this unreasonable amount from the Printer. An organized resistance would effectively stop this.[6]

There is no record of any such resistance ever having taken place. What seems more likely to have happened is that the auctioneers lost their ability to behave in this fashion as the increasingly heavy promotion of consumer products relegated them to the lesser ranks of advertising spenders.

Auctioneers certainly appear to have advertised over an extremely wide area. For example, *Felix Farley's Bristol Journal* for 7 July 1810 contains details of auctions in Plymouth of French and American ships seized as prizes, together with their cargoes, while Winstanley & Son have notices relating to the sale in London of estates in Gloucestershire and Carmarthen. Similarly, the Lincolnshire paper, the *Stamford Mercury*, published the previous day, carries details of an estate in Somerset to be auctioned in London.

Legal and public notices constitute another important category, covering such matters as announcements by government departments, workhouse governors, turnpike trusts, commissioners of enclosures and local associations for the prosecution of felons, as well as notices concerning deserters from the military, committal to gaol, bankruptcies and the like. Often these would be of much greater than average length. The *Stamford Mercury* of 6 July 1810, for example, contains a notice concerning a proposed enclosure inserted by the Commissioners, which covers over three-quarters of a column, running to almost 160 lines; while the *Newcastle Chronicle* carries in its issue of 30 November 1855 a notice in connection with the North Shields and Tynemouth Dock, occupying over a column. The fact that an advertisement was headed 'Official' seems to have been no guarantee that it actually was, since Bish, the lottery contractor, used the word to headline his advertisement in *Bell's Weekly Messenger* on 20 August 1826.

Under the category of 'publications' we find notices inserted by publishers, booksellers and sometimes medical quacks. Among the advertisements in London papers may be found a few names which have survived until the present day, Hatchards and John Murray being notable examples. The length of publishers' notices varies enormously, usually according to the number of books included though the publisher of a magazine or review might go into great detail about one particular issue. The *Odd Fellow* for 16 January 1841, for instance, contains an advertisement occupying 125 lines, for a monthly music magazine called *The Flauticon*.

As with auctioneers, it may perhaps be suspected that this group's share of total advertising does not fully do justice to the influence it wielded. A number of provincial booksellers were newspaper proprietors, while their London counterparts set up their own papers, the *British Press* and *Globe*, after a disagreement on advertising policy with Daniel Stuart, proprietor of the influential *Morning Post*. They even engaged George Lane, Stuart's erstwhile assistant, to act as editor, and it was he who set out their grievances: '... that their advertisements were frequently thrown into the back of the paper, and there mixed with others of a gross and offensive character; that frequently their advertisements were refused insertion, or if received, their insertion was attended with injurious delay ...'[7]

Medical advertisements in the papers examined are notable not so much for their number as for their explicitness, the general impression being that they tend to grow longer and more detailed as the century advanced – something which it is difficult to reconcile with Victorian reticence. Typical of this species is an advertisement appearing in the *Morning Chronicle* in 1840:

> PUBLIC NOTICE TO THE UNHAPPY
>
> Dr. Eady continues to be consulted in all cases of Syphilitic Disease, and Derangement of the General Health, Nervous Disability, the effects of Malpractice, the free indulgence of Pleasure, and other causes ...

Cooper & Company, members of the Royal College of Surgeons, leave even less to the imagination, with their spectacular guarantee: 'The Cure Effected or Money Charged Returned', which covers 'every stage and symptom of Syphilis, Gonorrhoea, Gleets, Secondary Symptoms, Seminal Strictures, and weaknesses of the Urethra &c'.

To some extent, treatments offered by the quacks seem to have been tailored to meet the needs of particular strata of society, reflecting perhaps the complaints

MURRAY'S RAILWAY READING:

CONTAINING WORKS OF SOUND INFORMATION AND INNOCENT AMUSEMENT,

PRINTED IN LARGE READABLE TYPE,

SUITED FOR ALL CLASSES OF READERS.

ALREADY PUBLISHED :—

MUSIC AND DRESS, ...	1/.
LITERARY ESSAYS FROM 'THE TIMES,' .	4/.
NIMROD ON THE CHACE, ...	1/.
LAYARD'S POPULAR ACCOUNT OF NINEVEH, .	5/.
NIMROD ON THE ROAD, ...	1/.
LORD MAHON'S HISTORY OF THE FORTY-FIVE,	3/.
LIFE OF THEODORE HOOK, ...	1/.
GIFFARD'S DEEDS OF NAVAL DARING, . .	2/6
THE FLOWER GARDEN, ...	1/.
JAMES' FABLES OF ÆSOP. 100 Woodcuts .	2/6
THE HONEY BEE, ...	1/.
NIMROD ON THE TURF, ...	1/6

SHORTLY :

A JOURNEY TO KATMANDU (the Capital of **NEPAUL**), **with** the CAMP of JUNG BAHADER; including a SKETCH of the NEPAULESE AMBASSADOR AT HOME. By LAURENCE OLIPHANT.

'A series of cheap and healthy publications.'—*Athenæum.*

'The mixed character of the series is a good feature, and carried out with vigour and discernment.'—*Christian Remembrancer.*

'A good readable type for railway reading is the chief consideration.'—*Atlas.*

'A new series, destined to occupy a very distinguished position.'—*Sun.*

'Mr. Murray has deserved well at the hands of the travelling community.'—*Observer.*

'We hail Murray's "Reading for the Rail" as one of the many efforts to supply books at once cheap and good.'—*Economist.*

'We heartily wish this new undertaking the success which it merits.—*Morning Herald.*

JOHN MURRAY, ALBEMARLE STREET;

AND TO BE OBTAINED AT ALL BOOKSELLERS AND RAILWAY STATIONS.

Advertisement for John Murray's Railway Reading, 1852.

inherent in their respective lifestyles. Hence the fashionable pox-doctors used the *Morning Chronicle*, and weeklies covering the more prosperous areas. 'Jordan's Cordial Balm of Rakasiri', for example, claims in the *Bury and Suffolk Herald* (1 September 1830) that 'To the delicate female enfeebled by the fatiguing routine of the fashionable life, the careworn man of business, and those particularly whose constitutions sympathize with the effects of undue indulgence in early life, this remedy cannot be too confidently recommended'. Contrasting with this is an advertisement which appears in the *Stamford Mercury* on 30 November 1855 for 'Dr Roberts' Poor Man's Friend Ointment'. It claims to be '. . . a certain cure for ulcerated sore legs, if of 20 years' standing, cuts, burns, scalds, bruises, chilblains, scorbutic eruptions, and pimples on the face, sore and inflamed eyes, and cancerous tumours . . .'

Though a great deal of medical advertising consisted basically of outrageous claims, often backed up by dubious testimonials, some advertisers made unashamed use of emotional copy, as for example in this lamentation on behalf of Perry's Purifying Specific Pills: 'What a pity that a young man, the hope of his country and the darling of his parents, should be snatched from all the prospects and enjoyments of life by the consequences of one unguarded moment.'

Sometimes the claims made by the quacks are astounding in their effrontery. The suppliers of AK Balsam invited the reader to drive a nail into the head of a hen or ram, so that it pierced the skull, brains and tongue. If balsam were then applied, it was claimed, 'It will directly stop the blood and cure the wound in eight or nine minutes, and the creature will eat as before.'

It is not clear how far the public were impressed by the titles often assumed by the quacks such as 'Doctor' or – in the case of Holloway – 'Professor'. According to John Corry, writing early in the nineteenth century, the degree of Doctor of Medicine was available by post from the University of Aberdeen at a cost of £1.13s.3¾d. Among those to avail themselves of this facility were the celebrated Dr Brodum, previously a footman, and Dr Solomon, a former shoeblack. 'Will it be believed by posterity,' lamented Corry, 'that at the commencement of the nineteenth century Quack Doctors were enabled, by the credulity of Englishmen, to amass wealth; nay, that any pretender to the art of healing might for a few pence *purchase* the academic degree of M.D. in a Scotch University, and afterwards obtain a patent to slay his thousands and tens of thousands according to law.'[8]

Newspapers seem to have made little effort to 'hide' their medical advertisements, which can be found on most front pages. Even the coronation issue of the *Globe*, published on 28 June 1838, carried an assortment of quacks, one of whom was offering *An Historical and Practical Treatise on Primary and Secondary Syphilitic Diseases*. The only concession sometimes made was to put these advertisements at the foot of the page, giving the position at the tops of columns to more respectable advertisers such as auctioneers and publishers.

Probably the clearest trend revealed by the survey is the growth of consumer goods advertising, reflecting the changing pattern of life resulting from the effects of the Industrial Revolution. This may be seen from the increase in advertising by manufacturers and retailers, and even more clearly from the changing content of the advertisements. Initially, products were made and sold at the same address, with readers of the *Morning Chronicle* in 1825 being offered fashionable clothing for men and women, harness, guns, pheasant and poultry coops, pianos, ice-pails, furnishings and so on. Already, however, there are signs of tradesmen seeking wider distribution for their products. As early as 1806, the *Brighton Herald* in its issue of 25 October carried an announcement for 'Bowles Universal Essence for Soups and Gravies', stating that it was obtainable from Bowles Wholesale Sauce Warehouse in London and from eighteen named stockists in the south of England. By 1810, Day & Martin, the London blacking manufacturers, could quote twenty-one outlets in the circulation area of the *Stamford Mercury*, and some idea of the scope of their distribution area, and presumably their advertising expenditure, may be gained from the fact that their announcements also appeared in *Felix Farley's Bristol Journal.*

It is interesting to note the number of companies active at this time who have survived until the present day. Crosse & Blackwell, for example, 'Purveyors in Ordinary to Her Majesty', took advantage of the revelations of food adulteration to proclaim 'the practice of colouring pickles and tart fruits by artificial means has been discontinued, and the whole of their manufactures are so prepared that they are not allowed to come in contact with any deleterious ingredient' (*Morning Chronicle* 2 July 1855). It is significant that the company apparently considered its products to be sufficiently well-known and distributed to be able to omit any reference to local stockists. Schweppes is another company already operating on a large scale, and using the royal arms in the *Stamford Mercury* by 1840, while 10 February 1844 saw the first advertisement in *The Times* by Huntley & Palmers. By 1855, the Stamford paper was carrying anncuncements from Hornimans Tea, Robertson's Patent Barley, and Callard & Bowser's Infants Food.

In one notable instance, a supplier actually used the advertisement to try to win over a potential retail customer. John Rose extolled the merits of his teas and coffees in verse, following up with a second stanza aimed specifically at Mr C. Julyan of Peterborough:

> John Rose's Teas and Coffees too
> Will bring you buyers not a few.
> Yea, thousands will be glad to buy
> The articles which you supply,
> Since it is clearly understood
> That what you sell is cheap and good.

In other cases, companies were supplying customers direct, and bypassing the retailer completely. By 1855, for example, it was possible for readers of the *Morning Chronicle* to have Yarmouth bloaters sent by rail directly to their homes, and for readers of the *Stamford Mercury* to order their tea directly from Bradens of Islington, and their wine from Hedges & Butler.

Although in many ways both manufacturers and retailers showed flashes of surprising sophistication in their advertising, it would probably be a mistake to emphasise this aspect too strongly. In mid-century in the *Stamford Mercury* there were still small advertisements with the traditional heading 'A Card', while one can only wonder at the commercial logic behind the following announcement:

NOTICE

> The great demand for JACKSON'S ALBATA PENS has induced the proprietor to reduce the prices within the reach of all writers.

By mid-century, there were some obvious changes in the advertisement columns, reflecting the growing division between manufacturing and retailing. More retailers seem to have been using the newspapers, though they probably constitute only a small percentage of the total. Tailors, drapers and milliners are still much in evidence, along with watchmakers and jewellers, booksellers, a few coffee and tea merchants, grocers, and 'hair-cutting rooms'. There seems, at the same time, to have been a movement towards more general retailing, with advertisers offering a wide range of frequently unrelated goods, reflecting perhaps the origins of the department store. Sometimes this diversity seems to have been carried to bizarre lengths, as with W. Wright, who proclaimed his business in the Stamford paper (3 July 1840) as being 'Wholesale and Retail General Furnishing, and Agricultural Ironmonger and Printer'.

New scientific developments, too, were opening up fresh opportunities in the shopping streets, as with the appearance of 'photographic rooms'. Nevertheless, retailer advertising tends to reflect the lifestyle of the area in which the paper circulated. Hence, ships stores are to be found in the Newcastle paper, seed merchants in the *Stamford Mercury*, and Chubb's patent fire-proof safes in the *Morning Chronicle.*

Indications of the divorce of manufacturing from retailing may be seen particularly in the increasing complexity of some of the products advertised. For instance, the unstamped weekly *Cosmopolite* for 28 April 1832 carried an advertisement for Fryers washing machines, which, it was claimed, would launder up to one hundred shirts in thirty minutes. By mid-century, the inventive mind seems to have taken a number of directions, not always attended by ensuing commercial success. Announcements appear for such products as self-lighting sealing wax, Ayckbourne's patent folding portable boat, and Soyer's Magic Stove which could cook dinner for up to twenty persons but was small enough to be carried in the trouser pocket.

Curiosities of this kind, fascinating as they are to the modern eye, are far from representative of the mass of products being advertised, most of which were of a much more mundane nature. Towards the middle of the century, the *Morning*

Chronicle was offering Mechi's castellated toothbrushes, the new Post Office adhesive stamps at 1s 1d for twelve, and Plastow's patent gas moderator and burner ('as used at the Stamp Office') promising a fuel saving of 25 per cent; while in the *Stamford Mercury* are to be found agricultural suppliers such as the London Manure Company, and Samuelson & Company of Banbury, manufacturers of the Patent Turnip Cutter.

A typical advertisement for a novelty product.
(By courtesy of the Robert Opie Collection)

Other categories of advertisement, though of less importance in terms of volume, also reflect the pattern of life of their readers, and the way it developed as the century advanced. 'Personal' advertising in Stamford is concerned mainly with animals lost and found; in Bristol church-pews are offered to let; while in London anonymous noblemen mysteriously offer for sale their curtains and furnishings. Businesses for sale are mainly shops and inns – the latter particularly in the *Morning Advertiser* – though by 1840 a *Morning Chronicle* advertiser was seeking a purchaser for a gas-works. By this time, too, more advertisements for items of machinery were appearing, with steam engines being among the most frequently offered.

Entertainments advertised included theatre, opera, concerts, lectures, exhibitions and displays of various kinds such as dioramas. The Stamford paper carries notices for the Birmingham Music Festival, and in 1855 for Charles Dickens' reading of *A Christmas Carol* at the Peterborough Mechanics' Institute.

Theatre Royal, Covent-Garden,

This present WEDNESDAY, Dec 18. 1816, (17th time) the New Musical Drama of

The SLAVE.

The OVERTURE and MUSICK composed by Mr BISHOP.

Governor of Surinam, Mr. TERRY,
Captain Malcolm. Mr. SINCLAIR, Captain Clifton, Mr. DURUSET,
Lindenburg, Mr ABBOTT, Fogrum, Mr. LISTON,
Matthew Sharpset, Mr JONES, Sam Sharpset, Mr EMERY,
Gambia *(the Slave)* Mr. MACREADY,
Somerdyke, Mr TAYLOR. Officer. Mr Comer, Jailer, Mr. Simmons
Provost, Mr. ATKINS, Zelinda's Child, Miss PARSLOE,
Planter's Boy Master Barnett, Dutch Planters, Mess. Treby, King, Tinney

Slaves and Attendants,

Mess. I. Brown, Crumpton, Everard George, Guittart, Higman, Howell, Penn, Lee, Linton, Terry,

Mrs Lindenburg, Mrs. EGERTON,
Stella Clifton. Miss MATTHEWS, Miss Von Frump. Mrs DAVENPORT
Zelinda *(a Quadroon Slave)* Miss STEPHENS.
Indian Girls, Mesdames CAREW, STERLING, MAC ALPINE.

Female Slaves and Attendants,

Mesdames Bologna, Chipp, Coates, Corri, Finlay, Green, Grimaldi, Herbert, Hibbert, Iliff, Mortram.

With, *(FOR THE LAST TIME but Two,)*

BLUE BEARD;

Or, FEMALE CURIOSITY.

IN WHICH THE GRAND

EQUESTRIAN TROOP

WILL PERFORM

With new Scenes and Embellishments.
And the Original Musick by Michael Kelly, Esq.

Abomelique, Mr. BARRYMORE,
Ibrahim, Mr. SIMMONS, Selim, Mr. DURUSET,
Shacabac by Mr. FAWCETT, Hassan by Mr. MENAGE,
Fatima, Miss MATTHEWS, Irene, Mrs. BISHOP,
Beda, Mrs LISTON,

The Dance by Mrs. PARKER, and the Corps de Ballet.

No Orders can be admitted.

E. Macleish, Printer. 2, Bow-street, Covent-Garden — Vivant Rex et Regina.

☞ *On account of a Domestick Affliction which has befallen*

MISS O'NEILL

She will not be able to perform till Monday next, when she will appear in JULIET

Mr. KEMBLE

For his Last Time of acting before Easter, will Tomorrow, perform CORIOLANUS

The All-Attractive Musical Drama of THE SLAVE,

Will be performed on Friday

Mr. HENRY JOHNSTON having again been received with universal applause in Sir Archy Macsarcasm, will repeat that character shortly.—And on Friday the 27th, will perform the part of SIR PERTINAX MACSYCOPHANT

The Grand Romance of BLUE BEARD,

to accommodate the numerous FAMILIES, will be performed on Saturday and Monday—*(the Last Times of the appearance of the* EQUESTRIAN TROOP.*)*

From the overflow from every part of the Theatre, GUY MANNERING, and BLUE BEARD will be repeated on Saturday next.

Tomorrow, Shakspeare's Tragedy of CORIOLANUS. Coriolanus, Mr. KEMBLE.
With (18th time) the Melo-Drama of The BROKEN SWORD.

On Friday, (18th time) The SLAVE.
With the Farce of LOVE, LAW and PHYSICK.

On Saturday, (9th time this season) the Opera of GUY MANNERING.
Lucy Bertram by Miss STEPHENS.

On Monday, Shakspeare's Tragedy of ROMEO and JULIET,
Romeo, Mr. C. KEMBLE, Juliet by Miss O'NEILL.
[Being the Last Night of performing till the Holidays.]

The New Grand CHRISTMAS PANTOMIME,

which has been in preparation since the su[mme]r, will be produced *On Thursday* the 26th.

The development of railways is reflected by the offer of shares in railway companies, the appearance of railway timetables in the advertising columns by mid-century, and by invitations to tender for the supply of such items as wagons, sleepers and fence posts. Shipping announcements also tend to be for steam packets rather than sail. The pressure thus put on other forms of transport is probably indicated by the announcement in *Felix Farley's Journal* in November 1840 that the coach fare from Bristol to Swansea had been reduced.

Taken overall, it is clear that advertising was being increasingly used by a wider range of businesses. This in turn led to a demand for suitable media and in particular was to help stimulate the development of the British national press.

Advertising media

1 The press

It is remarkable that the interests of commercial advertisers and newspaper proprietors should have been so closely identified at a time when the success of each depended upon the growth of the other. In the early years of the century, technological advances in the printing industry were making possible the production of newspapers with much larger circulations than hitherto. While this would eventually bring economies of scale, it meant that larger amounts of capital were needed for the purchase of new machinery. In order to obtain a reasonable rate of return on that capital, the newspaper proprietor needed to generate profits at a level virtually impossible without advertising, which in turn would be attracted by the higher circulation which his new machinery helped him to attain. Advertisers needed such a vehicle for their messages at the very time its production became technically feasible.

At the beginning of the nineteenth century, printing had changed little since the time of Gutenberg. The normal method of producing a newspaper was on a wooden hand-press, giving a maximum output of about 250 impressions per hour. The first notable improvement was Lord Stanhope's iron press, on which it was possible to print a large forme in one pull instead of the two pulls necessary on the normal wooden press. The major innovation, however, was the application of steam power to printing. Friedrich Koenig patented his mechanical press in 1810, and it was used the following year to produce a page of the *Annual Register* at a rate of 400 sheets per hour. By 1814, *The Times* was using steam presses installed by Koenig and Bauer, and capable of 1,100 sheets per hour. The four-cylinder press developed by Applegarth and Cooper, installed by *The Times* in 1828, could produce 4,000 sheets per hour, while by 1857 it had rotary presses giving 20,000 impressions per hour.

The value of higher printing speeds was limited so long as type still had to be cast by hand and set separately for each press. Notable improvements here included the letter-founding machine invented in 1822 by Dr William Church, which could cast up to 20,000 letters in a day, compared with a maximum of 7,000 per day working by hand; and stereotyping which, after being introduced commercially by Lord Stanhope in 1805 using plaster of Paris moulds, was later made more efficient by the use of papier mâché.

The ability to print at faster speeds meant an increased demand for paper, which itself was made entirely by hand until the end of the eighteenth century. In 1803, paper-making machines were set up at Frogmore, Hertfordshire, by the Fourdrinier brothers, and at St Neots by John Gamble. These machines were capable of producing up to 1,000lb of paper per day, compared with 60lb to 100lb per day by hand. By 1843 the price of some kinds of paper had fallen by nearly 50 per cent, and by 1860 it was down from 1s 6d to 6½d per lb. At the same time, the annual paper production of the United Kingdom had risen to 100,000 tons, compared with 11,000 tons in 1800.

Although mass publishing on the Northcliffe scale was still many years ahead, the technological advances in the first half of the nineteenth century, allied to a reduction in the stamp duty in 1836, helped to bring about considerable increases in newspaper circulations.[9] In 1801, *The Times* had a daily sale of between 2,500 and 3,000 copies; the *Morning Herald* and *Morning Advertiser* sold about 2,500; the *Morning Chronicle*, *Oracle* and *True Briton* between 1,500 and 2,000; and the *Morning Post* and *Public Ledger* about 1,000. Twenty years later, while *The Times* with its new steam presses was selling 7,000 copies a day, the *Morning Chronicle* had reached about 3,100, the *Morning Advertiser*, *Morning Herald* and *New Times* between 2,700 and 3,000, and the *Morning Post* around 2,000, the *Oracle* having ceased publication. *The Times* in fact dominated the field to an increasing extent, its daily sale by 1855 nearing 60,000 copies, while none of its rivals even approached 10,000.

These examples all relate to London newspapers published daily. There was an enormous difference between them and the provincial papers which, with very few exceptions, were published weekly and had considerably smaller circulations. A typical example is the *Cambridge Chronicle* where Thomas Catling, aged twelve, went to work in 1850:

> The paper was printed one side at a time, the motive power of the machine being supplied by a couple of sturdy navvies turning a wheel. One of the compositors stroked the sheets singly on to a large upper cylinder; my duty was to 'take off' each one as it came through the machine. When the completed papers appeared, the first issues were folded, packed into wrappers, and taken in washing baskets through the churchyard of Trinity to the neighbouring post office. Albeit the entire issue did not quite reach two thousand, the work went on through the whole of Friday night.[10]

In 1832–3, of the 130 provincial papers, 69 had circulations below 1,000, while only two sold more than 4,000. By 1849, out of a total of 289 papers, 148 were selling under 1,000 per week and 27 over 4,000. As a comparison with the scale of newspaper publishing today, the total number of provincial papers sold in

1823 was about 5.4 million, which is only some million more than is sold on a single Sunday by the *News of the World.*

Our knowledge of newspaper circulation at this period is based on the returns of stamp duty payable by each paper. The stamp was impressed upon each sheet of paper at the Stamping Office in London, in Edinburgh after about 1831, and later in Manchester. Stamping was done by hand, a good stamper being capable of some 8,000 sheets per day, which was as fast as the machinery which was tried for a time at the beginning of the century. However, reliance on a hand operation, and the concentration of stamping into three centres at the most, meant that country papers faced considerable administrative inconvenience. Rather than send blank sheets to London for stamping, they would buy ready-stamped sheets from agents, or from papermakers. As a country newspaper proprietor was sometimes the local stationer, he might hold stocks, and sell in small quantities to other local papers. This kind of dealing seems to have been relatively popular since papermakers in particular would supply on credit, whereas at the Stamping Office, payment was made at the time of purchase.

Trading in stamps seems often to have made it impossible to determine the relationship between the number credited to a particular paper and the actual copies sold. In Manchester, for example, the *Manchester Times* admitted selling 8,000 stamps to the *Blackburn Gazette*, though the *Manchester Guardian* accused it of using only 80,000, while being credited with 185,000 (i.e. illicitly disposing of 105,000). The *Manchester Times*, in its turn, found the *Chronicle* had bought many more stamps than it needed, printed several hundredweight of extra copies and sold these to grocers for use as wrapping paper. The evidence was displayed in the *Manchester Times* shop window.

In London, *The Times* was reputed to be turning over its unused stamps to the *Evening Mail*, or selling them to country papers. But while some of its rivals were almost certainly indulging in such practices, *The Times* was apparently not.

The effect of the trading in stamps upon the accuracy of the official figures is described in detail by Mr Wood, Chairman of the Board of Stamps, in a note attached to the return for 1832:

> In the instance of the London newspapers, the account may approach to tolerable correctness as the stamps are usually obtained by the parties directly from this office; but it may be observed that these papers borrow from each other and we also have reason to believe that agents of country papers have been induced by London printers to take out stamps in the name of the latter which were intended for country use; so that, even with regard to London papers, perfect accuracy cannot be attained.
>
> But in the case of country papers still less reliance can be placed on these accounts. The supply of stamps to country papers is effected through country stationers. These persons take out large quantities of stamps and furnish them, from time to time, to the respective newspapers as required. It is only from the returns made by those stationers that the numbers of stamps obtained by each country paper are

known to this office. The stationers are bound to make these returns but furnish them with much reluctance and irregularity, and frequently omit them altogether. It is well known that the Board have no means of detecting or punishing any mis-statement, and it is therefore believed that, even when furnished, little regard is paid to accuracy.

To combat such abuses, the 'distinctive die' was introduced in 1836, under a provision of 6 and 7 William IV c 76. What this meant in effect was that every stamp incorporated the name of the publication for which the paper was destined, which presumably put an end to the kind of practices deplored by Mr Wood.

The stamp was not levied upon publications containing what was called 'class news' – i.e. relating only to one particular trade or profession – or on 'private news' – i.e. personal libels, family transactions and the like. The basis for this was the statutory definition of a newspaper as 'Any paper containing public news, intelligence or occurrences . . .' The line between what was a newspaper and what was not was indeed a fine one, and as the Select Committee on Newspaper Stamps noted, '. . . The Board of Inland Revenue, as it appears from the evidence of their Secretary, recognise a difference hard to be understood between public and private news, and draw a distinction unknown to the law between public and class news.'

The kind of anomalies to which this situation gave rise are described by John Crawfurd:

One man prints a paper giving theatrical news and criticism and the Stamp Office directs him, at his peril, to desist, or pay the tax. Another, gives news of literature and the fine arts, the theatre excepted, and no one thinks of meddling with him. Any man who would give periodical reports in terms of statute, of the proceedings of our magistracy and courts of justice, things which all men ought to know, yet giving no other intelligence, would, undoubtedly, produce a taxable article; and failing to pay the tax, be deemed a smuggler. A man who gives news of comets, thunder storms, droughts and deluges, may publish at what interval he pleases, and in what shape he pleases with impunity. A man may publish in what shape and at what time he thinks proper, an account of the price of merchandise in all countries of the world; but should he presume to give intelligence of the political state of the countries where the markets for such commodities existed, and without which knowledge, his dry price current would be of little value, he would be at the mercy of the Stamp Office . . . but it must always be recollected, that it is not common sense, but the Stamp Office which is the arbiter.[11]

One important result of this distinction between public and class news was the appearance of a number of trade and professional magazines which, because of their limited editorial appeal, were not liable to stamp duty – among them the *Farmer's Journal* (*c.* 1806), the *Lancet* (1823), *Mining Journal* (1835), *Chemical Gazette* (1842), and the *Builder* (1843). This not only made it much easier for advertisers to reach economically the trade or profession in question, but also laid the basis for what today is possibly the best-informed and most comprehensive trade press in the world.

The stamp duty was responsible for the generally unattractive appearance of newspapers in the first half of the century, since it was levied upon each printed sheet, which effectively limited a paper to four pages – that is to say a single sheet folded once. Although in 1825 the duty on supplements containing only advertisements was halved, it was really only *The Times* which benefited from this provision. Other papers could not attract advertising in sufficient volume to be able to sell at the same price, and dared not raise the price to cover the cost of an extra sheet. The result was a growing pressure of news and advertisements upon a fixed area of space, which led to proprietors adopting such measures as reducing the size of the type and increasing the number of columns per page.

THE PRIZE CHAMPION REAPER.

SOLE PROPRIETORS—WM. DRAY & CO.

PRICE, £18.

WM. DRAY and Co. have received the PRIZE for the **BEST REAPER** at the Bath and West of England Society's Show at Taunton. The trial is thus described—"The word was given, and Mr Stevens, Engineer to Messrs Wm. Dray and Co., took his station on their Machine, and away it went at a fearful pace, clearing everything before it, and taking off the green rye as short as a corn stubble.

The next Reaping Machine ordered out was GARRETT'S, but it had scarcely gone a dozen yards before its knives clogged, and then forced down the crop, and was dragged over it. YOUNG'S Reaper was tried with no better effect."—*Somerset and County Herald, June 12th*, 1852.

This Implement gained the Championship at the Great Challenge Trial at Cleveland, beating its competitor on the Seven Points named; it has all the improvements suggested by the Inventor, to the present Proprietors; and has been patronized by Prince Albert, the Dukes of Marlborough, Cleveland, &c., &c., and Orders have been received for it from numbers of the most influential Prop.ietors in the kingdom.

FOR WATERING GARDENS, DISTRIBUTING LIQUID MANURE, BREWERS' USE, ETC.

PATENT VULCANISED INDIA-RUBBER HOSE-PIPES.

JAMES LYNE HANCOCK,

(SOLE LICENSEE AND MANUFACTURER),

GOSWELL ROAD, LONDON,

THESE Pipes are well adapted for watering gardens, conveying liquid manure, racking beer and cider, and all purposes where a perfectly scund waterproof and flexible pipe is required. They are particnlarly suitable for fire-engines, and are found exceedingly useful in dwelling-houses for conveying hot or cold water to baths, &c. Hose-reels for winding up and wheeling away long lengths of the Vulcanized Rubber Garden Hose, are now manufactured by J. L. HANCOCK, of light and cheap wicker work.

N.B.—Vulcanised India-rubber Garden Hose, fitted up with roses, jets, and branches complete, with union joints ready to attach to pumps or water-cisterns. All letters or orders addressed to J. L. HANCOCK, Goswell-mews, Goswell-road, London, will meet with immediate attention.

N.B.—Vulcanized India-Rubber Washers and Sheet Rubber for Joints and Steam Engine Packings, cut any Size to Order—and THURSTON'S Patent Vulcanized Rubber Billiard Cushions.

Early examples of illustrated newspaper advertisements.
(*Darlington and Stockton Times*, 1852. By courtesy of the Public Record Office)

A further effect was to force illustrations out of the pages of many newspapers, particularly in London. This was true of the advertisements as well as the editorial columns. A writer in 1825 commented, 'I like the country papers because they do not object to a picture or cut'; while by 1855 the *Quarterly Review* was observing: 'Twenty years ago some of the daily newspapers admitted illustrated advertisements into their columns; now it would be fatal to any to do so.' The *Manchester Guardian*, founded in 1821, carried illustrations for the first ten years or so of its life, these being mainly in the advertisement columns. After this, however, they disappeared, not to return until 1866. Illustrations certainly continued to appear throughout the period in some country papers, generally well away from London, as for instance in the case of the *Newcastle Chronicle*. They were usually emblematic in nature, and very small, taking up a tiny space at the lefthand side of an advertisement. Their purpose was not to distinguish a particular advertiser, but to differentiate between various categories of product or service, since advertisements were not normally grouped under classified headings. Hence suitable emblematic devices denoted items related to shipping, railways, music, coursing, steeplechasing, wood auctions and so on. An exception to these generic motifs is the insignia used by insurance companies, which occur widely in their advertisements, notable examples including the British Fire Office, the Phoenix, the Norwich Union, the Royal Exchange and the Guardian.

The problem of illustrations is an example of the dilemma which confronted the newspaper proprietor in his relations with advertisers. In general terms, they enjoyed an identity of interests, since advertisers needed newspapers, and newspapers needed advertising revenue. Yet while gladly accepting the advertisers' money, the proprietors wished to subject them to restraints which were becoming increasingly irksome, as is evident from this comparison in the *Westminster Review* between English and American advertising:

> The accumulation of advertisements, even at the enormous price charged for them in the well established journals, is so great as to prevent all possibility of displaying them properly, so as to catch the eye of the public. In the American papers scarcely an advertisement appears without some engraving of a character adapted to the nature of the announcement, and the practice, although not very chaste to us, who are accustomed to see advertisements set in the smallest type, and crowded together so as to be almost lost, is found to be very useful to the advertiser.[12]

It is in many ways surprising that advertisers put up with such restrictions for as long as they did, in view of the extent to which newspapers depended on advertising revenue. This dependence was well known, James Perry in 1807 and Cobbett in 1809 giving the breakdown of costs involved in publishing a sixpenny paper as being:

Stamp*	3½d
Paper	1d
Newsman	1d
	5½d

*This was effectively three and one-fifth pence net, but the discount was barely enough to cover spoilages and returns.

Thus ½d per copy was left to cover operating costs, including the interest on any borrowings, and to give the proprietor a suitable return on his investment. To raise the selling-price was presumably out of the question, since this would lose sales to rival papers able to hold their price at 6d by virtue of the volume of advertising they attracted.

The Periodical Press of Great Britain and Ireland, published in 1824, by which time both the stamp and advertisement duties and the selling-price of papers had been raised, complained that '. . . after making allowance for the cost of materials used, the loss of stamps and the usual risks of trade, the publisher has scarcely more than three farthings per sheet to pay the interest on his capital, and provide for his family'. This kind of return was clearly insufficient. Cobbett allowed 3½d per copy of his *Political Register* (selling at 10d) for printing, spoilages, carriage, warehousing and wages. Furthermore, anyone setting up a newspaper had to make a considerable capital outlay. No one was allowed to publish or print pamphlets or newspapers before entering into recognizances to the value of £300 in London and £200 elsewhere, to cover a possible charge of blasphemy or seditious libel (60 Geo. III c 9). These sums were later increased to £400 and £300 respectively, and extended to cover libel suits brought by individuals. Under I Will. IV c 73 a further bond had to be furnished as security for the payment of advertisement duty, the amount being fixed in each case by the Commissioners of Stamps and Taxes. In addition, working capital was required to finance stocks of stamped paper, which had to be paid for at the time of purchase, and for the granting of quarterly credit to advertising agents. Unless the proprietor could find such sums for himself, or had a rich patron or backers, he might be tempted to borrow, hoping to pay the interest out of the profits. Meanwhile, newspapers were demanding ever heavier capital investment. The *Westminster Review* estimated in 1829 that some £250,000 was invested in the London dailies and £100,000 in the weeklies, while Crawfurd in 1836 believed that since the sale of the *Morning Chronicle* in 1823, the expense of running a paper had doubled.

Obviously the proprietor's gross margin of ½d to ¾d per copy had to be supplemented from some other source. During the eighteenth century, they had received payments from government or party funds, and advertisements from government departments, in return for favourable editorial treatment. They had also extracted bribes, payments for suppressing unfavourable paragraphs, and 'contradiction fees'. In the nineteenth century, however, the growth of commercial advertising provided a new and infinitely bigger source of revenue which made bribes and subsidies of little relevance for newspaper finance. *The Times*, when accused of enjoying a monopoly position, replied: 'Our monopoly is the monopoly of BARCLAY and PERKINS' porter, TWININGS teas; of Mr COBDEN'S agitation; and of FORTNUM and MASON's hams.'

There was a substantial difference in the relative financial positions of London and provincial newspapers. The important London papers had bigger circulations, appeared daily, and carried much heavier editorial overheads. Charles Knight described the finances of a London newspaper in *The Newspaper Stamp and The Duty on Paper*:

> The permanent expense incurred for the literary production alone of a first-rate morning paper, disbursed in the salaries of editor, sub-editors, reporters, translators, foreign correspondents, travelling expenses, is not less than £15,000 per annum. This gives a cost, for each number published, of about £50. The daily printing expenses, exclusive of paper and stamps, would amount, upon average, to £25 for each number. Here, then, is an expense of £75 to be incurred every time a daily morning paper goes to press, whether it sell 1,000 or 10,000 copies. If it sells a thousand copies only, those thousand bear an expense of £75. The actual receipt for 1,000 newspapers is about £24. Here is a loss, therefore, upon the sale of 1,000 copies of above £27; the paper and stamps not yet being reckoned. These, for 1,000 copies, cost nearly £18. Here is a positive loss, therefore of £68 per number – £408 per week – of £21,216 per year, for a daily morning paper that sells only 1,000 copies, and has no advertisements . . . How, then, will it be said, do morning papers thrive under such circumstances? The answer is easy. In this, as in every other case of literary enterprise, the permanent expenses are diminished as the circulation of a work is increased. The expenses that told as £75 upon a sale of 3,000; and so, when a sale of 12,000 is reached, they will only tell as £6.5s per 1,000 and the costs of 1,000 stamps and paper being about £18, the returns from the sales exactly meet expenses. But then comes the great item of advertisements. One hundred advertisements a-day will give a profit of £8,000 per year, 200 of £16,000, 300 of £24,000, and so on. This is the golden dream which some newspapers have realised; but, for all new experiments, there is the frightful certainty of very considerable if not enormous loss before any material sale can be established, and consequently, before advertisements can be obtained.

The advertising profits of the *Morning Chronicle* rose from £4,300 in 1800 to £12,400 in 1819, while Daniel Stuart estimated the profits of his *Courier* for 1806 as being about £8,000, and put those of the *Morning Post* over the previous four years at around £35,000. No paper, however, could approach *The Times* as an advertising medium. By 1838, it was paying £11,238.3s.0d duty, which at the current rate of 1s.6d per insertion means it carried 149,842 advertisements – about 10 per cent of all the newspaper advertisements appearing in Britain that year. The average number of advertisements per issue of *The Times* was approximately 480. In comparison, its nearest rival, the *Morning Chronicle*, paid £4,619.0s.6d, equivalent to 61,590 advertisements and an average of 197 per issue.

Although certain papers became extremely profitable as a result of the advertising they attracted, investment in newspaper publishing also involved a high degree of risk, probably because many ventures had insufficient capital to tide them over the initial period of 'very considerable if not enormous loss' to which Knight refers. The failure of the *True Briton* was said to have cost Lord Kenyon £7,000; the owner of the *Representative* lost £15,000; the collapse of the

Morning Journal in 1831 left its two proprietors bankrupt; and Knight mentions 'the common report that a celebrated bookseller lost £20,000 in a very short time by a speculation of this nature'. In London, smaller local papers appeared and vanished again with such rapidity that a writer in 1824 could only put their number as being between 50 and 60.

The economics of publishing a country paper were quite different from those of the London press, the following costing based on 1,000 copies being given by Charles Knight:[13]

Editing	£ 4. 0. 0	
Composition	8. 0. 0	
Office expenses (including interest on capital)	6. 0. 0	
'Permanent expenses'	£18. 0. 0	£18. 0. 0
Paper and printing	4. 10. 0	
Stamps	13. 7. 0	
	17. 17. 0	17. 17. 0
Cost of producing 1,000 copies		35. 17. 0
Income from sales of 1,000 copies		22. 18. 0
Loss		£12. 18. 8

Assuming this level of costs, Knight estimated the break-even point without advertisements would have been about 3,500 copies sold. On the other hand, on a sale of 1,000, a newspaper would probably have needed to carry at least 60 advertisements to cover its operating deficit. If further proof were needed of the precarious nature of country newspaper publishing, the return of duty for 1849 shows that 238 newspapers carried between them 804,268 advertisements. This is an average of under 65 per issue (compared with Knight's break-even point of 60) and assuming a rate of 5/- per insertion, would produce an average weekly income from advertising of only about £16.

It is therefore scarcely surprising that many country newspapers were controlled by printers, (Mitchell's *Newspaper Press Directory* of 1846, which lists the occupations of the proprietors, shows that some 107 local newspapers out of more than 230 were under the control of the printing and allied trades). While a small circulation paper might not generate sufficient revenue to exist as an independent enterprise, it could furnish a useful source of additional income for a jobbing printer, with overheads carried by the printing business as a whole rather than by the newspaper alone, though it must be doubted whether even the most economically produced paper could make a profit without some measure of advertising support.

As well as being important in terms of revenue, advertisements had a second value to the publisher in that they helped to boost a paper's circulation. According to Daniel Stuart:

> Numerous and various advertisements attract numerous and various readers, looking out for employment, servants, sales, and purchases, &c &c. Advertisements act and re-act. They attract readers, promote circulation, and circulation attracts advertisements.[14]

Advertising space in newspapers was bought by the line, with an advertisement of average length in the London papers costing 6s.0d. before 1833, and 5s.0d. after this when the duty was reduced. In addition, there were extra charges for particular categories and special positions, which varied from paper to paper.

Sometimes advertisements were apparently booked on a barter basis. In 1825, William Hone sent out to provincial newspaper proprietors a printed advertisement for his *Every-Day Book*. The recipients were invited to insert it in their columns on the understanding that payment would consist of 100 copies of the *Every-Day Book* number one for the first insertion, and 100 of either number one or number two for the second. It is not known how many proprietors availed themselves of this offer.

The duty certainly seems to have helped keep British rates far higher than those in continental Europe or North America. In 1829, the cost of a ten-line advertisement in a London paper was about 1s.0d. per line, whereas in New York the charge was only 3d per line, with a discount for repeat insertions. Two years later, *L'Office-Correspondence* of Paris issued its *Tarif*, showing rates in papers as far afield as Vienna and St Petersburg. The charge for French papers is generally 30 centimes per line, for those in other continental countries 50 to 60 centimes per line, and for those in London 1 franc 60 centimes a line, with a minimum charge of 10 francs per order.

Before leaving the question of newspaper rates, it is worth emphasising that they were related solely to the length and characteristics of the individual advertisement. Most stamped newspapers charged roughly the same regardless of how many copies were sold, and though, as Daniel Stuart observed, circulation attracted advertisers, it was not until later in the century that proprietors began to gear their rates to the number of people likely to see an advertisement as well as to the space it occupied.

There can be no doubt that the stamp duty held down sales of newspapers. In the twenty-one years preceding the reduction of the rate to 1d, the total number of stamps issued rose by 20 per cent. In the fifteen years following, the increase was 300 per cent. Just how this affected advertisers is not clear, since the value of newspapers as an advertising medium depends not only on the circulation but also on the number of people reading each copy. It is apparent from the evidence available that the average number of readers per single copy of a paper must have been far higher than is the case today. So few people could afford a newspaper to themselves, especially between 1815 and 1836 when the stamp duty was at its highest, that a number of methods were evolved to enable would-be readers to share the cost. One of the most common, described by *Fraser's Magazine*, was for a group to club together, sharing the cost of the purchase:

> It was only by clubbing together little subscriptions, and transferring an occasional journal from hand to hand, and from post-office to post-office, till its news became a tradition before it reached final destination, that the artisans in towns and the bulk of the rural population, were able to obtain the luxury of having a newspaper all to themselves in their own chimney corner.[15]

The second method in general use was to pass papers from one reader to another, with each succeeding member of the chain paying slightly less. W. H. Smith, in evidence to the Select Committee on Newspaper Stamps, described this as happening particularly in the case of *The Times*, with the paper eventually changing hands at 2d or even 1d, and reaching its final reader on the second morning after publication.

It was always possible to buy used copies of newspapers at a reduced rate without belonging to a chain. Some readers simply resold them, and according to the *St James Chronicle*, as many as nine out of every ten copies of *The Times* were passed on by their original purchaser. A would-be reader might advertise in the paper of his choice for someone to pass copies on to him, in the manner of the following announcement in *The Times* on 18 January 1825: '*The Times* wanted, to be posted same day as published. Apply stating lowest cash price to Mr Lawrence, Post-office, Market Rasen, Lincs.' Reading-rooms and coffee-houses also often sold their old copies of newspapers as the new copies arrived. Charles Lamb, for instance, contracted to buy *The Times* from William Hone's Coffee House the day after publication. Even after the reduction in the stamp duty in 1836, reselling seems to have continued on a large scale, as is indicated by the following advertisement in the *Morning Chronicle* on 24 November 1843:

> NEWSPAPERS at LESS than HALF PRICE
>
> *N. Serjeant*, Newspaper Agent, 2 Bell-Yard, Temple Bar, begs to inform town and country gentlemen, they can have *The Times*, *Herald*, *Chronicle*, *Sun*, *Globe* or *Standard* served in town, or sent into the country by the morning mails, the morning after publication, at 14s per quarter, cash in advance, or 15s.6d on credit. *The Times*, *Chronicle*, or *Post* on the day of publication, cash in advance, 23s per quarter, or on credit, 25s. The morning papers sent by the morning mails at £1.12s.6d. NB all letters, to be prepaid.

A fourth method of obtaining newspapers cheaply was through hiring, even though this had been made illegal as early as 1789. In that year, the Secretary to the Treasury stated that a single copy of a newspaper would be hired out to as many as twenty or thirty readers before being sent to the country at a reduced rate, while *The Times* complained that papers which had been hired out were included among 'returns'.

Charles Barker was another early entrant to the advertising agency field. (By courtesy of Charles Barker ABH International Ltd)

Two photographs by John Thompson from *Street Life in London* (1875), one showing the depths to which the sandwichman had sunk at that time. The other shows a pair of billposters at work.

WORLD-WIDE
Circulation
VINTAGE
RESTORER
WILLIAM

PERSPECTIVE VIEW *of the* COFFEE MART *and* SUGAR WAREHOUSES,
& COLONIAL COFFEE HOUSE *and* SUBSCRIPTION ROOMS,
Skinner Street, Snowhill
LONDON.

Colonial
COFFEE-HOUSE,
No. 1,
SKINNER STREET, LONDON,
ADJOINING THE COFFEE MART,
Opened this Day,

HANDSOMELY FITTED UP,

For the accommodation of the Public, and also in the view of promoting the welfare of the British Coffee and Sugar Plantations

---

COFFEE, &c. for Breakfast, &c. 1s. each.
SINGLE CUP, &c. - - - 6d. each.

Morning and Evening Papers will be provided.

A Subscription Room, **on the First Floor, is fitted up in an elegant Style, with private Entrance, for the use and amusement of Ladies and Gentlemen, and will be opened in a few Days, liberally supplied with Magazines, Reviews, Gazette, Morning and Evening Papers, Lloyd's List, Price Current, Shipping Intelligence foreign and domestic, *&c.*—Subscribers to be allowed to take Coffee in this Room.—A sitting Room for the use of Ladies (Subscribers) exclusively.**

Tablets, in gilt Frames, descriptive of the various Professions in the Fine Arts, Trades, Manufactures, &c. may be put up in the Coffee Room and Subscription Room. Also Bills of Sales by Auctioneers, *&c. &c.*

*** As it is intended the number of Subscribers shall be limited, and as select as possible; it is requested that Ladies and Gentlemen who may feel disposed to support this superior Establishment, will leave their Address with Mrs. Allen, at the Bar of the Colonial Coffee-House, who will in due time transmit to them the Rules, &c. to be observed regarding the Subscription Room.

***February* 1, 1812.**

W. Wilson, Printer, 4, Greville-Street, Hatton-Garden, London.

Samuel Deacon's business as an advertising agent grew out of his coffee house, the opening of which is announced on this bill. (By courtesy of Mr Richard Deacon and the Guildhall Museum)

The practice seems to have continued unchecked, however, since according to 'An Old Printer', writing in 1898:

> It was customary for news-vendors to lend the morning papers for an hour each day for from sixpence to a shilling per week, and to solicit orders from provincial customers to whom these same papers would be dispatched by the evening post, the usual charge being twenty-four shillings per quarter.[16]

A man who did not wish to hire a paper to read in his own home might subscribe to a reading-room. According to the *Edinburgh Review* in 1829:

> Every large, and indeed almost every small town in England, and several in Ireland, have now subscription reading-rooms, at which all the leading London papers are taken, so that no person who can afford to pay a guinea or so, annually, needs be without the means of gratifying his curiosity, or desire, for improvement.

In 1833 the Manchester Coffee and Newsroom, which carried ninety-six newspapers every week, including some unstamped, together with the *Edinburgh* and *Westminster Reviews* and several monthly magazines, charged one penny for reading, while coffee cost another twopence. There were also a number of other reading-rooms in Manchester, notably the Exchange which offered 130 papers on weekdays, and 186 on Saturdays, including the leading foreign journals.

Another method of obtaining a newspaper to read was to borrow it. At one end of the social scale, country-house guests seem to have had them provided as a matter of course. According to Prince Pückler-Muskau, '. . . that half a dozen newspapers must lie on the table for every one to read who likes is, of course, understood'. Among the working classes, borrowing was possible in coffee-shops and public houses. The *Westminster Review* in 1829 attributed the growth of newspaper readership to 'the establishment of little coffee-houses or shops in which most daily papers are taken', noting that 'no man who can read (and how few there are of those who go to coffee shops who cannot read), thinks of calling for his cup of coffee without at the same time asking for a newspaper'. According to 'An Old Printer', a similar situation existed in public houses:

> If a person of humble means desired to become acquainted with what was going on around him, he would have to go to a public house and borrow *The Morning Advertiser* for five minutes. A placard was generally hung up in the bar requesting gentlemen not to monopolise the current day's paper for more than that time. *The Weekly Dispatch* (price sixpence) was also a publican's newspaper, and this used to be borrowed by regular outside customers.

It is clear that each individual copy of a newspaper attracted a considerable number of readers. Contemporaries varied widely, however, when they came to make more precise estimates. The Secretary of the Treasury's view in 1789, already mentioned, was that twenty or thirty people read a single copy in London, the paper then being sent to the country. The *Westminster Review* similarly reckoned 'that every newspaper is read by thirty persons, a very fair calculation considering how great a proportion of newspapers goes into reading rooms and coffee-rooms, and other public places' but it mentions for the Manchester press a rather higher figure of between fifty and eighty, adding, 'This is more than we should be disposed to credit from calculations generally adopted; but as it has been communicated by persons likely to be well acquainted with the fact, it is but fair to state it.'[17]

These estimates refer to weekly papers. With regard to the daily press, W. H. Smith stated in evidence to the Select Committee on Newspaper Stamps: 'I have no doubt that every daily paper in London is read by three or four distinct persons.'

The press was clearly of tremendous importance as an advertising medium. It is impossible to say with any accuracy, however, what proportion of the population was reached, and with what degree of frequency. To begin with circulation figures, the inaccuracy of the stamp returns has already been noted. In addition, there were a number of influential and widely read unstamped journals such as *Punch*, and in the 1820s and 1830s a considerable volume of unstamped papers, for both of which categories no figures are available at all. There are further problems in relating stamp returns to the number of issues of a paper per year. This would have to be calculated separately for every title since, while most were weeklies, there were also dailies, twice dailies, twice weeklies, thrice weeklies, fortnightlies, quarterlies and some listed simply as occasional. As regards the number of readers per copy, we have seen the difficulties involved in arriving at a satisfactory estimate. In addition, we do not know what proportion of those readers were regular, and how many might by chance see the very occasional copy. Lastly, there is no evidence at all as to the degree of readership duplication – i.e. the extent to which the average reader saw more than one title. Even supposing, therefore, that it were possible to calculate the number of readers in gross terms in an average week, to attempt to express this as a proportion of the total population would be meaningless since if, for example, each reader were to see two different titles, this would reduce the coverage by 50 per cent.

The first half of the nineteenth century provides the first two known instances of research into the effectiveness of advertising media. Their importance lies not so much in the methods involved as in the fact that questions of this kind were being asked at all. In the first case, the merits of three different publications were assessed in terms of the number of replies received when advertising a harp – good in principle, but scarcely meaningful for the business advertiser.[18] In the second, a writer in the *Quarterly Review* tried to measure the kind of impact to be gained from an advertisement in *The Times*. Taking the depth of the insertion (one inch), he multiplied it by the number of copies sold (170,000) to arrive at a figure of 2¾ miles, exclaiming in triumph, 'Thus we have at a glance the real amount of publicity which is procurable in a great journal.'[19]

2 Posters

The poster was the second advertising medium throughout the nineteenth century and well into the twentieth. Before 1855, there were three main reasons for its popularity. Firstly, it was not subject to the advertisement duty. As Crawfurd observed, 'In short, "Bill-sticking" has become a regular profession in every considerable town in the kingdom, under the patronage of the stamp-duty, which in its liberality allows of the publication of a single advertisement on a single scrap of paper without taxation.' As a result, newspapers lost advertising revenue and the walls of Britain's towns and cities became increasingly defaced.

The second reason derives from the policies pursued by newspaper publishers. Advertisements were confined between column rules, crowded together, and were not allowed to include illustrations. The poster, in freeing the advertiser from such constraints, offered him enormous creative scope.

Thirdly, the poster provided a means of disseminating information with remarkable rapidity. As early as 1808 a writer observed that 'within six hours, by means of printed bills, the inhabitants of a great city can be advertised of a thousand things necessary to be publicly known; and in cases of fugitive robbers, traitors, spies, etc., the hue and cry, or notice of their apprehension, is circulated throughout the kingdom in four or five days.'[20]

Although the full potential of the poster was not to be exploited until the second half of the century, the demands made by advertisers were already leading to technical advances in poster printing. Large displays could be assembled from separately-printed sheets posted edge-to-edge, up to thirty-six sheet size, but this meant that the type needed for headlines was far bigger than anything printers normally used. Large letters were therefore cut individually by hand by skilled craftsmen, using a close-grained wood such as apple or pine. The same men also produced the 'pictorial embellishments' which gradually began to appear on posters at this period.

The *bonhommie* which originally existed in the poster trade was shattered, according to Dickens' 'King of the Billstickers', by the abolition of the National Lottery in 1826. Previously, there was no over-sticking of anyone else's bill. Now it became normal practice as may be seen from contemporary illustrations of street scenes. Fighting broke out among bill-stickers, as freelance vied with freelance, and as together they fought off early efforts to organise poster companies with exclusive rights to certain hoardings such as those in Trafalgar Square. When Livesey, proprietor of the *Moral Reformer* magazine, went to Chester in 1830, he found that bills for the latest issue of his publication had been covered by others advertising lectures on astronomy and astrology. As he noted, 'It appeared probable that it arose out of the rival feeling of the different men who post bills in that city.' The result of such competition must surely have been to reduce the effectiveness of the poster as an advertising medium.

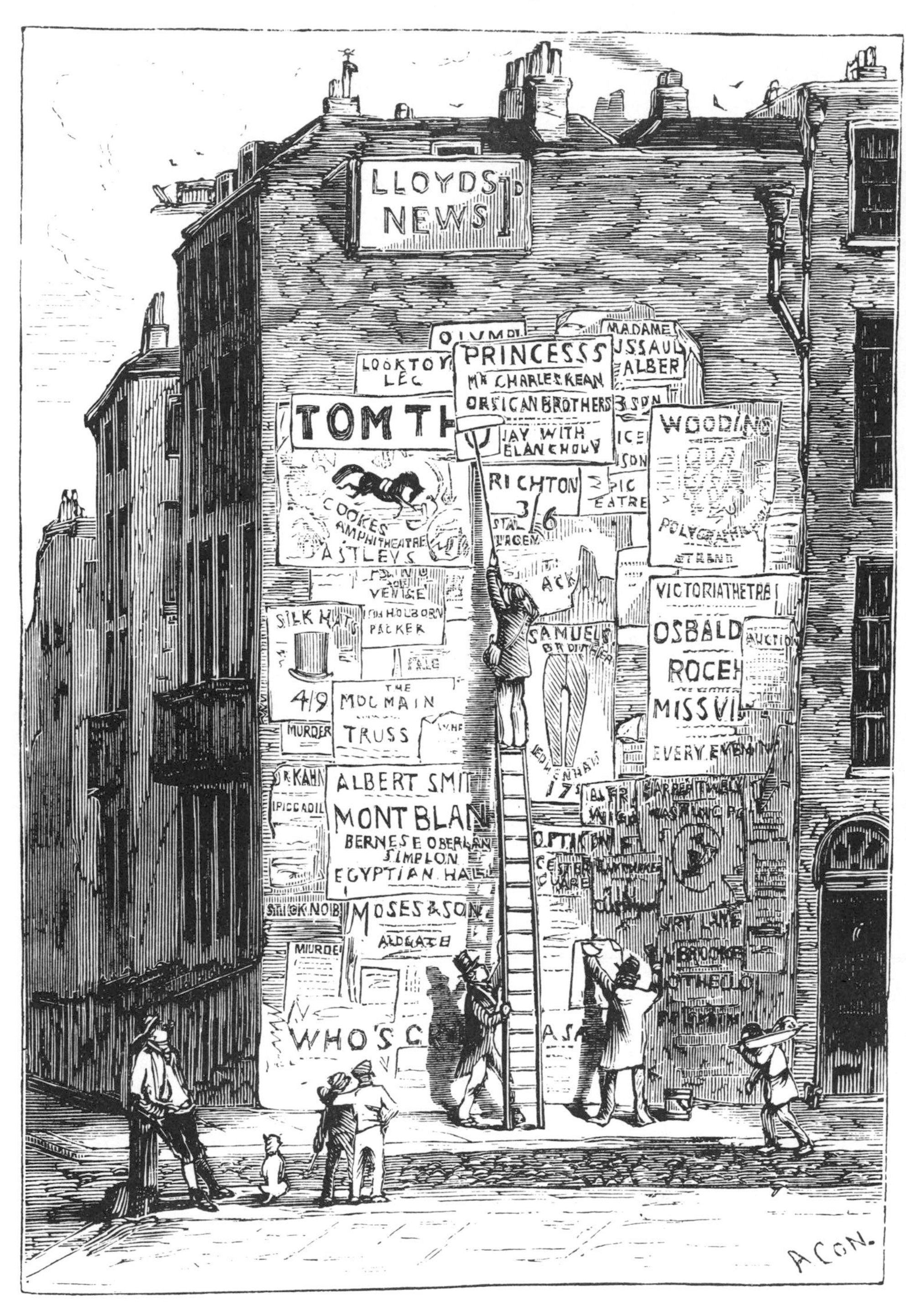

An Old Bill Station, from Henry Sampson's *History of Advertising* (1874)

A further aspect of the rivalry between bill-stickers was the way they made themselves a public nuisance, bringing the trade into disrepute by their excessive zeal in seeking out sites. *Tait's Magazine* observed in 1834:

> If a house by any chance becomes tenantless, on a given day, the next shall see its walls covered to the very chimney tops with posting bills, not a square foot unprofaned by paste. How they become possessed of the knowledge, no one may divine, excepting it be by intuitive perception.

There was, however, a lighter side to bill-posting, as when the trade became the subject of a popular song, quoted by Henry Sampson:

> I'm Sammy Slap the billsticker, and you must all agree, Sirs,
> I sticks to business like a trump while business sticks to me, Sirs,
> There's some folks call me plasterer, but they deserve a banging,
> 'Cause yer see, genteelly speaking, that my trade is paper hanging.
>
> With my paste, paste, paste!
> All the world is puffing,
> So I'll paste, paste, paste.

Posters at this time were mainly printed notices, though illustrations were by no means unknown. Woodcuts were used for emblematic and heraldic devices, and in some instances to portray a striking scene of some theatrical event or exhibition, with the illustration taking up virtually the whole area. They were used by a wide range of advertisers, as is clear from the collection at the William Salt Library, Stafford. To some extent, the material is similar to that to be found in the columns of local newspapers: advertisements for inns and local tradesmen; official announcements about elections; details of entertainments such as balls, concerts, and ploughing matches; appeals for funds to help the working classes celebrate the wedding of Queen Victoria; and collections for the wounded of the battle of Alma. It is clear, however, that posters were also used in cases where advertisements would probably have been refused by the local press – for example, a defence of the Roman Catholic church and attack on Guy Fawkes night, and various notices concerned with trade union activities.

Some advertisers were using illuminated signs lit by lanterns, and later by gas. An instance is mentioned by Mayhew who was told by an informant: I had a transparency done and stretched on a big frame and lit up by gas, on which was written –

MAY THE
DESTROYER OF PEACE
BE DESTROYED BY US
TIFFIN AND SON
BUG-DESTROYERS TO HER MAJESTY.

We have very little information about the effectiveness of posters, apart from the 'King of Billsticker's' assertion that some 150 stickers were working in London (in 1851) and that they could post an average of one hundred bills per day. This would mean that in a week they could post $150 \times 100 \times 6 = 90{,}000$ bills. With a London population of about 2.3 million, this is equivalent to one bill for every twenty-five people per week.

It seems unlikely that such a high ratio was achieved elsewhere, except perhaps in a few densely populated urban areas. Even in London, we have no idea of how long a bill was likely to be on view to the public before another was plastered over it, though it is worth bearing in mind that it was the custom of the trade never to cover another bill while it was still wet. In short, it is probable that poster advertising was widely used but extremely inefficient.

By way of variation, and presumably for reasons of cost, some advertisers still used the time-honoured method of writing directly on to walls. This was true in the early years of the nineteenth century, especially in the case of publishers, quack-doctors and blacking manufacturers, who were among the first national advertisers of consumer goods. According to the *London Magazine* in 1825:

> Colburn and Warren surprise you with the variety, brilliancy and country-circulation of their advertisements. The former of the two has not yet, I believe, like the other, had his name whitewashed in letters twice as long as his Magazine upon the walls of the Metropolis and the Park-palings of the country. This is, however, a popular and striking mode of advertising . . . more extensively patronised by gentlemen in the blacking and medical line.

Macaulay, too, referred acidly to 'all the wall-chalkers of Day and Martin', another firm selling blacking.

It would appear that this method of advertising must have been practised on a scale sufficient to constitute a nuisance, since provisions aimed at curbing it are included in the Metropolitan Police Act of 1839.

3 Mobile Displays

The desire to escape the advertisement duty, together with the increased competition faced in poster advertising, seemed to point to the solution of carrying messages around the streets. Prince Pückler-Muskau gives a graphic description of how this technique was employed in London in the 1820s.

> Formerly people were content to paste them up; now they are ambulant. One man had a pasteboard hat, three times as high as other hats, on which is written in great letters, 'Boots at twelve shillings a pair – warranted'. Another carried a sort of banner on which is represented a washerwoman and the inscription, 'Only three-pence a shirt'.

The impression made by these boards and banners must have depended in large measure upon the appearance of the men carrying them. While a sketch by George Scharf shows a group in the 1820s quite smartly attired in fancy costumes, Mayhew indicates that such work was the last resort of men fallen on hard times. A bankrupt draper told him, 'I have tried to get work at carrying placard boards, but I can't. My clothes are now too bad for me to do anything else.' Photographs and caricatures from about the middle of the century also tend to depict the sandwich-man as shabby and down-at-heel, which can hardly have helped to enhance the appeal of the advertiser's product.

A further means of transporting an advertising display around the streets was to have it drawn by horses. Prince Pückler-Muskau describes how 'Chests like Noah's Ark, entirely pasted over with bills, of the dimensions of a small house, drawn by men and horses, slowly parade the streets, and carry more lies upon them than Münchausen ever invented.' Probably the most sophisticated version is to be found in a patent filed in 1824 by George Samuel Harris of Caroline Place, Knightsbridge. The application refers to:

> A Machine for the Purpose of giving the most Effective and Extensive Publicity by Day and Night, to all Proclamations, Notices, Legal Advertisements, and other Purposes to which the same may be applicable, destined for Universal Information, and which will henceforward render unnecessary the Defacement of Walls, and Houses in the Metropolis and its Vicinities by Bill-Sticking, Placarding, and Chalking, which latter Practices have become a Great and Offensive Public Nuisance.

Harris described his advertising machine as follows:

> My invention consists in the use and application of a machine or lantern of cylindrical, octagonal, or any other convenient shape, and of suitable size, composed of slight framings of wood, or other material arranged in such a manner as to form a number of openings or pannels [sic] adapted to receive the bills or notices which are desired to be proclaimed or advertised. The said machine I denominate 'The Royal Patent Ambulatory Advertiser'. It is intended to be mounted upon a carriage of any convenient description . . .
>
> I construct the said machines or lanterns of such magnitude as to render the bills, notices or advertisements legible to a considerable distance during the day time; and in foggy or dark weather, or when notices are desired to be exhibited at night, I place lamps or lights of any convenient description within the machine or lantern in such a manner as to render the bills, notices or advertisements legible in the manner of transparencies, the said bills or notices being written, printed, or otherwise rendered visible upon paper or other sufficiently transparent material, and afterwards oiled or varnished for the purpose of rendering them more transparent, and to protect them from the effects of the weather.[21]

There were two main drawbacks to the use of carts for advertising. Firstly, the advertiser's innate tendency to make everything as big as possible meant that the messages carried by the carts became increasingly difficult to read. According to *Punch*, 'They are now on so gigantic a scale, that no ordinary vision can take in more than half a letter at a time – and thus the perambulating van must fall into the rear by the excess to which it has been carried.' Secondly, the carts also aroused considerable public antagonism, causing congestion in the street, and becoming a source of danger to pedestrians. As *Punch* complained, 'Go where you will, you are stopped by a monster cart running over with advertisements, or

Drawing from George Harris's patent application of 1824.
(By courtesy of the Patent Office)

are nearly knocked down by an advertising house put upon wheels, which calls upon you, when too late, not to forget "Number One".'

There was also an irate reaction from *Times* readers, such as *Civis*, writing in April 1846:

> It really seems that the proper authorities to abate any nuisance in the city are in a state of torpor, or they would bestir themselves and prevent the entire destruction of

> the retail trade which is taking place through the walking placards and advertising vans being allowed to perambulate through the great thoroughfares. At this moment, half-past 12 o'clock, the bottom of Cheapside is nearly choked in consequence of the snail pace of one of these nuisances – a van – with a large globe on the top, and a man blowing a trumpet sitting beside the driver. Surely, sir, something ought to be done to remedy so crying an evil; but I feel quite convinced that nothing will until you give your powerful aid as the great reformer of every abuse . . .

Eventually the outcry against advertising carts was such that they were effectively suppressed by the London Hackney Carriage Act of 1853; and by 1874, Henry Sampson could write that, 'The huge vans, plastered all over with bills, which used to traverse London, to the terror of horses and the wonder of yokels, were improved off the face of the earth a quarter of a century ago.'

To some extent they had already been superseded, since by the 1840s advertisers were displaying their messages on the sides of omnibuses. Here again, however, the public reaction seems to have been unfavourable, due to the way the omnibus proprietors put the interests of the advertisers before those of their passengers. *Punch* launched a vigorous attack:

> Not content with the ordinary vans, the Advertisers have commenced plastering the omnibuses with their placards. It is too bad that the windows of these vehicles should be obstructed during the hot weather with the announcements that put a stop to wholesome ventilation. Is there no other way of raising the wind than by preventing the free passage of air, and must a cheap tradesman's outrageous puff keep off anything in the shape of a pleasant blow from the riders in the omnibus?

In 1847, an even worse prospect loomed when it was proposed to allow advertisements also to appear inside omnibuses. *Punch* was outraged:

> How will you like sitting for an hour opposite to a pleasant list of wonderful cures by some Professor's Ointment? or how will ladies like being stared in the face all the way from Brentford to the Bank with an elaborate detail of all the diseases which Old Methuselah's Pill professes a specific for? . . . We say most emphatically to the gentlemen who have announced their advertising omnibuses – 'We prefer your room to your company'.

The problem of advertisements obstructing light and ventilation seems to have been a very real one, and was tackled by Section 15 of the London Hackney Carriage Act of 1853. From an advertising point of view, those inside seem often to have been singularly ineffective, to judge from another comment by *Punch*: 'We have advertisements in omnibuses, placed in such a position, that unless you can turn your eyes upside-down, or sit upon your own head, there is no possibility of reading them'.

4 Other media

A widely used form of advertising was the handbill, which seems to have evolved from the earlier tradesman's card. Bills were handed out to passers-by in the street, either by sandwich-men, or by some specialist in the art. William Weir, writing in Charles Knight's *London* (1843), was told by one bill distributor: 'Any man can stick a bill upon a wall, but to insinuate one gracefully and irresistibly into the hands of a lady or gentleman, is only for one who, to natural genius, adds long experience.'

Bills could also be delivered direct to people's houses. This method of operation was already well established by the 1820s as is apparent from the *Royal Blue Book*, a detailed guide which lists the occupant of every house, street by street; the 'nobility and gentry' with their town and country residences; and the principal types of business. According to an announcement in the 1829 edition:

> Many ladies and gentlemen who have been engaged in visiting and canvassing in the Western part of the Town, have found considerable inconvenience, and their progress much retarded for want of correct information, with regard to the Houses in Squares and long Streets; so to obviate, in some measure, this difficulty and to offer a suitable Guide, was the inducement to commence this Publication, and has been a considerable object during its progress; hoping it will prove useful not only to persons so engaged, but also in delivering Cards, Letters etc.

This kind of activity was apparently a last resort in terms of employment. A ruined grocer told Mayhew, 'I had a few days work at bill delivery – that is, grocers' circulars. I was at last so reduced that I couldn't pay for my lodging.'

The potential offered by the penny post was quickly grasped, the volume of advertising material carried being sufficient to produce this complaint, again from *Punch*: 'We are haunted with advertisements enough in all shapes, tricks, and disguises. The Penny Post has increased the distribution of them most prolifically. Half our *billets-doux* end with an eloquent appeal to run to some cheap grocer's and buy a pound of his best Hyson.'

Another new medium which became available towards the middle of the century was railway advertising in the form of notices placed in second- and third-class carriages, in station buildings, and on platforms. The possibilities here were enormous, the total number of passenger journeys made in 1850 reaching some 73 millions. But while a few contractors, notably W. H. Smith, were buying concessions from railway companies and renting out the sites to advertisers, the full potential was not to be recognised for some years, and at least one speculating contractor was ruined when he could not dispose of the sites which he had acquired.

From an early date, advertisers were obviously aware of the value of the publicity stunt. Prince Pückler-Muskau describes an early and highly successful example:

> The notorious Hunt deals in shoe-blacking; a large sort of wagon filled with it and drawn by four fine horses, which the young gentleman his son drives 'four-in-hand', daily traverses the city in all directions. The young Hunt betted a hundred pounds that he would drive the equipage in question at full speed across the 'Serpentine', and won his wager in brilliant style. A caricature immortalised this feat, and the sale of his blacking, as is reasonable, increased threefold.

As many parts of the country were still without a local newspaper, the bellman or crier was still being used for advertising items of local interest. According to an article in the *Leisure Hour*:

> Among ourselves, the most ancient medium of advertising now extant is, without doubt, the town crier . . . though he has long vanished from London, driven away by the arts of the bill-sticker and the cheap printer, yet he survives in country places; and in those smaller places where the printer has not condescended to settle, he is still not only the medium but the monarch of publicity . . . Notwithstanding he is such a piece of antiquity, it is like that he will survive many novelties as yet unborn, because he adapts himself to the exigencies of the moment, and does what is to be done on the instant . . .

The evolution of the advertising agent

One result of the increasing scale of production, as we have seen, was that manufacturers needed to advertise over wider areas of the country. This meant that for each town where his goods would be sold, a prospective advertiser needed to know the newspapers which were published and their respective circulations. Assuming he could obtain this information, he would then have to negotiate with them regarding price, position and dates of insertions, and often pay cash in advance. While papers were quite understandably unwilling to extend credit to advertisers whose bona fides they had no means of checking, it meant that the advertiser was taking the paper on trust, assuming that everything would appear as agreed, and indeed that the publisher would still be in business when the due dates arrived. What the advertiser needed, therefore, was someone who could keep track of the rapid changes taking place in the newspaper world, advise on the suitability of a particular journal, write the copy if required, simplify accounting procedures, and ease cash flow problems by granting credit. These were the services offered by the early agents; and as newspapers began granting them commission, advertisers were able to benefit in effect free of charge.

At the same time, the London agent met a commercial need on the part of the provincial press. He channelled London advertising to the country papers, taking upon himself the responsibility for payment. He facilitated the exchange of information between newspapers which otherwise would have had virtually no contact with each other. He sent them copies of the London papers which were their main source of news. And he often kept them supplied with stamped paper, all stamping prior to 1831 being carried out at Somerset House.

Although the early agents normally allowed their clients one month's credit, they did not necessarily have substantial financial backing. They themselves usually had quarterly accounts – often overdue – with newspapers, so they would have expected to be paid by their clients well before their own quarterly payments became due.

The earliest agent of whom any record remains is William Tayler, who in

1786 described himself, in an advertisement he took in the first issue of the *Maidstone Journal*, as 'Agent to the Country Printers, Booksellers &c.' He also offered to supply accounts of parliamentary proceedings, proclamations and royal speeches, as well as prices current, Lloyd's List, and various foreign gazettes. In 1790, Dr Trusler's *London Adviser and Guide* noted that advertisements for country papers could be sent through Tayler, who charged a handling-fee of sixpence or one shilling plus the cost of the letter. He seems to have concerned himself almost exclusively with country newspapers, dealing apparently with only one London evening paper and no mornings at all. It is interesting to note the way he supplied both advertising and news, for as will be seen, Charles Barker's agency evolved in similar fashion some thirty years later.

Although Tayler is the first recognisable advertising agent, newspapers at this time were taking advertisements from a variety of intermediaries. Newsagents accepted them on behalf of the papers they sold (as is still the case in some country areas today) and tradesmen of various kinds handled advertising in addition to their normal business. The *Derbyshire Mercury* paid commission to a printer in Nottingham and, apparently, to the local innkeeper and undertaker in Ashbourne. *Felix Farley's Journal* in Bristol accepted advertisements placed through the London firm of Thompson and Co., described in the *Post Office Directory* as 'stock and share brokers and general agents'. *Baldwin's London Weekly Journal and Surrey and Sussex Gazette* announced that advertising could be submitted through the Clerks of the Roads in London, and many country papers informed their readers that advertisements could be handed in at the leading London coffee-houses.

One of the most important figures on the advertising scene at the beginning of the nineteenth century came from the unlikely background of the counting-house at Christ's Hospital School. James White, friend of Charles Lamb, and mentioned in the *Essays of Elia*, founded an agency in 1800 which has continued in business until the present day, though its name has changed several times over the years. Tradition has it that Jem White was called upon to place occasional advertisements for the school, and was thus drawn into the world of newspapers and advertising which had long centred upon the taverns and coffee-houses in and around Fleet Street. Before long, White found himself also handling advertisements for other people, and for a time acted as agent while still retaining his post in the counting-house – a feat by no means impossible since his own house, from which he operated the agency, was next door to the school. Eventually, however, his advertising activities became so lucrative that he decided to devote himself to them full time. Quite apart from the contacts he made in the coffee-houses, White would not have been short of influential connections in the newspaper world. As well as being married to a New Bond Street bookseller's daughter, he was a frequent guest at suppers given by Charles and Mary Lamb, which were attended by many of the best known literary and newspaper figures of the time.

Jem White provides an early indication that agents were actually involved in the writing of advertisements, as distinct from just passing on to various papers copies of something written by the advertiser. White himself was an author of some little note, his *Falstaff Letters* having been highly praised by Charles Lamb, and it is hard to believe that he would not have used this talent to advantage in his business. He also apparently used Lamb himself as a copywriter, since Mary Lamb wrote to Sarah Hazlitt in 1809: '. . . White has prevailed upon him to write some more lottery puffs'. The agency still has a copy of a similar item which it placed in *Bell's Weekly Messenger* three years earlier and which is reputed to be Lamb's work, although there is no direct evidence of any connection.

> A SEASONABLE HINT. – Christmas gifts of innumerable descriptions will now pervade this whole kingdom. It is submitted whether any present is capable of being attended with so much good to a dutiful son, an amiable daughter, an industrious apprentice, or a faithful servant, as that of a SHARE of a LOTTERY TICKET, in a scheme in which the smallest share may gain near two thousand pounds?

Another intriguing hint comes in a mention in the *London Magazine* in February 1825 of a 'certain prose writer of the present day' having been commissioned to write lottery puffs, but having his work returned as too modest.

A single ledger from this period survives, giving details of White's transactions with country newspapers, and turnover here alone was in excess of £10,000 per annum. Tradition has it that another ledger was kept for London papers. If this were so, and if advertising placed by White's followed the same pattern as national expenditure, this would put the agency's total turnover from newspaper advertising at around £18,000 per annum. This figure would have been supplemented by income from the supply of stamped paper and possibly of newsletters, the offering of a confidential reply service, the sale of newspapers, the sending out of review copies for authors and publishers and, within a few years, printing and engraving. What little we know about Jem White's private life supports this impression of prosperity. He was one of three bondsmen in the sum of £500 for Charles Lamb at the East India House, and was able to commission miniatures of himself and his wife from Sir William Newton, later court miniature painter to William IV.

For two years after his death in 1820, the agency was run by his widow. She remarried in 1822, the business then trading under the name of her second husband, Richard Barker. William Tayler, meanwhile, had taken Mr Newton into partnership, and by the 1820s, the firm had become known as Newton and Company. Newtons and Richard Barker together dominated the London advertising scene at this period, as is evident from an article in the *Edinburgh Review* in 1829:

> The means of communication between the provincial papers and the metropolis, are very simple. There are two newspaper agency offices; the respectable and old established firm of Newton and Co, formerly Tayler and Newton, in Warwick-square, and that of Barker and Co. in Fleet-street. At these offices, advertisements

> are received for all the country papers without increased charge to the advertiser, the commission of the agent being paid by the newspaper proprietor, and these agents also send to the country the stamps necessary for the papers, and undertake the collection of accounts owing in London.

Although only Newtons and Barkers are mentioned, it is certain that other agents were operating by this time. Deacons, for example, grew out of the Colonial Coffee-House opened by Samuel and Thomas Deacon in Skinner Street in February 1812. They produced for the occasion an illustrated bill which provides ample evidence of the brothers' interest in advertising:

> A Subscription Room on the First Floor, is fitted up in an elegant style, with private Entrance, for the use and amusement of Ladies and Gentlemen, and will be opened in a few days, liberally supplied with Magazines, Reviews, Gazettes, Morning and Evening Papers, Lloyds List, Prices Current, Shipping Intelligence foreign and domestic &c, &c . . . Tablets, in gilt frames, descriptive of the various professions in the Fine Arts, Trades, Manufactures &c may be put up in the Coffee Room and Subscription Room. Also Bills of Sale by Auctioneers, &c &c.

The Deacons probably also accepted newspaper advertising, as was usual with coffee-houses, because people who came to read the papers found it convenient to hand in their advertisements at the same place. In 1822 the brothers moved to Walbrook, but soon afterwards parted company after a quarrel, which – so family tradition has it – arose from the loss of an important advertising client. As a result, Thomas kept the coffee-house, while Samuel took the reading-room, together with the advertising business which was growing increasingly important, and moved to Bond Court nearby.

In an advertisement in 1842, Samuel announced that he had available not only the country papers but '. . . a perfect copy of the *London Gazette* from 1665, and the daily London Newspapers for upwards of 100 years past.' In addition, 'From these sources he has collected and formed an Index of Upwards of Forty Thousand Notices to HEIRS, NEXT OF KIN, and persons entitled to property. The BANK EAST INDIA and SOUTH SEA COMPANY'S Dividend Books are also kept at the above Office.' Deacon charged a search fee of five shillings. If he found the required notice, a copy was sent to the enquirer at a further fee of between £1 and £5.

Another early entrant into the field was the firm of Lawson and Barker, known after the dissolution of the original partnership as Charles Barker (not to be confused with Richard Barker, to whom Charles was apparently unrelated). From its foundation in 1812, the firm had a very close connection with *The Times*. Lawson was in fact *The Times* printer, receiving a share in the paper of half of one-sixteenth under the terms of the will of John Walter I. The agency's office at 12 Birchin Lane was used by Alsager, *The Times*' city correspondent, and Barker was able to describe it as '. . . a branch of *The Times* where various articles are written . . .'. Lawson and Barker acted originally as a press agency, sending parliamentary and financial newsletters to country papers, and receiving reports from them on behalf of *The Times*. With a wide network of contacts, it is not surprising that the firm also became involved in advertising, and this gradually developed into its main activity. Barker worked much as might be expected, placing advertising on behalf of his clients, negotiating on rates, and giving an opinion when requested. Mr Stuckey of the Albion Hotel in Brighton wrote to him, supplying precise details of the papers he wished to use, the number of insertions in each, and the copy. The General Steam Navigation Company asked him to query the rates it was being charged by some of the national papers, and requested his opinion on whether to include the *Public Ledger* in its schedule. He also undertook the collection of overdue accounts on behalf of publishers as far afield as Dublin, Glasgow, Edinburgh and Newcastle, apparently receiving a commission of three per cent on large amounts and five per cent on smaller ones.

While agency activity naturally centred on London, the success of the early agents induced David Robertson, an Edinburgh newspaper proprietor, to set up a business on the same lines. In an advertisement in 1819 he 'begs leave to acquaint his Friends and the public, he has commenced business on the plan of Newton and Co. and J. White of London, at this Office, where he will receive ADVERTISEMENTS for every newspaper in the united kingdom.'

ADVERTISING AGENCY.

DAVID ROBERTSON, one of the Proprietors of the Edinburgh Weekly Chronicle, begs leave to acquaint his Friends and the public, he has commenced business on the plan of Newton and Co. and J. White of London, at this Office, where he will receive ADVERTISEMENTS for every newspaper in the united kingdom.

In announcing this establishment, it is unnecessary to particularise the advantages it presents to every class of advertisers. To the gentlemen of the law in this city and throughout Scotland, it will afford great facilities, *without any addition whatever to the expence*; as by one order their advertisement may be conveyed to every newspaper in the empire, and their account for the whole settled with one individual. The terms will be exactly those charged by each paper, without any commission or extra expence to the advertisers. The accounts of each will be produced at settling, and files of the respective papers regularly preserved for the satisfaction of all concerned.

EDINBURGH WEEKLY CHRONICLE OFFICE,
210. HIGH STREET, EDINBURGH.

By the 1830s and 1840s, a number of agents were producing lists of newspapers, either as posters to be pinned up in the counting-house, or – as the number of papers increased – in the form of reference books. They gave what was thought to be the information needed by the advertisers, including the day and place of publication, political stance, and in some cases the average circulation and the number of advertisements carried per copy, calculated from the latest official returns. The lists appear to contain virtually all the papers in the country, and in some cases overseas journals as well.

It is clear from the picture which emerges of the early agents and their activities that they were not, as is often asserted, agents of newspapers rather than advertisers, and did not have arrangements with certain papers only. As Charles Mitchell, a leading agent, wrote in his *Newspaper Press Directory*:

> . . . it is clear that if an advertising agent were in fact the agent of any one newspaper in particular, instead of transacting business with all, the main object of his business would be lost sight of, viz., the affording to the advertisers the opportunity of making arrangements at once for a simultaneous and universal system of advertising in ALL the provincial newspapers, or in as many of them as may be necessary or advantageous.

Mitchell went on to explain that the agent acted in advertising transactions in effect as a principal, '. . . and becomes himself responsible to the provincial proprietors for the payment, instead of their having to look to the many separate individuals or firms who send their announcements through them'. This view, although generally accepted in advertising circles, was not shared by the courts, and the legal status of the advertising agent was not settled beyond doubt until as late as 1957.

The Great Expansion 1855–1914

The Growth in Expenditure

IN 1853 THE advertisement duty was abolished, and 1855 saw the end of the newspaper stamp. The result was a tremendous expansion of the press, coinciding with a vast increase in advertising. Although there are no longer any official returns on which to base calculations of national expenditure, the indications of growth are plain. Firstly, there was an ever growing demand for advertising media, which was matched by an increase in the volume of advertising space available. In terms of the press, this meant a growth in the number of newspaper titles published, an increase in the number of pages per issue, and the development of consumer magazines, particularly those aimed at women. At the same time, there was a search for alternative methods of bringing advertising messages to the notice of the public, which produced a host of ingenious inventions of doubtful commercial value.

Secondly, more companies were advertising, and individual budgets were increasing in size. The many new inventions which appeared were made known to potential customers and had their benefits extolled by means of advertisements. The second half of the century also saw the widespread introduction of branding into the area of basic household commodities and foodstuffs, and though many manufacturers still resented the intrusion of advertising into commercial practice, it seems to have been true that in any particular product field, the first firm to begin promotion on a substantial scale would see a dramatic increase in sales which would force its competitors into employing the same weapon in retaliation.

The second half of the century saw business reservations about the respectability of advertising largely overcome, with an increasing number of firms being tempted into the field. Virginia Berridge, who has examined the changing character of advertising in the popular Sunday press, notes how in the 1870s

TRAIN YOUR MOUSTACHE
IN THE WAY IT SHOULD GO.

CARTER'S
THRIXALINE
is a unique transparent fluid for training, fixing, and beautifying the Moustache of all sorts and conditions of men. Has never been equalled for holding the Moustache in any position. *Prepared only by*
JOHN CARTER,
HAIRDRESSER,
At the Old Palace of Henry VHI.
17, FLEET STREET, E.C.
Price, post free, 2/9, 5/9, and 10/9.

CLAXTON'S
DOUBLE CHIN CURER.
Patent 19381/04.
ForIrestoring contour of face tin advancing years.
Gives an even support under chin; will fit any size or shape head.
No measurements required.

Price One Guinea, Post Free.
Please cross Cheques and Orders "Coutts & Co."

P. CLAXTON
(Patentee of Ear Cap),
108, STRAND, LONDON, W.C.

TO BE WORN THREE TIMES IN THE WEEK.

Madame A. T. ROWLEY'S
TOILET MASK
(OR FACE GLOVES)
Is a **natural beautifier** for **bleaching** and **preservin** the **skin** and **removing complexional imperfections.**
It is **soft** and **flexible** in form, and can be **WORN** witho **discomfort** or **inconvenience.**
It is recommended by eminent physicians and scientists as a substitu for injurious cosmetics.
COMPLEXION BLEMISHES may be hidden imperfectly by co metics and powders, but can only be removed permanently by the Toil Mask. By its use every kind of spots, impurities, roughness, etc., vanis from the skin, leaving it soft, clear, brilliant, and beautiful. It is harr less, costs little, and saves pounds uselessly expended for cosmetic powders, lotions, etc. It prevents and removes wrinkles, and is both complexion preserver and a beautifier.
Illustrated Treatise, with full particulars, post free, 3 stamps.
MRS. A. T. ROWLEY,
THE TOILET MASK CO. 139, OXFORD STREET LONDON, W.

The rising standard of living allowed an increasing number of men and women to spend time and money in pursuit of facial perfection.
(By courtesy of the Robert Opie Collection)

consumer-choice began to expand for the working class.[1] Initially, products were mostly limited to such utilitarian fields such as washing and cleaning, and livening up food – sauces, relishes and meat extracts – though there are indications of an improving standard of living in the appearance in the advertising columns of such items as plated cutlery and more elaborate furnishings. By the 1880s, rising incomes were reflected in advertisements for sets of furniture offered on credit terms, ready-to-wear clothes for men, and paper patterns and sewing machines for women.

The beginning of the twentieth century was to see the popular dailies carrying announcements for cigarettes, sweets and large-scale retailers (notably carpet- and menswear shops, and department stores). Railway excursions also seem to have been growing in popularity.

THE
BELT DRAWERS,
A SPECIALITÉ IN
GENTLEMEN'S UNDERCLOTHING.

The Article is formed on a principle that affords to the wearer a nice, gentle, and uniform support to the loins, abdomen, &c., imparting therewith a sense of remarkable comfort, as also a pronounced healthful influence.
Moderate price and excessive durability, rendering the article an economical garment withal.

Makers and Originators of the Article,
SANDLAND & CRANE,
Gentlemen's Hosiers,
55 REGENT STREET,
LONDON.
(The Quadrant section of the Street, and next to Swan & Edgar's.)
Illustrated Prospectus & Price List on application.

WHITE'S PATENT. **Corset Attachment** WHITE'S PATENT.
The "TITAN" (Regd.).
Indispensable with the present tight-fitting skirt. Produces straight front without increasing size of waist or impeding action in walking, as it does not require stocking-suspenders to keep it in position. Guaranteed not to ride up or wrinkle. Idealises the symmetry of the figure and gives indescribable elegance to the simplest gown. Reduces High Figures and Large Hips. Restores the Figure after Confinement. Affords great support with perfect ease, and gives permanent satisfaction to the wearer.
Can be attached without sewing to any corset. Under skirts can also be attached without sewing to the lower edge, thus further reducing size. **Worn by Royalty.** Recommended by the Medical Profession. Thousands of unsolicited testimonials.
N.B.—When ordering, the size round largest part of hips should be given. Every Attachment is stamped "TITAN."
In Black, White, and Ecru, price 5/9.
Of all the best Drapers and Ladies' Outfitters,
Or of the Patentee and Sole Manufacturer,
A. WHITE, 1, 2, & 3, Langley Court, LONG ACRE, LONDON. W.C

WITHOUT ATTACHMENT.

WITH ATTACHMENT.

With the decline of Victorian reticence, advertisers were able to show not only the latest fashions but also the secrets of what lay beneath.
(By courtesy of the Robert Opie Collection)

In a paper such as the *Daily Telegraph*, the emphasis in the 1870s and 1880s was far more commercial, the advertisements being broadly related to such matters as banking, insurance, business and property sales, company prospectuses, and sales by auction, as well as such middle-class interests as education, charities, entertainments, and horse and carriage sales. By the early years of the twentieth century, while the balance was still generally commercial, there are display advertisements in such consumer fields as soft drinks, carpet and fashion retailing, department stores, medicines, foods and holidays.

In 1909 *The Times* noted that 'A variety of staple products are now chiefly or largely sold through advertising of specific brands', and that advertising had also been used to introduce to the public a number of new inventions including in the previous quarter of the century 'type-writers, fountain-pens, calculating machines, piano-players, phonographs, cameras, safety-razors, patent book-cases, and motor-cars'.

The third indicator of advertising growth lies in the estimates of people working in the business in various capacities, and in the prospects for employment. Thomas Russell, writing in the *Evening News* in 1910, declared 'Today probably 100,000 people in this kingdom are occupied exclusively with advertising in one branch or another', while G. W. Goodall four years later put the total at around 80,000 employed directly and indirectly, this being comparable with the number employed in grocers' shops. The continued expansion of advertising was still creating a demand for able people and offering excellent chances for advancement, since according to Russell, 'A young man of intelligence and ambition can earn a better salary in the advertising business than in any other career except those professions which are more or less closed to all except the wealthy . . . Men of four or five years' experience readily command salaries of £5 to £15 per week.'

In the early years of the twentieth century, contemporaries began to make estimates of the total national expenditure on advertising. The trade journal *Advertising World* put the figure at around £10 million, which was subsequently quoted by Howard Bridgewater, Advertisement Manager of the *Financial Times*, in his book *Advertising* (1910). Two years later, *The Times* carried an article by Thomas Russell in which it was asserted that the figure was £100 millions. G. W. Goodall in 1914 put the expenditure somewhere between £80 and £100 millions, with £40–£50 millions of that being spent in the press. Sir William Crawford, writing in 1931, estimated that press expenditure in 1906 (the year he entered the business) had been around £15 millions, rising to £25 millions in 1913. Wareham Smith, Advertisement Director of the *Daily Mail*, contented himself with remarking that '. . . it is no exaggeration to say that millions of pounds are spent annually in applying the power'.

David Dunbar has produced the following estimates based on the Census of Production together with indices of advertising space volume published by *Advertising World*:[2]

Year	*£ Million Press*	*£ Million Posters and Transport*	*£ Million Total*	*As % of Gross National Product at factor cost*	*As % of Consumers' Expenditure*
1907	10.5	1.5	12.0	0.55	0.66
1910	11.5	2.0	13.5	0.61	0.71
1912	13.0	2.0	15.0	0.62	0.74

Even though these figures fall well below the wild guesses of contemporaries, they still represent a massive increase since the repeal of the taxes. The pattern of growth in the second half of the nineteenth century must, however, remain a mystery for lack of data on which an estimate could reasonably be based.

There is rather more information to be gleaned regarding the growth of individual advertisers' budgets. An early indication of what was considered a high level of expenditure comes from William Smith in 1863, who mentions two firms (unnamed) spending £6,000 to £8,000 per annum, and a large tailor (also unnamed) who spent in excess of £5,000. By the beginning of the twentieth century, writers were recommending particular levels of spending as being the minimum necessary for a successful advertising campaign. Clarence Moran, for example, writing in 1905, declared that an expenditure of £200 to £300 on 'an article of general consumption' was so insignificant as to be money wasted. The same year Turner Morton, writing in *Pearson's Magazine*, quoted the same minimum level, but estimated £2,000 to £3,000 to be a reasonable figure, with £20,000 to £30,000 being needed for 'anything like a sensation'.

It is interesting to compare these figures with the sums being expended by patent medicine vendors, who appear to have been the heaviest advertisers of the period. Beecham's advertising budget, for example, rose from £22,000 in 1884 to £95,000 in 1889, and £120,000 in 1891. In 1895 Joseph Beecham told a party of visiting journalists at the St Helen's factory that the firm's annual expenditure on advertising was £100,000. Thomas Holloway, another celebrated figure in this field, saw his expenditure grow from £5,000 in 1842 to £30,000 in 1855, £40,000 in 1864, £45,000 in 1882, and £50,000 in 1883, the year of his death. Another medicine vendor, F. J. Clarke, began advertising a blood mixture which he made up in his Lincoln chemist's shop. For three months he advertised at the rate of £500 per month, and then for the remainder of the first year spent an average of £1,000 per month. Advertising and printing together cost him £15,000 in his first year, later to be increased to a level regularly exceeding £20,000 per year. Clarke's business prospered, and he was eventually to become four times Mayor of Lincoln.

Nevertheless, heavy advertising was not an infallible road to commercial success. In 1905 the annual meeting of A. J. White and Co, manufacturers of Mother Seigel's syrup, was told that profits had fallen in the six years since the company's flotation from £80,000 to £13,000, while advertising expenditure over that period totalled over £900,000. Even Thomas Holloway, successful though he was in later life, overspent on advertising in his early years and was forced to compound with his creditors. If 'Cryptus', writing in 1906, is to be believed, such an experience was not uncommon: 'The fundamental rule is that you must never spend more than you get back. This sounds so obvious as to make its statement unnecessary. Yet many an advertiser has ruined himself by overshooting the mark.'

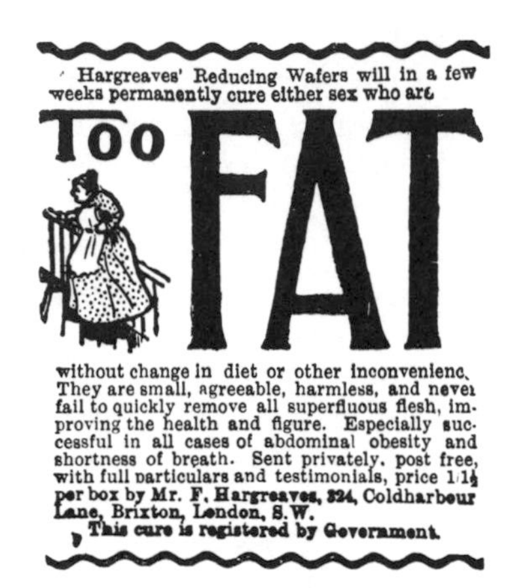

Patent medicine vendors were some of the heaviest advertisers at the end of the nineteenth century. (By courtesy of the Robert Opie Collection)

Newspaper and magazine publishers were often among the leading advertising spenders, with Amalgamated Press spending £100,000 promoting its various publications in 1903, and cheap periodicals frequently promoting 'boom' issues carrying serials to the extent of £10,000.

Manufacturers of repeat-purchase household products rapidly developed into some of the heaviest advertisers, with the soap market being one of the first to be exploited. The house of Pears, founded in 1789, had its business methods revolutionised by Thomas Barratt who became a partner in 1865. Expenditure on advertising, which had previously been negligible, was raised by Barratt to £80,000 per annum by the time that Pears became a limited company, and was

JAN. 23, 1892 THE ILLUSTRATED LONDON NEWS 121

FOR CLEANING ARTISTS' BRUSHES AND PALETTES.

MAKES COPPER LIKE GOLD. MAKES TIN LIKE SILVER. MAKES PAINT LOOK NEW.
MAKES MARBLE WHITE. MAKES BRASS LIKE MIRRORS.

FOR POTS AND PANS. FOR KNIVES AND FORKS. FOR KITCHEN TABLES. FOR BATHS AND WINDOWS.

FOR GLASS GLOBES. FOR KNIFE HANDLES. FOR EVERYTHING. REMOVES RUST FROM STEEL AND IRON.

Sparkling Glassware. Shining Pots and Pans. White Marble. Clean Hands. Polished Stair Rods. Paint like New. For Scrubbing Floors.

SOLD BY IRONMONGERS, GROCERS, AND CHEMISTS EVERYWHERE.

(By courtesy of the Robert Opie Collection)

to reach £126,000. Lever, too, was a prodigious advertiser, his expenditure totalling some £2 millions over twenty years. Tobacco was another repeat-purchase product to be extensively promoted, major factors here being the growing importance of branding, and the decline of the specialist tobacconist. In the case of Wills, while sales rose from 958,000lb to 2,895,000lb between 1871 and 1880, advertising expenditure was only equivalent to 0.2d per lb – i.e rising from about £800 to £2,400. By the end of the century, however, the company was spending more heavily on the promotion of individual brands, with £2,000 going on Diamond Queen cigarettes in Birmingham and Liverpool in 1897, £5,000 on Gold Flake tobacco and cigarettes in 1898, and £4,000 on Capstan cigarettes in 1900. Other major cigarette advertisers included John Player, spending in 1898 at a rate exceeding £20,000 per annum, and Ogdens, who were reported that year to have spent over £100,000 in recent years in promoting threepenny cigarettes.[3]

Firms which had never before advertised were beginning to do so, not only to exploit the full potential of markets or to resist the activities of competitors, but also in order to counter natural fluctuations in demand. The level of expenditure needed to undertake such remedial action could be relatively modest, as is indicated by the following statement by the Chairman of Spratts and Co in March 1885:

> Twelve months ago, when the directors began to find business dropping off in consequence of the bad times among country gentlemen, sportsmen and other customers, they resolved on a heroic remedy, which has been completely successful. They flooded the country with advertising at a cost of between £4,000 and £5,000. Now they are beginning to reap the reward of their courage and enterprise, having gained by the past two months two-thirds of all the business they lost last year.

Retailing was an area which witnessed a considerable change in attitude as regards advertising, particularly with the appearance of the department store. Robinson and Cleaver, who began by using small one-shilling advertisements, were by 1900 spending around £500 per month. Thinking on advertising, however, as with many other aspects of retailing, was changed drastically by Gordon Selfridge, who spent £36,000 on promoting his Oxford Street shop even before it had opened. By 1910, Thomas Russell could write of retailers making 'a respectable showing', with expenditure of between £10,000 and £15,000 per annum. Nevertheless, there still remained some stores which refused to advertise at all. John Lewis remained throughout his life steadfastly opposed to the concept of advertising, and Bourne and Hollingsworth, which opened in 1894, advertised for the first time in 1952.

At the end of the period, expenditure was growing notably in two further areas. The first was the motor car and related products, with an estimated £250,000 being spent in one week by exhibitors at the 1907 Motor Show. The second was advertising by the government, particularly on army recruitment which saw £6,000 spent in the spring of 1913 and a further £20,000 in a campaign running through autumn and winter.

(By courtesy of the Robert Opie Collection)

Individual advertising budgets, as has been seen, varied considerably according to the attitude of the advertiser, the state of development of the market in which he was operating, and the degree of competition he was facing. It is hardly surprising, therefore, that there was little public appreciation of the kind of sums being expended. According to Thomas Russell, 'The uninformed public always exaggerate the aggregate expenditure of the large advertisers, and always under-estimate the expense of small advertisers.' He believed, however, that no advertiser spent anything like £1 million per annum, that an expenditure of £250,000 would be exceptionally high, and that several companies in the United Kingdom were spending around £150,000 which again indicates a considerable rise in levels of expenditure since the middle years of the previous century.

Advertising media

1 The Press

Although the press expanded at a tremendous rate in the period up to 1914, the trends which can be observed were only accentuated versions of those already apparent in the first half of the nineteenth century. The increased cost of news-gathering, together with the higher production costs resulting from longer and faster printing runs on more elaborate and expensive machinery, meant that newspapers became even more financially dependent on advertising. Advertisers, for their part, with the more widespread introduction of nationally-distributed branded products, needed a means of promoting them to the increasingly discerning mass of the population. While the interests of advertiser and publisher coincided to this extent, it was the advertiser who held the advantage, since there was always the possibility that he might divert money into other media. The end of the century, therefore, saw publishers gradually giving way to pressure to run advertisements across more than one column, to permit the use of bold type and illustrations, and to provide accurate circulation figures.

Because the stamp duty had been abolished, there were no longer any official returns to give an indication of newspaper circulations. When a figure was given, it often related to the number of copies printed rather than the number sold – a distinction of major importance, since as early as 1859, it was claimed in a court case that the *London Journal* was selling its excess copies as scrap to the extent of forty tons at a time.

Louis Collins, a well-known advertising agent, took a firm stand on the subject in 1885:

> But as to the EXTENT of the circulation, an outsider has no adequate means of judging; on this head the publisher alone can give reliable information. It is much to be regretted that such information is seldom given by publishers. Vague statements are often made, and, unfortunately, in not a few cases, the actual figures are studiously concealed. This is not only unfair to the advertisers, but it is also positively injurious to the newspaper proprietors themselves . . . Advertising without a knowledge of circulation is really dealing in the dark.

The solution, according to Collins, was for advertisers to ask for a firm statement from the publisher, and to insist on some form of confirmation of its accuracy. This, he says, was being provided in some cases by making available account books or auditors' certificates, or by reference to paper-makers or printers. Moreover, in Collins' view, any publisher overstating his circulation would be guilty of fraudulent misrepresentation.

Lack of reliable information was the main reason behind the formation in 1900 of the Advertisers' Protection Society. In May 1905 the Society's monthly *Circular* to its membership included: 'We urge all members of this Society to demand before placing orders with any publication, a clear statement of circulation, and to stipulate in their orders that they are placed on the basis of the circulation named.'

Inviting members to send details of correspondence, verbal statements and refusals, the article continued:

> Bear in mind you should know *how many copies reach readers*. That is what you are *supposed* to pay for. Printers' certificates include all copies they *hope to sell*, also the returns that are *sold* to the paper mills, and other waste, but these do not help *you* to sell *your* goods.

In October 1906 the *Circular* carried for the first time a slogan which was to be its battle cry for some years to come: 'What we want is net sales. Pulp Mill Circulation does not sell goods.' The pressure exerted by the Society seems to have had some effect, since the following year, the Chairman was able to state at the annual dinner that 'guaranteed circulations were becoming quite common'.

Such activities were hardly likely to foster amicable relations with publishers, many of whom steadfastly refused to admit either the right of advertisers to know net sales, or the importance of the figures, insisting that 'quality' of circulation was of more importance. There seems, in fact, to have been a closing of the ranks against the Society, for in November 1911 the *Circular* reported: 'They are frightened of any combination among advertisers . . . the large publishers have come to an understanding among themselves that we are to be treated as if we did not exist. They have not even the courtesy to acknowledge the receipt of any letters we write to them.'

In pursuance of its aims, representatives of the Society called on the new circulation manager of *The Times* in December 1912. The *Circular* reported, 'He takes up the position that to give figures of circulation does harm to the advertiser as they only mislead him, and that it is therefore in his best interest that he should not know them.'

Some papers went a little further in trying to accommodate their advertisers. The *Liverpool Daily Post and Mercury*, for instance, published the following certificate signed by a firm of Chartered Accountants: 'We hereby certify that the net sale of each of the three papers, the *Liverpool Daily Post and Mail*, the *Liverpool Echo*, and the *Liverpool Weekly Post*, were greater for the twelve months ending 31st December 1908, than during the twelve months ended 31st December 1907.' This illuminating document was issued in 1911.

Where publishers refused to furnish details, it was only natural that the Society should wish to provide some kind of guidance on circulations for the benefit of its members. This it appears to have done on the basis of the response reported by members to advertisements in particular media – something which many publishers attempted to thwart by refusing to accept any advertisement with a 'key' telling the advertiser the source of an enquiry.

Not surprisingly, the Society's estimates were on occasion far from accurate. In particular, it put the sales of the *Observer* at 5,000 instead of 77,000, which so outraged the paper's publishers that they brought an action for damages – unsuccessfully – against the Society, and the editor of the *Circular*. The judgement in this case, together with the Society's obvious intention of pressing ahead with the publication of circulation figures, seems to have undermined the resistance of publishers. In October 1911, Associated Newspapers began producing figures certified by a chartered accountant in respect of the *Daily Mail*, *Daily Mirror*, *Evening News* and *Weekly Despatch*. By the beginning of 1913, they had been followed by the *Chronicle* and the *Daily News and Leader*. The latter declared its intention of publishing every day the sales for the previous day. Although there was still far to go, it was with some justification that Frederick Oetzmann, one of the founders of the Society, wrote in the *Circular* in February 1913: 'My experience is that the advertising business can be done in a far better and more satisfactory manner now than say, ten years ago, in fact each year there has been a steady increase in the number who are willing to give guarantees of sales.'

Even though there is a lack of accurate information, it is clear that the repeal of the stamp duty signalled the start of an era of dramatic press expansion. In the next five years, 120 papers were established in 102 towns where previously none had existed. By 1864 it was estimated that the combined sales of English daily papers had reached 511,000, with 248,000 of these being published in London and 263,000 in the provinces. A further 176,000 were produced daily in the rest of Britain, giving a total of 687,000. The sales of London weekly papers were put at 2,263,000, and those in the remainder of the United Kingdom at 3,907,000, giving a total of 6,170,000.

While no comparable figures exist for the end of the period, the claimed circulations of individual publications indicate the rate at which expansion had continued. For example, that of the *Daily Telegraph* rose from 27,000 per day in 1856 to 300,000 in 1880; *Lloyds Weekly* claimed one million in 1896 and the *Daily Mail* reached that figure during the Boer War. At the same time, the number of titles was increasing, daily papers published outside London rising from 5 in 1854 to 52 in 1864, and 129 in 1889, with 52 of these being mornings and 77 evenings.

Magazine publishing grew in similar fashion. The number of women's magazine titles increased from 4 in 1846 to 50 by 1900, though in terms of individual circulation they could not compare with the popular family journals such as *Titbits*, which was selling 900,000 per week in the eighties, and *Answers* which reached similar levels in the following decade.

This rapidly changing picture had considerable implications for advertisers. The appearance of mass-circulation penny and later halfpenny dailies meant that there was now a means of bringing nationally distributed consumer goods to the notice of the vast majority of the consuming public in a quicker and more effective manner than had hitherto been possible. The penny dailies seem to have tapped a new source of readers, since their combined circulations were greater than the volume of sales lost by their older rivals, though it may be that many of the people now buying a cheap paper for themselves had previously been hirers or joint purchasers of other papers. *The Times*' advertising monopoly, which had depended upon its circulation lead, was broken. As the new popular dailies forged ahead, 'The Thunderer' was left far behind, reaching a peak of 66,000 in the mid-sixties and then falling to a mere 38,000 by 1908. At the same time, the press was becoming a more flexible instrument for the advertiser, who could now select virtually any town or region for special coverage by means of the expanding provincial press, and isolate particular population segments or interest groups by using magazines.

The massive increases in circulation during the second half of the century could not have been achieved without considerable technological advances in the field of newspaper production, with improvements coming at each stage of the process. The hand casting of type, still common at mid-century, meant one man could produce 4,000 characters per ten-hour day; by the eighties *The Times* was casting by machine at a rate of 6,000 characters per hour. By 1900, Linotype machines for the mechanical setting of type were in use at 21 London dailies and 250 other papers and periodicals. Vast increases in printing speeds were possible with rotary presses such as the Hoe, particularly when allied to the use of curved stereotype plates and the feeding of paper on the reel instead of in separate sheets. Thomas Smith, looking back in 1899 over his twenty-one years as an advertising agent in Fleet Street, noted the profound changes which had taken place and what they meant for advertising:

> Twenty one years ago the newspaper advertisements were old-fashioned, stereotyped and conservative. Since that period a great change has taken place, arising from various causes. The cheapening of papers and new methods of its [sic] production, specially in surface papers, the cheapening of process blocks, the invention of a rapid process in production of blocks by electric light, and the printing of blocks by up-to-date machinery – all these things have aided the enterprising advertiser. To a large extent also newspapers have admitted blocks where they did not before.

In the case of many hundreds of small local papers, these developments seem to have taken effect slowly, if at all. The *Middlesex Chronicle*, a typical example, had a circulation of just under 3,000 at the turn of the century. It was only in 1870 that it had acquired a steam press, printing until then having been done with power supplied by a man turning a handle attached to a large flywheel. The printed sheets were rolled up and passed to the newsagents, who had to lay them out on the shop-floor and fold them. As late as 1908, the *Chronicle* was still being set entirely by hand. The novelist William le Queux worked on the paper for a time as a young man, and in *Scribes and Pharisees* (1896), he gives a daunting description of life on the so-called *Hounslow Standard* (the office of the *Chronicle* being situated in Hounslow). The frontage was . . .

> a small mouldy-smelling shop in a bad state of repair . . . behind in the garden was a shed in which half-a-dozen youths set type, while further on was a small outhouse, originally built for a stable, but now euphemistically termed the 'machine room', containing, as it did, an old-fashioned press worked by a grunting gas engine, which very often failed or had to be turned by hand. This interesting piece of machinery was broken in places, and had been repaired with string.

As late as 1915, the Advertisers Protection Society *Circular* commented:

> Advertisers sometimes wonder how small country weekly papers – in some of which space can actually be bought at less than a penny an inch – manage to exist, but it is an open secret that these papers do not exist through the profits they actually make themselves; they are actually run in conjunction with jobbing printeries, and it is because of their influence on the printing business that they are carried on.

The technological advances introduced by the national press meant that enormous differences developed between the circulations of various newspapers. In the first half of the nineteenth century, *The Times* outstripped its rivals by a considerable distance, but the variation among the remainder was often to be measured in hundreds rather than thousands. By the beginning of the twentieth century the difference between the ailing *Times* and the *Daily Mail* was in the region of a million copies per day, with other papers at various points between. The reaction of major advertisers, wishing their announcements to be seen by as many people as possible, was to favour those publications with the biggest circulations. *Lloyd's Weekly*, the *Daily Telegraph*, the *Graphic*, and the *Illustrated London News* were said in 1882 to be attracting more business than they could handle, in spite of substantial rate increases. To realise their advertising potential to the full, they needed to print more pages per issue, while to keep ahead in terms of circulation meant printing more copies and selling at the lowest feasible cover-price. This in turn involved constant investment in expensive new machinery. Little wonder, then, that newspapers in this vicious circle gradually gave way to advertisers' demands for greater freedom.

In earlier years, as we have seen, advertisers were confined within the column rules, and illustrations were rarely allowed, except in the case of small emblematic woodcuts in some of the country papers. By 1897 H. J. Palmer, editor of the *Yorkshire Post*, could write: 'During the last year or two there has been a marked expansion in advertising enterprise, and an equally striking change in advertising methods.' Even four or five years earlier, according to Palmer, it had been impossible to induce any leading London or provincial paper – 'with one or two exceptions' – to accept an advertisement set in display type. 'Yet today *The Times* itself is ready, subject to certain conditions, to clothe advertisements in type which three years ago would have been considered fit only for the street hoardings.' Leading papers were now even accepting 'that once intolerable monstrosity, the picture block'. He therefore believed that 'In newspaper history the year 1896 will be said to have witnessed the successful revolt of the advertiser from the stifling bondage in which he has been enchained for over a century.'

A striking example of the importance of advertising revenue for a particular newspaper is provided by the changing fortunes of *The Times*. Printing House Square had always adopted an extremely highhanded attitude towards advertisers. In 1857 one who complained was told by Mowbray Morris, *The Times* Manager, that 'One of the most stringent rules in that [advertisement] office is not to guarantee the publication of an advertisement on any named day', and in 1862 Morris wrote to tell another advertiser that 'It has never been the practice of *The Times* to receive trade advertisements under any conditions whatever either of time or place.' As yet, the circulation and prestige of the paper were still such as to attract a surfeit of advertising. According to Morris in September 1860, 'We suffer always at this period of the year, for a space of full

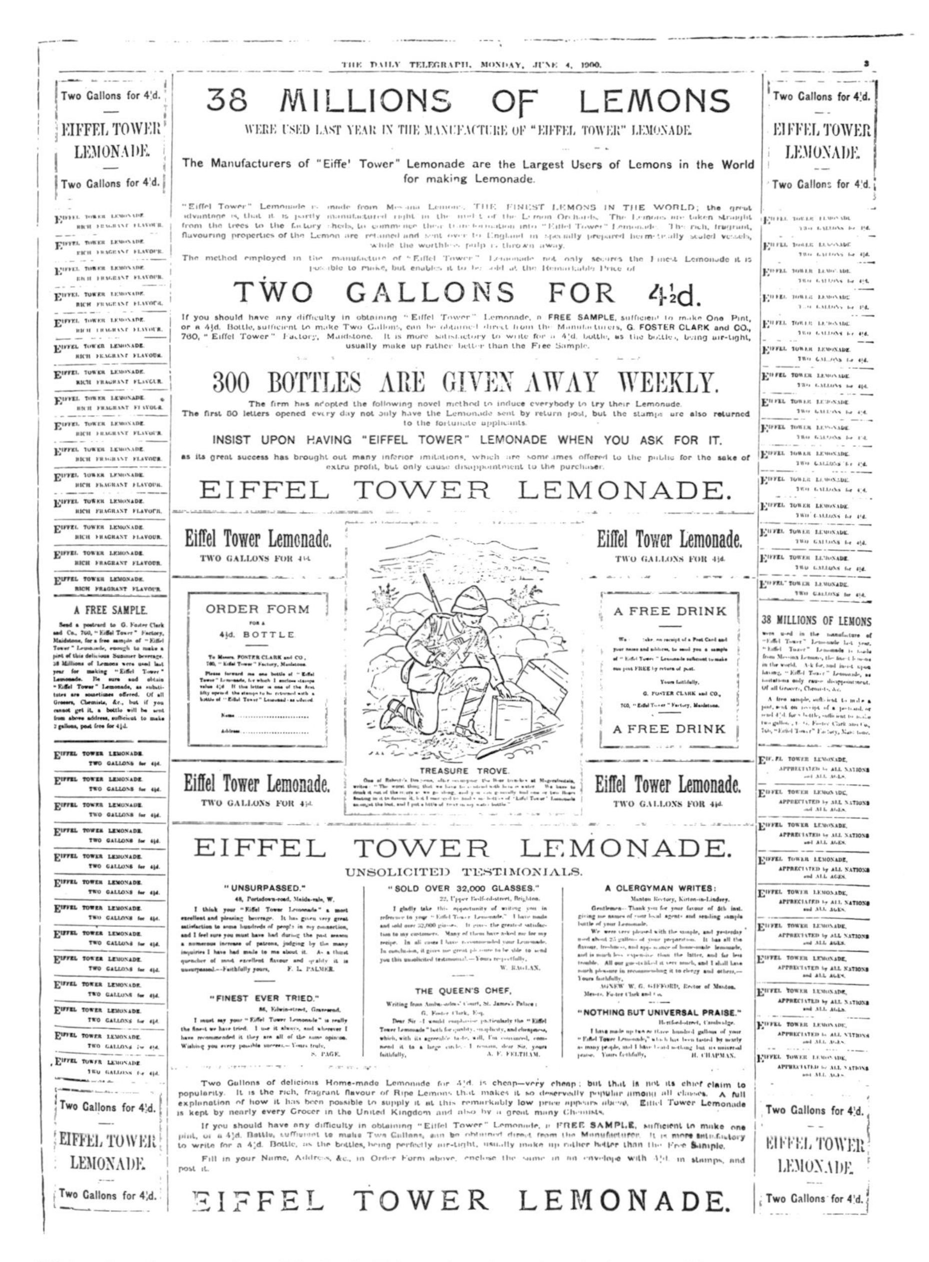
THE DAILY TELEGRAPH, MONDAY, JUNE 4, 1900.

Two Gallons for 4½d.

EIFFEL TOWER LEMONADE.

Two Gallons for 4½d.

38 MILLIONS OF LEMONS

WERE USED LAST YEAR IN THE MANUFACTURE OF "EIFFEL TOWER" LEMONADE.

The Manufacturers of "Eiffe' Tower" Lemonade are the Largest Users of Lemons in the World for making Lemonade.

"Eiffel Tower" Lemonade is made from Messina Lemons, THE FINEST LEMONS IN THE WORLD; the great advantage is, that it is partly manufactured right in the midst of the Lemon Orchards. The Lemons are taken straight from the trees to the factory sheds, to commence their transformation into "Eiffel Tower" Lemonade. The rich, fragrant, flavouring properties of the Lemon are retained and sent over to England in specially prepared hermetically sealed vessels, while the worthless pulp is thrown away.

The method employed in the manufacture of "Eiffel Tower" Lemonade not only secures the Finest Lemonade it is possible to make, but enables it to be sold at the Remarkable Price of

TWO GALLONS FOR 4½d.

If you should have any difficulty in obtaining "Eiffel Tower" Lemonade, a FREE SAMPLE, sufficient to make One Pint, or a 4½d. Bottle, sufficient to make Two Gallons, can be obtained direct from the Manufacturers, G. FOSTER CLARK and CO., 760, "Eiffel Tower" Factory, Maidstone. It is more satisfactory to write for a 4½d. bottle, as the bottles, being air-tight, usually make up rather better than the Free Sample.

300 BOTTLES ARE GIVEN AWAY WEEKLY.

The firm has adopted the following novel method to induce everybody to try their Lemonade.
The first 50 letters opened every day not only have the Lemonade sent by return post, but the stamps are also returned to the fortunate applicants.

INSIST UPON HAVING "EIFFEL TOWER" LEMONADE WHEN YOU ASK FOR IT.

as its great success has brought out many inferior imitations, which are sometimes offered to the public for the sake of extra profit, but only cause disappointment to the purchaser.

EIFFEL TOWER LEMONADE.

Eiffel Tower Lemonade.
TWO GALLONS FOR 4½d.

ORDER FORM
FOR A
4½d. BOTTLE

A FREE DRINK

A FREE DRINK

Eiffel Tower Lemonade.
TWO GALLONS FOR 4½d.

TREASURE TROVE.

Eiffel Tower Lemonade.
TWO GALLONS FOR 4½d.

Eiffel Tower Lemonade.
TWO GALLONS FOR 4½d.

A FREE SAMPLE.

38 MILLIONS OF LEMONS

EIFFEL TOWER LEMONADE.

UNSOLICITED TESTIMONIALS.

"UNSURPASSED."

48, Portadown-road, Maida-vale, W.

I think your "Eiffel Tower Lemonade" a most excellent and pleasing beverage. It has given very great satisfaction to some hundreds of people in my connection, and I feel sure you must have had during the past season a numerous increase of patrons, judging by the many inquiries I have had made to me about it. As a thirst quencher of most excellent flavour and quality it is unsurpassed.—Faithfully yours, F. L. PALMER.

"FINEST EVER TRIED."

86, Edwin-street, Gravesend.

I must say your "Eiffel Tower Lemonade" is really the finest we have tried. I use it always, and wherever I have recommended it they are all of the same opinion. Wishing you every possible success.—Yours truly, S. PAGE.

"SOLD OVER 32,000 GLASSES."

22, Upper Bedford-street, Brighton.

I gladly take this opportunity of writing you in reference to your "Eiffel Tower Lemonade." I have made and sold over 32,000 glasses. It gives the greatest satisfaction to my customers. Many of them have asked me for my recipe. In all cases I have recommended your Lemonade. In conclusion, it gives me great pleasure to be able to send you this unsolicited testimonial.—Yours respectfully, W. RAGLAN.

THE QUEEN'S CHEF.

Writing from Ambassadors' Court, St. James's Palace:
G. Foster Clark, Esq.

Dear Sir,—I would emphasise particularly the "Eiffel Tower Lemonade" both for quality, simplicity, and cheapness, which, with its agreeable taste, will, I'm convinced, commend it to a large circle.—I remain, dear Sir, yours faithfully, A. F. FELTHAM.

A CLERGYMAN WRITES:

Manton Rectory, Kirton-in-Lindsey.

Gentlemen,—Thank you for your favour of 5th inst. giving me names of your local agents and sending sample bottle of your Lemonade.

We were very pleased with the sample, and yesterday used about 25 gallons of your preparation. It has all the flavour, freshness, and appearance of home-made lemonade, and is much less expensive than the latter, and far less trouble. All our guests liked it very much, and I shall have much pleasure in recommending it to clergy and others.—Yours faithfully,

AGNEW W. G. GIFFORD, Rector of Manton.
Messrs. Foster Clark and Co.

"NOTHING BUT UNIVERSAL PRAISE."

Hertford-street, Cambridge.

I have made up two or three hundred gallons of your "Eiffel Tower Lemonade," which has been tasted by nearly as many people, and I have heard nothing but its universal praise. Yours faithfully, H. CHAPMAN.

Two Gallons of delicious Home-made Lemonade for 4½d. is cheap—very cheap; but that is not its chief claim to popularity. It is the rich, fragrant flavour of Ripe Lemons that makes it so deservedly popular among all classes. A full explanation of how it has been possible to supply it at this remarkably low price appears above. Eiffel Tower Lemonade is kept by nearly every Grocer in the United Kingdom and also by a great many Chemists.

If you should have any difficulty in obtaining "Eiffel Tower" Lemonade, a FREE SAMPLE, sufficient to make one pint, or a 4½d. Bottle, sufficient to make Two Gallons, can be obtained direct from the Manufacturer. It is more satisfactory to write for a 4½d. Bottle, as the bottles, being perfectly air-tight, usually make up rather better than the Free Sample.

Fill in your Name, Address, &c., in Order Form above, enclose the same in an envelope with 4½d. in stamps, and post it.

EIFFEL TOWER LEMONADE.

Two Gallons for 4½d.

EIFFEL TOWER LEMONADE.

Two Gallons for 4½d.

This advertisement from *The Daily Telegraph* utilises the whole area of the page, combining the old technique of repetition with the possibilities of illustration, and exploiting current interest in the war in South Africa five months, from what our neighbours call an embarras des richesses. There is a daily average remnant of 60 columns of advertisements, nearly enough to fill another Times. Advertisements are often kept standing for more than a week, to the great injury and dissatisfaction of advertisers.' By 1893, however, the position had changed so drastically that the paper's management had to break with tradition, swallow its collective pride, and engage two canvassers to sell advertising space.

It seems to have been broadly true that publications founded towards the end of the century often enjoyed a financial advantage over many of those which appeared soon after the repeal of the taxes. According to Henry Sell, a leading agent, in the scramble to sell their advertising space in the 1850s, many publishers offered it at very low terms to major advertisers, who accepted provided they had a permanent option to renew at the same rate. This would have meant that as circulations grew and costs rose, the potentially most profitable advertisement positions in those papers were becoming increasingly uneconomic.

The uneasy relationship between publisher and advertiser is well illustrated by the case of Northcliffe. Newspaper profitability depended upon income from advertisements which in the case of Associated Press in 1904, for example, was £264,000. Even so, Northcliffe retained a highly dictatorial attitude regarding the kind of advertisements he was prepared to accept in the papers he controlled. In 1900 he set up the advertisement department of the *Daily Mail* during a five-minute interview with Wareham Smith, telling him, 'Don't go out after your advertisers. Wait for them to come to you.' According to Smith, 'Advertisements had to conform in appearance to the rest of the paper, his view being that people bought a newspaper primarily for *news*, and that advertisements should not swamp the news, either actually or apparently.' This probably explains why he was so keen on classified advertisements, promoting them vigorously with the slogan, 'Twelve words for sixpence, same price as a telegram.'

It was said that he would have done without advertising completely had it been possible. His brother Leicester wrote, 'He was rigid in excluding more than a certain number of advertisements from the *Daily Mail.* On one occasion, further capital had to be raised as a result of that policy.' Yet at the same time, when major advertisers were slow to take space in the *Mail*, he ran advertisements free of charge for his great rival, George Newnes, so as to make the paper appear such a valuable advertising medium that even Newnes could not avoid using it.

The following examples give some idea of Northcliffe's highhanded attitudes towards those advertisers on whose patronage he depended:

> Most strongly protest against your injuring my newspaper by use of such type as in OXO advertisements please send me written explanation why you disobey my orders. (Telegram to Wareham Smith 1914)

Painting by John Orlando Parry of a poster site near St Paul's in the 1840s. This shows the development of poster advertising, particularly the use of illustrations and colour, and the extent of overposting. (By courtesy of Alfred Dunhill Ltd)

These watercolours by George Scharf, dating from the 1820s and 1830s, indicate the wide variety of advertisers and placards. The assorted liveries of the men bearing placards contrast strongly with their conditions later in the century. (By courtesy of the Trustees of the British Museum, London)

Soap manufacturers became major advertising spenders towards the end of the nineteenth century. The 'Bubbles' advertisement for Pears is the most celebrated example of an academic painting used for advertising – much to the chagrin of the artist, Sir John Millais. Searching for a novel means of advertising, Hudsons used a balloon to promote their name and later celebrated this exploit in advertisements through the more usual media. (By courtesy of Unilever Ltd)

An example of the distinctive technique employed by the 'Beggarstaff Brothers', James Pryde and William Nicholson, as applied to advertising. (Victoria & Albert Museum)

> The appearance of the front page is marred by a large number of display advertisements in the lower half. (To *The Times* 12 January 1909)

> Deal firmly with advertising people plastering *The Times* with advertisements, to the disgust of many readers. (To Wickham Steed 18 December 1909)

> Leave out all top-heavy advertisements which ruin the paper, such as the bottle in Johnson's Prepared Wax, and the large heading of Quaker Oats. If you do not leave them out, I shall ask the printer to do so. (To the *Daily Mail* February 1922)

Northcliffe was by training and temperament a journalist, and his sensibilities do seem to have been offended by some of the advertisements appearing in his papers. On one occasion, he wrote, 'Opening the paper, I felt like a bird wounded by an arrow.' Genuine if misguided concern is probably shown, too, in the way he refused to allow the inclusion of words such as 'rupture' or 'constipation'. He was prepared to tolerate advertising because it gave him the freedom to run the kind of newspapers he wanted, though he was fortunate in that the large circulations of his papers kept them in constant demand by advertisers, the cost in terms of a thousand copies sold often being cheaper than in competing papers, despite the higher advertisement rates. (The original rate of 8s.0d. per single column inch in the *Daily Mail* had risen to 40s.0d. by 1906, while in 1910 a full page cost £350 in the *Mail* and £130 in the *Evening News*.) He was, nevertheless, well aware of the danger inherent in such a situation, as is clear from the following message to *The Times* on 30 November 1920:

> It is not pleasant to think that, owing to the gigantic wages paid in newspaper offices and the high price of paper, newspapers are now for the first time in their history, *entirely* subordinate to advertisers. I see no way out of this impasse, other than by maintaining a great daily net sale and thus keeping the whip hand of the advertiser.

Advertising rates were generally fluid as a result of the way the advertising business was conducted, the whole emphasis being on bargaining and trading rather than scientific appraisal of the media available. According to Moody's Agency, some publishers adhered rigidly to their stated rates, some varied them slightly for special reasons, and others accepted the best price they could obtain, on the basis that if there were no advertisements, they would have to pay for editorial matter to fill the space. Even after World War I, Thomas Russell was estimating that only about 10% of publications had absolutely fixed rates, though many of the remainder endeavoured to conceal their reductions in some way. Publishers must in fact have been under constant pressure from the variety of middlemen – contractors, canvassers and farmers – who made a living by offering the advertiser lower prices than he could obtain if booking direct, and from advertisers and agents who seem to have developed a system of bidding for space, making low offers to rival publications and giving an order to whichever accepted the biggest reduction on its normal rate.

By this time, too, advertisement space was being sold not only by the line, in the traditional manner, but also by area, calculated in terms of column inches (i.e. depth expressed in inches and width in terms of the number of columns). This introduced still more variables. Advertisers would pay more than the equivalent of the classified rate in order to enjoy the greater creative freedom which display space offered, and publishers, by careful handling of the make-up of a paper, could charge higher rates for special positions – for example, 'solus' on a page, or next to or surrounded by editorial matter. While this latter principle was accepted, publishers had no guide as to how great the extra charge ought to be, and seemingly fixed their rates according to what they thought advertisers would be prepared to pay for the privilege of appearing in a specified position on a particular page. In addition, an agreed rate was still subject to the complicated tangle of discounts and allowances which publications used as inducements to obtain series bookings, to secure prompt payment, to push expenditure above a given figure, or simply to offer bigger apparent reductions than their competitors. To increase the confusion yet further, some advertisers were also trying to claim the 10% agency commission, and even setting up their own 'advertising agency branches'.

There seems to have been little attempt to link rates to the number of copies of a publication which were actually sold. The principle was certainly propounded by a few agents, but it was to have little validity until accurate circulation figures became generally available. In short, while circulation was becoming a more important factor in deciding what rates should be charged, the situation was as yet too chaotic and the other influences too numerous for it to win general acceptance.

The second half of the nineteenth century saw enormous changes take place in the structure and influence of the press. Reductions in the prices of newspapers and magazines, together with increases in wages, meant that hiring and clubbing together by would-be readers became a thing of the past. Improvements in transportation and in printing technology made possible the great national daily newspaper in the modern sense, printed at high speed in enormous quantities in London and distributed throughout the country overnight. Local requirements were met by the greatly increased number of small local newspapers. Special-interest groups, too, saw the appearance of magazines designed to cater specifically for their tastes. These changes were bound to increase the effectiveness of the press as a medium for advertising. Magazines carried the advertiser's message to important new market groups (such as motorists), and the many publications aimed at women opened up a whole new field for the promotion not only of fashion and beauty products, but also for the household goods and branded foods which were becoming widely distributed in the last quarter of the century. National newspapers meant that national advertising campaigns for nationally distributed products could be organised far more efficiently than hitherto. An advertising agent could make a single advertisement booking, send a single block to the newspaper, and reach millions of readers with one insertion, rather than trying to supplement the thin coverage of the London press with a selection from the hundreds of local newspapers. Local traders and shopkeepers, on the other hand, were able to choose the paper covering the particular town or district on which they drew for their customers.

Press readership can only be discussed in general terms, since most of the evidence available is of a very general nature. There is for instance no indication as to what proportion of the population were regular newspaper readers by 1914 compared with 1855. More papers were certainly sold, but it is impossible to estimate how far this was simply offsetting the enormously high readership per copy of their more expensive predecessors. Nor can we say what proportion of families saw more than one newspaper per day, or how far there was an overlap in readership of daily and weekly papers, or of newspapers and magazines.

Those publications which first appeared in the last quarter of the century were certainly in keeping with changes in public taste. For example, in 1878 interest in cricket gained considerable impetus from the first visit of the Australians, particularly when they beat England in a single day at Lords in front of 5,000 people. The eighties also saw the beginning of professional football and a marked increase in working-class betting on horse races. Such developments may be seen reflected in the increased coverage which the new papers gave to sport, as with racing tips from 'Captain Coe' in T. P. Connor's *Star*. In the case of women's magazines, as Cynthia White has pointed out, editorial

Advertising in ladies' periodicals reflected editorial concerns.
(*The Young Ladies' Journal*, 1889)

coverage was often concerned with problems being faced by women at that particular time, such as household management, coping on a small budget, make-up, employment, personal relationships and child care.

It used to be thought that the success of the press was based on a new working-class readership created by the Education Act of 1870. The expansion of the press was taking place, however, long before the results of the Act could have been felt, and there are ample indications of an existing working-class demand for newspapers and magazines. Apart from the evidence of multiple readership in the first half of the century, William Smith wrote in 1863: 'Now, a cheap press circulating all over the kingdom, the price of advertisements within the reach of all, and but a few, even down to the very errand-boy, I am glad to say, who cannot read . . .' An article four years later in the *Newspaper Press* also describes newspapers as being 'scattered around not merely in the mechanics institutes, but read by the side of the loom, in the workshop, in the mine, and even in that most benighted place of all, a labourer's cottage'.

By the first decade of the twentieth century, the predominant position of the press was beyond any doubt. Whatever the product and whatever the audience, it was almost certainly the best advertising medium. According to Clarence Moran in 1905:

> Every rank of society, from the highest to the lowest, reads newspapers. For those who cannot aspire to *The Times*, or even the penny dailies, a multitude of halfpenny journals is published every morning and evening. And if the price even of these is out of reach, there are always the free libraries. More easy of access still, the advertisement sheets of some papers are pasted up at labour bureaux and elsewhere. Another medium is offered by the weekly and monthly press, from the *Nineteenth Century* and its half-crown rivals to the 'half-penny comics', while a wider publicity probably than that of these is offered by the 'popular monthlies' and 'weeklies'. There is, in fact, no class of consumers which cannot be affected through the medium of some section or other of the press.[4]

2 Posters

In the second half of the century, poster composition gradually evolved so that the woodcut developed into a coloured design dominating the whole area, and the textual element became so reduced that in some cases it was omitted completely. Selling messages, it was found, could be put across by means of visual symbols as well as by words.

These changes were made possible by improvements in printing technology, particularly the development of lithography. With relief-printing, the impression of tone could only be imparted by stippling or cross-hatching on the woodcut. In lithography, however, the drawing was made on a stone – later a zinc plate – which itself provided texture, and which made possible gradation effects. The process had been invented by Senefelder in 1793, being originally intended for the cheap reproduction of works of art; but during the period of political upheaval in France it was used for the printing of notices and proclamations. Something of its potential was also foreshadowed in the lithographs produced by political caricaturists such as Daumier, Gavarni and Doré. Some technical improvements were introduced, notably the invention of the rotary lithographic press by Brisset in 1833, and the development of chromolithography by Engelmann in 1836. It was now possible to produce illustrated posters in colour by lithography, instead of the crude method sometimes used earlier of stencilling flat colours on to a woodcut. In France the technique was soon adopted by such artists as Gerard Grandville (*Scenes de la Vie des Animaux*, *c.*1840) and Gavarni (*Le Juif Errant*, 1845). As yet, however, the printing machines were rather cumbersome and it was not until the partnership between Chéret and his printer Chaix in the seventies that the process became really practicable for large-scale commercial use, with production costs low enough for it to be used for long runs of colour posters. A further development of note was the introduction of photographic half-tone illustrations. Again the lead seems to have come from Paris, with Leopold Reutlinger using the technique in a poster for the *Théâtre des Variétés* in 1897, produced on special waterproof paper.

The first English poster in the modern sense is generally regarded as having been Frederick Walker's *Woman in White* (1871), which was engraved on wood by W. H. Hooper. Walker is quoted as saying, 'I am impressed on doing all I can with a first attempt at what I consider might develop into a most important branch of art', though he was to die in 1875 with this as his only excursion into the field. The importance of his single design often seems to be overestimated. Illustrations covering the whole printing area of a poster were by no means new, and the process employed by Walker was woodcut, and not lithography. In that sense it marked the end of an era rather than the beginning of a new one, since relief-printing became much less used for posters until the half-tone process was developed at the turn of the century. Certain aspects of the design are, however, worthy of note. Firstly, it was successful, measured in terms of the attention it attracted, in a way that no poster before had ever been, due presumably to the air of mystery it managed to create. Secondly, it was probably the first poster to be designed by a Royal Academician. And thirdly, it demonstrated the impact which could be achieved by a visual theme derived from, and integrated with, the basic idea behind the poster. However, the precedents thus created were by no means universally accepted. Walter Crane, for example, probably spoke for much of the artistic establishment when he declared:

> I feel that there is something essentially vulgar about the idea of the poster unless it is limited to simple announcements or directions, or becomes a species of heraldry or sign-painting . . . The very fact of the necessity of shouting loud, and the association with vulgar commercial puffing, are against the artist and so much dead weight.[5]

It is strange that advertisers failed to perceive the benefits of integrating the illustration with the central theme of the poster, the impact of which was so strongly emphasised by *Woman in White*. Instead, they proceeded in another direction, generally treating the visual element as something quite separate from, and often quite unrelated to, the main message. Rather than commissioning artists to produce designs, as was the case in France, they often spent large sums of money on buying 'academic' paintings, the most celebrated instance being Millais' *Bubbles*. Outraged Academicians felt that their names were being used to help promote sales.

This method of operation in turn had an effect on the way that poster artists worked. The pictorial element, having a separate existence, was something to which a brand name – anybody's name – could be added later. The result was to bring the poster nearer to pure than applied art, so that from an aesthetic point of view, poster illustration in Britain reached a higher standard in the last years of the nineteenth century than at any time before or since. Consequently, the curious position was arrived at where, on the one hand, critics of advertising were decrying the way that cities were becoming defaced by bill-posting, while on the other, the poster became a cult object, bought secretly from printers or peeled from hoardings while the paste was still wet.

Poster collecting was at its peak from about 1894 onwards, by which time it was widely regarded as an art form in its own right. That year, the *New Review* carried articles on 'The Art of the Hoarding' by Chéret, Hardy and Beardsley. Books on the subject were produced by critics such as Maindron (1895), Hiatt (1896) and Sponsel (1897). International poster exhibitions were mounted between 1893 and 1897 in Hamburg (twice), London (twice), Brussels, Dresden, Rheims and St Petersburg, and in 1898 a monthly magazine, *The Poster*, made its appearance in London. The enthusiasm of collectors indeed reached such a pitch that Dudley Hardy had printed at the foot of his Savoy posters 'This poster is the property of Mr R. D'Oyly Carte, London, and any person selling or receiving the same is liable to prosecution.' All this was, of course, far removed from the harsh realities of the street hoarding. What it meant, however, was that posters in themselves were universally accepted, and that what was traditionally 'the poor man's picture gallery' now had a new consistent audience, though how much value this had from an advertising point of view is difficult to say.

Something of the crusading zeal of the poster enthusiast for this fusion of art with commercial interest comes across in the following passage from the *Catalogue* of the 1896 Hamburg Poster Exhibition (my own translation):

> Art should be accessible to everyone, and joy and enrichment should be granted to all; not only to those who can afford to buy works of art or have the time to seek them out in galleries. To accomplish this end, art must go on to the streets, where chance will bring it to the notice of many thousands on their way to work who have neither time nor money to spare. These high ethical ideals are fulfilled by posters created for everyday practical purposes – provided they are good posters . . .

Advertisers seem to have had strictly limited objectives in their use of posters. The job of the poster designer appears to have been to attract attention and to ensure that the company's name was remembered in association with a particular type of product. This explains why the visual element was related to the product in only the most general way. Thomas Barratt, for example, apart from buying established works of art to advertise Pears Soap, also commissioned a series of posters in the form of optical illusions, which were reported to have attracted crowds of forty or fifty people who would stare at them for up to twenty minutes at a time.

This concept of the poster's function was reflected in the way that poster artists worked. James Pryde, one of the celebrated 'Beggarstaff Brothers', described how one of their designs eventually found its way on to the British hoardings:

> Among the tragedies of that time which, happily, we can now laugh at as comedies, was a poster of a Beefeater – a suggestive design printed in red, black and yellow, which we thought particularly appropriate for a beef extract. We took it to the office of the firm in question and pinned it up on the wall of the very small room into which we were shown. After a while, the art editor or manager or whatever he called himself, a dear old gentleman rather like Father Christmas in appearance, came into the room; he gave the poster one glance and went out of the room without saying anything. Later, it was offered to Sir George Alexander, who had a Beefeater on the hoarding of St James' Theatre, but he did not find it suitable. Still later, that poster was redeemed by the proprietors of Harper's Magazine, who reproduced it freely in the United States, where it had a great success in advertising that publication, and it also had a vogue here for the same purpose.[6]

Even when the artist received a direct commission from the advertiser, the product itself was treated as being of only minor importance, as is clear from the following explanation by Dudley Hardy, one of the most outstanding British poster designers of this period:

> When designing a pictorial advertisement, the object to be kept in view should surely be to produce something novel and striking, which will attract the passer-by and compel his attention. But though I do not consider it necessary that the design should have any distinct relation to the newspaper, drama, or merchandise, the existence of which it is supposed to publish, I think it is well to introduce, if possible, something into the design which directly or indirectly refers to the matter in hand.[7]

The posting of printed bills on walls must be considered entirely separately from the designing and printing aspects considered so far. At one level we are in the realms of Royal Academicians, of critics, exhibitions and salons. At the other, we come face to face with the hard commercial realities of the street hoarding and poster contractor.

In *Street Life in London* (1877) Adolph Smith estimates that some 200 men were working as bill posters, with a number of foremen and superintendents being employed in addition to supervise their work. 'Ladder-men', working a twelve hour day, could earn up to £1.15s.0d. per week, though some contractors who recruited from lodging houses or the workhouse paid as little as 16 shillings. Fly-posters, whose trade was supposedly illegal, earned 4 shillings a day but worked only during the summer months. Their employers seem to have despatched them in waves with instructions to paste over bills put up by competitors. Smith was told by one firm that on Boat Race day men were sent out at two, six, eight, and ten o'clock in the morning.

By the turn of the century, statutory controls ensured that fly-posting in towns was almost a thing of the past, at least as far as bill posters of standing were concerned. This in turn meant that the bill posters were competing fiercely for permitted sites. In the case of hoardings surrounding building works, theatre tickets for the site-foreman were originally enough to ensure sole use. Then the builders, seeing the possibilities, began to charge rent for the use of the hoarding. Finally, the building's owner assumed control of advertising himself, so that if the builder wanted to let the hoarding, this had to be included specifically in his contract.

Meanwhile, considerable efforts were being made to improve the appearance of poster hoardings, and to achieve higher standards of display. Standard poster sizes were agreed by the trade, and surrounds of neutral-coloured paper were introduced. While the more orderly arrangement which resulted seems to have

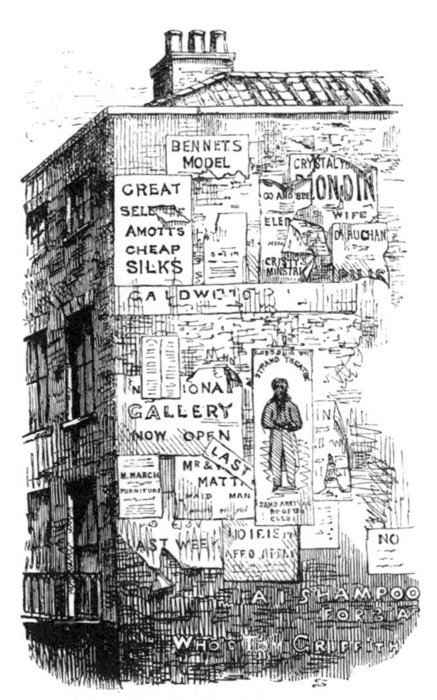

WALL-POSTING AS IT IS.

WALL-POSTING AS IT OUGHT TO BE.

Billposting As It Is and As It Ought to Be.
From William Smith: *Advertise How? When? Where?*, 1863.
(By courtesy of K. C. Matthews)

been visually desirable, it had the effect of limiting still further the number of posters which could be displayed, with the result that the rents of sites were forced upwards to the point where the best positions could only be afforded by the biggest advertisers.

For the advertiser wishing to use posters, the problems were formidable. There were hundreds of contractors who controlled poster sites in various locations, and billposters who carried out the actual posting. Then the sites themselves were graded into three categories, according to the type of town or district, the kind of street, and the size and situation of the individual hoarding. Advertising agents, when handling poster campaigns, were not prepared to accept information from the contractor at its face value, but used their own inspectors to make reports on the various sites under consideration. Some idea of the general atmosphere pervading these aspects of poster advertising may be gained from Thomas Beecham's refusal to consider using the medium unless he owned the site, since he believed he would otherwise be cheated by the bill poster.

Advertising agents seem generally to have acted as contractors, sub-letting the work in turn to local contractors and making their profit that way. In London, most large agents handled their own posting, even though there was keen competition among billposting firms to work for them and for large contractors. According to Moran, by the early years of the twentieth century major advertisers were growing dissatisfied at the agent's making a profit by squeezing others further down the line, since there was always the suspicion that in order to save money, he might be skimping on inspection. They were therefore themselves paying the agent a commission of 10 per cent on the value of the posting contract. The following figures taken from Moran give some idea of a provincial poster campaign, using 5,000 × 16-sheet bills in four colours:

Artist's sketch[a]	£25. 0. 0
Printing 5,000 at 1s.4d.	£333. 6. 8
Posting at £1 per 100 d/c units per month[b]	£800. 0. 0
Agent's services at 10 per cent on posting contract	£80. 0. 0
	£1,238. 6. 8

[a]The cost of the design could vary between £5 for an unknown artist and £100 for someone of the calibre of Hardy, Hassall or the Beggarstaffs.
[b]Posting includes the rental of the site. Damaged posters were replaced free of charge.

The effectiveness of the poster was limited to a large extent by the way it was used. As we have seen, advertisers looked on it as a means of achieving repetition. Not only did this put it at a disadvantage compared with the newspaper advertisement, which could carry a more lengthy message, but it also caused considerable irritation to many members of the public. For this reason, W. Teignmouth Shore, writing in *Saturday Review* in 1907, doubted its value:

'The effect of posting is often over-estimated; in many cases the money had better be spent in other directions. The chief, if not the sole, effect of posters is to familiarise the public with the name; it is the dreary drip of constant iteration'.

Repetition, however, may be a perfectly valid advertising tactic, both for reminding consumers about an existing product, and for ensuring that the name of a new product is known and remembered. To that extent, poster advertising was probably highly successful. How far it was socially responsible will be discussed in a later chapter.

3 Other media

While the press and posters were the dominant media, the balance between the remainder was constantly changing, as new methods of carrying messages were devised, and the deficiencies of older ones became apparent. The poster was vulnerable to weather, small boys, and oversticking by competitors. These disadvantages were overcome by the use of the enamel sign, which at the same time carried the subtle implication that the product advertised, the manufacturer, and the claim being made were as permanent as the sign itself, rather than transient like the printed poster. Enamel signs became exceedingly popular in the second half of the century, particularly after Benjamin Baugh of Birmingham took out a series of patents for enamelling and metal fabrication from 1859 onwards. The earliest advertisers included makers of animal foods, confectionery, and soaps, high-class retailers and some luxury products, though the latter categories disappeared as the method became more widespread and subject to criticism. Among the most popular sites were the approaches to railway stations, stair-rises, seat-backs and outer bodywork of omnibuses, shop-fronts, gable-ends, walls and fences.

The circular delivered to the house seems gradually to have been going out of favour, with William Smith leaving no doubt as to the reason:

> At the present time, Linendrapers send out the usual flimsy bills, announcing 'Great Sale', or 'Bankrupt Stock to be Cleared', by the boys or men (who take no interest except to reduce the bulk in the pocket-handkerchief of their arm) to Brixton, Dulwich, Dalston, Islington, Holloway, Highgate &c; and the general plan is to put bills under the door or knocker, when, if they are not surreptitiously taken away by the boys, how many of them, may I ask, are looked at or read? It is a waste of money, and so is the envelope directed 'To the Mistress of the House'.

The use of the postal service, meanwhile, was becoming increasingly popular, not only because of its greater reliability, but also because it allowed advertisers to reach prospective customers as a group wherever they lived, instead of having to deliver their messages to every house in a particular street regardless of suitability. This was of special interest to those firms wishing to advertise technical or industrial products, who might want to contact companies in a particular line of business at various addresses in different parts of the country. The introduction in 1855 of a halfpenny postal rate for circulars gave advertisers a further reason for selecting this particular medium.

As an indication of the sophisticated use being made of the postal service by the end of the period, the Reliable Advertising and Addressing Service had in 1907 a register of nearly 30,000 private car owners, arranged in geographical order and constantly revised, as well as London and suburban rental lists, with 170,000 names graded according to the value of the rent. The company could handle 250,000 circulars or catalogues in 24 hours, despatching in that year over 400 tons of mail, and addressing over nine million envelopes on behalf of a range of clients which included leading London department stores; manufacturing companies such as GEC, Dunlop, and the Columbia Phonograph Company; the Middlesex Hospital; the Franco-British Exhibition, and the Railway Benevolent Institution.[8]

Advertisers also produced their own mailings, with duplicated letters being used extensively in the last quarter of the century. In 1879 Lord John Manners, Postmaster General, reported to the Commissioners of the Treasury on the widespread use of circulars by leading City merchants, stating that 'not a few of them actually possess and have in habitual use either a Papyrograph or an Electric Pen Machine or both'. The latter device was described in his memorandum as 'a kind of stencilling by means of a perforated sheet of paper'. The other method mentioned, Lewthwaite's 'Papyrography', had been in use for some five years, would produce up to 250 copies, and was normally used by firms wanting quantities of between 50 and 100.[9]

The introduction of the telegram gave the advertiser an opportunity of delivering his message with considerably increased impact. Its potential was quickly realised, a *Times* reader complaining as early as 1864 that he had received the following communication:

> Messrs. Gabriel, dentists, Harley-street, Cavendish-square. Until October, Messrs. Gabriel's professional attendance at 27 Harley-street, will be 10 till 5.

By 1875 'An Adept' was reporting how a large furnishing firm had undertaken 'one of the boldest advertisements carried out in modern times'. Five thousand telegrams had been despatched from various offices, all timed to arrive 'at the fashionable dinner-hour, when most of the best families would be assembled', and telling the recipient that 20,000 bedsteads were now ready at the advertiser's store.

Telegrams, as will be seen later, could provoke a great deal of angry criticism, especially when sent out by advertisers to arrive during the night. Properly used, however, they could be an extraordinarily effective weapon in the advertiser's armoury. On 17 and 18 June 1914, the Spottiswoode, Dixon and Hunting advertising agency despatched 40,000 pre-paid telegrams on behalf of *Punch*, the message reading:

> Do not see your name on our Guinea Concession List for Pictures from Punch. Is this oversight on our part? Shall we reserve your set before closing Guinea Concession List? Kindly wire yes or no on enclosed prepaid form.

By 4 p.m. on 19 June, they had received 21,036 replies. Out of the total sent, only four were returned as untraceable.

Multiple-address telegrams used in this way were relatively cheap, the cost being 2d per copy delivered after the first copy, plus ½d for each word in the address. They were much employed by news agencies and betting tipsters, and were used in the 1913 LCC elections when 87,000 were sent out with the same text.

The sandwich-man was still in use, though contemporary illustrations generally show him as a miserable character whose appearance must have been a considerable hindrance to the products he was advertising. According to William Smith,

> The present style of sandwich-men is not up to the standard of the age. It is not to be expected, out of the small remuneration they receive, that these men should create a great sensation in the way of personal appearance, by parading the streets in evening dress; still an improvement might be made in their style. For instance, let the advertisers supply the men with a good strong suit of clothes, hat, and boots, and all complete, and a neat board.

A few years later, 'An Adept' commented in similiar vein, 'The animated sandwiches are only moveable hoardings or walls, and are usually the wretched sweepings of the workhouse', while Henry Sell described them as 'unmistakeable denizens of Whitechapel and St Giles'. Sometimes they were dressed in some kind of fancy garb, with Thomas Lipton, for example, using men in Indian dress to advertise his tea. Even military uniforms were worn, though this practice was restricted by the Uniforms Act of 1894.

Adolph Smith portrays the sandwich-man in the most dismal terms. Advertisers paid two shillings per day for his services, from which the contractor who hired him out took a commission of 25%. For this he was subjected to humiliation at the hands of small boys, who flung mud at him and tickled him with straws. He was kicked and knocked over by the conductors of passing omnibuses. He was pushed into the gutter by police, whipped by coachmen, and sprayed with dirt by passing traffic. In short, as Smith commented, 'Few men who earn their living in the streets are better abused and more persistently jeered at than the unfortunate individuals who let themselves out for hire as walking advertisements.'

In spite of this generally depressing picture, there are some signs of efforts being made to improve the lot and the appearance of the unfortunate sandwich-men. The Reliable Advertising and Addressing Service had a section handling this kind of work in addition to its postal operations, a photograph in the firm's prospectus showing the men clad relatively smartly in white uniform coat and cap. It is interesting to note the claim that 'With an improvement in the appearance of both men and boards, this form of publicity has now advanced in popularity with many firms whose business allows of outdoor advertising.'

Handbills were still in widespread use in the second half of the century, though again the kind of person engaged in distributing them can have done little to further the advertiser's cause. William Smith gives this pathetic description:

> 'You will occasionally on a wet or snowy day, when you would not even turn out a stray cat, see a poor and not too warmly clad old man, standing on the corner of a street, mechanically offering a bill, when not a single person is seen, except a wet policeman, plodding along his damp and dreary beat.'

Alternatively, bills were flung by the handful through the windows of cabs and carriages as they left railway stations.

From William Smith: *Advertise How? When? Where?*
(By courtesy of K. C. Matthews)

William Smith recorded in detail a walk he took through London during Cattle Show Week in 1861, and made calculations based on the number of bills he was handed en route:

> I started on the Thursday morning from the Elephant and Castle to the railway station, London-bridge; over the bridge, down Cannon-street, to the office of The Times; through the Temple gardens, along the lefthand side of the Strand, to the Adelphi Theatre. From there to the bottom of Parliament-street, through the Park and Sloane-street, returning down Piccadilly, Coventry-street, across Leicester-square, Longacre, Great Queen-street, Holborn-hill, along Smithfield, to the (then) Eastern Counties Railway; back down Bishopsgate-street, Cornhill, Cheapside, Ludgate-hill, Fleet-street, along the right-hand side of the Strand, Waterloo-place, Regent-street, Oxford-street, Baker-street, to the Bazaar; and then returned to the Adelphi Theatre by the same route, but on the opposite side of the road.

> During my journey I took every bill, book, or pamphlet that was offered to me, and on my arriving at my destination, I had in all two hundred and fifty. The average number of pedestrians that would pass the bill-deliverers in the route given, from 10a.m. to 7p.m., would amount to 40,000 – (that is certainly under the mark). If only one-half of the passers-by took half of the bills, &c., given away, the number distributed would amount in the nine hours, to two millions three hundred thousand!
>
> If we make the calculation on the same scale for the year, allowing for Sundays, wet and foggy days, out of the 365, they would amount to the almost incredible number of 575,000,000! Then we have to take into consideration besides, that I did not in my walks pass more than half of the London bill-deliverers, and only touched at one of the railway stations – (at the South Western Station, Waterloo-road, 1,500 bills are given away during the summer); so if we double the number, 1,150,000,000 are distributed.

Considerable ingenuity was exercised in the search for novel means of advertising. The Great Northern Railway received an application to instal advertising gas lamps. *The Times* reported in 1911 that 'auto-advertising cabinets' were to be set up along London tramway routes. Advertising panels were placed in public houses and luncheon-rooms. Bill-boards and samples were introduced into the harlequinades at theatres, and advertisements were later shown in cinemas. Advertisers put their announcements on matchboxes, menu-covers, horses, airships, balloons, paving-stones, an elephant, and anywhere else where they were likely to attract attention. In one case a man was equipped with a pair of boots, the soles of which were cut in the form of stencils supplied with ink by a tube running down his trouser leg.

To reach the public at night as well as by day, methods were developed for projecting messages on to the sides of buildings. An article in *The Times* in 1876 (reprinted from the *Globe*) recounted how traffic in the Strand was brought to a standstill by

> . . . a gratuitous exhibition of dissolving views, exhibited on a large screen on the second floor of a house on the north side of the street. The subjects exhibited have been facsimiles, on an enlarged scale, of the posters which appear on street-hoardings, and give in attractive forms, rapidly succeeding each other, gratuitous advice as to the best sewing machine, the cheapest hatter, where to dine, the most popular newsagent &c.

Projected advertisements were later used in railway stations, theatres and music halls, though in the latter instances there were complaints from advertisers that the displays took place before the audience in the most expensive seats had arrived, and sometimes even began before the doors had been opened.

The advertising stunt remained a favourite tactic throughout the period, its popularity seemingly increasing after the visits of the American showman Phineas T. Barnum in the 1840s and 1850s. The theatrical approach to advertising had an obvious appeal for William Smith, who at the time of writing his book was acting manager of the Adelphi Theatre. He promoted a play entitled *The Dead Heart* by the extensive use of sticky labels, the effect of which was that, in his words, 'Omnibuses, cabs, carriages, Windsor Castle, the Old Bailey Court, waiting-rooms far North; refreshment-rooms at the opposite extreme; steam-boats, bottles, glasses, and measures at the public-houses both in London and the country got these labels mysteriously stuck upon them.' In spite of complaints from irate members of the public who were unable to wash the labels off again, Smith regarded the effort as a great success on the grounds that it would be talked about, pronouncing it to be 'a capital mode of publicity'. What effect it had upon the sale of seats for the play he does not say.

Barnum-style tactics seem to have been employed particularly by retailers. When Jesse Boot opened a new shop, he hired a brass band, sandwich-men to parade the street, a Salvation Army man (normally employed by the company as a packer) to walk around with a bell proclaiming the merits of Boots products, and sometimes a coach-and-four carrying advertising placards, quite apart from using the more normal methods of bill distributing and festooning the upper storeys of his shops with signs.[10]

David Lewis, who opened his first shop in Liverpool in 1856, was another to adopt unorthodox publicity techniques. In 1869, he began issuing the halfpenny 'Pass Book', a notebook with a stiff cover and cash rulings, and some advertisements on inside pages. Twenty million copies were sold in ten years. In 1882, Lewis launched his *Penny Readings*, 250,000 of which were cleared in eleven weeks, and 3,500,000 over the next ten years. The opening of Lewis's Manchester branch in 1880 was celebrated by the release of balloons each carrying a list of the merchandise available and a request to the finder to notify the store where it was recovered. One reply came from Northern Italy.

Perhaps Lewis's most spectacular exploit, however, was the chartering of the *Great Eastern* as a floating exhibition and fair. Although he himself devised the plan, he died before it could be put into effect as part of the Liverpool International Exhibition in 1886. The ship, anchored in the Mersey and dressed out with banners advertising Lewis's stores, attracted some half million visitors.

The techniques used in Glasgow by Thomas Lipton, another highly successful retailer, were said to owe much to Barnum. Pigs were driven through the streets under a banner proclaiming 'Lipton's Orphans'. Thin men were paraded carrying signs inscribed 'Going to Lipton's', and fat men were proclaimed as 'Coming from Lipton's'. Monster cheeses were hauled through the streets to Lipton's shops, there to be stuffed with sovereigns and sold. He even tried to present the Queen with a five-ton cheese to mark her Jubilee in 1885.

Barnum-style tactics were by no means the exclusive preserve of the retailer. Henry Sampson relates, for instance, what happened when the manufacturer of a patent umbrella made use of the occasion of 'a great boat-race' on the Thames:

> Skiffs fitted with sails, on each of which were printed the parapluie, and a recommendation to buy it, dotted the river, and continually evaded the efforts of the Conservancy Police, who were endeavouring to marshall all the small craft together so as to leave a clear course for the competitors. Every time one of these advertising

> boats broke into mid-stream carrying its external umbrella between the dense lines of spectators, the advertisement was extremely valuable, for straying boats of every kind are on such occasions very noticeable, and these were of course much more so.

A few years later, Thomas Beecham adopted a similar means of advertising his medicines at seaside resorts, supplying local boatmen with free sails which carried a suitable slogan, and supplementing this by painting advertisements on the hulls of boats and on bathing vans.

By the turn of the century, consumer goods companies and some of the leading newspapers were following similar promotional policies. Competitors in a London to Brighton walking race were served with cups of hot Oxo, by courtesy of that company, from a fleet of twenty-five motor cars. Mellins Food spent £4,000 on balloons, the finders of which were entitled to prizes, while Lemco, another food company, dropped into the sea thousands of wooden bottles, the finders of which might receive anything from a quarter-pound jar of Lemco to a free seaside holiday. Newspaper and magazine proprietors, spurred by Harmsworth, offered even more extravagant prizes for the winners of competitions designed to boost their circulation. *Answers* offered a pound a week for life, while others ran buried treasure competitions in London's parks. Around the turn of the century, some of the most spectacular promotional schemes were dreamed up by S. H. Benson, the advertising agent, for the benefit of his clients. On a given day in 1897, he arranged for 1,000 grocers in London to give away a penny stamp and a sample of Rowntree's Elect Cocoa in exchange for that day's *Daily Telegraph*. In the same year a number of London omnibuses decorated with flags and cocoa-pods carried specially dressed conductors who gave each lady passenger a free sample of cocoa. During the South African War, Benson also organised the Bovril War Cable Scheme, in which 1,000 Bovril stockists in London had special bulletin boards, and ninety cyclists kept them supplied with despatches as soon as they arrived, much to the annoyance of newspaper publishers. The cost of the scheme to the advertiser was said to have been £10,000.

It is possible to trace examples of the theatrical approach to advertising throughout the period, with many of its proponents seeing the creation of excitement as an end in itself. At the same time, however, this concept was being questioned by writers thinking more deeply about the role of advertising in business. As early as 1875, 'An Adept' was already sounding a cautious note:

> We are free to admit that a Barnum-like course of publicity may occasionally be attended with success, and chiefly by the amusing absurdity by which such a system is generally accompanied; but we maintain that unless the object or matter advertised before the public has a sub-stratum of truth, honesty and propriety, then loss and not gain will ensue. Moreover, the super-structure and promise held forth to the world must be capable of bearing reasonable and even rigid enquiry.

The same writer commented specifically upon the use of sticky labels recommended so enthusiastically by William Smith: 'There was a short rage for a kind of adhesive label which, if moistened like a postage-stamp, would take much scraping to remove when once it was attached to any object. It gave rise to many practical jokes, and so deservedly went out of use.'

The advertising agent

As the volume of advertising expanded in the second half of the century, so did the number of advertising agents in business, particularly in London. However, all manner of people on the fringes of advertising began using the term to describe their operations with the result that it is virtually impossible to tell which of them were agents in the true sense of the word. S. H. Benson, a leading member of the profession, wrote in 1909 that advertising agent was 'a nondescript term incapable of definition', used as it was by frame-makers, news-vendors, railway companies, and refreshment contractors, as well as by two types of agent – those who simply handled space bookings on behalf of their clients, and those who in addition provided creative and other services.[11]

Two years earlier, Paul Derrick, head of a well-known agency, stated that there were 336 firms calling themselves advertising agents:

> A close scrutiny of the list would prove that according to the modern accepted definition of the term, fully 300 of 336 are not to be considered as advertising agents.
>
> Of the remaining 36, by far the greater number would prove to be only glorified examples of the submerged 300, inasmuch as they are brokers, or buyers and sellers of advertising space, rather than advertising specialists. They are more concerned in selling space than in studying the needs of the advertiser.[12]

To complicate matters still further, individual firms carrying on some or all of the agent's functions might also be involved in other business activities. Thomas Smith, for instance, as well as being a successful advertising agent, ran a printing business, was chairman of Dr Tibbles' Vi-Cocoa, proprietor of Newham and Co. (bedding manufacturers), and a director of Page Woodock Ltd. and the Omega Oil Co., in addition to which his agency acted as the advertisement department of *Great Thoughts* and *Christian Aid*. Rowland Brown, a notorious 'farming' agent of the period, was also a barrister with chambers in Lincoln's Inn.

Table VII (p. 100) gives some idea of the growth of agencies and other services in London during the second half of the century. It must be treated with caution, however, since the categories shown change over the years, firms may appear in more than one category, and their descriptions of themselves seem sometimes to be rather less than accurate.

While London was the hub of the advertising business, it did not by any means have a monopoly. H.A.B. wrote in 1880 that '. . . What are known as "Advertising Agencies" have sprung up like mushrooms in the principal towns, and in many instances have developed into flourishing businesses during the last 50 years.' Goodall, quoting *Advertising World*, put the number of provincial

TABLE VII

The Growth of Advertising Services in London, 1866–1906.

Date	*Category*	*No.*
1866	Advertising Offices	6
	Newspaper and Advertisement Agents, Town and Country	92
1876	Advertising Offices	56
	Newspaper and Advertisement Agents, Town and Country	125
	Advertisement Contractors	3
1886	Advertisement Contractors	76
	Advertisers' Agents	17
	Advertising Expert	1
	Advertising Offices	76
	Advertising Office (Indian)	1
	Advertising Office (Provincial)	1
	Newspaper and Advertisement Agents	127
1896	Advertisement Agents	83
	Advertisement Contractors	132
	Advertisement Offices for Prospectuses	11
	Advertisers' Agents	34
	Advertising Artist	1
	Advertising Offices	60
	Advertising Offices (American)	15
	Advertising Offices (Continental)	10
	Advertising Offices (Foreign)	11
	Advertising Offices (Indian)	8
	Advertising Offices (Provincial Newspapers)	9
	Advertising Offices (Scottish Newspapers)	2
1906	Advertisement Agents and Contractors	339
	Advertisement Offices for Prospectuses	25
	Advertisers' Novelty Manufacturers	26
	Advertising Artists	7
	Advertising Balloon-makers	2
	Advertising Offices (American)	8
	Advertising Offices (Colonial)	22
	Advertising Offices (Continental)	15
	Advertising Offices (Foreign)	21
	Advertising Offices (Indian)	13
	Advertising Offices (Provincial Newspapers)	17
	Advertising Offices (Scottish)	5

N.B. This table is intended to indicate the growth in the range of services offered. Year-by-year comparison is impossible because of changes in the categories employed. There is also considerable duplication within the figures for any particular year, with some names appearing in virtually every category.

Source: Post Office Directories

agencies at around seventy. They seem, however, to have handled relatively little of the growing volume of advertising. According to the *Circulation Manager* magazine in 1914, 'The proportionately small amount of business done by provincial agents does not matter very much. The bulk of it – probably five-sixths – is done from London.'

Many of the so-called agents outside London were probably little more than stationers and newsagents, who accepted advertisements from country retailers, and drove the hardest bargain possible with the local newspapers. One example is J. W. Savill of Dunmow, who described himself on his letterhead as 'Printer, Bookseller, Newsagent & c', and signed himself 'advertising agent & c'. On 16 May 1865, he wrote to the *Herts and Essex Observer*:

> Gentlemen,
>
> I enclose you an Advt. – 'Dunmow Building Society' for insertion in the 'Observer' next Saturday – make out an a/c with full price to the Society, and a similar one to myself with the usual commission of twenty five per cent which I deduct as an advertising Agent – send both a/c's to me and I will remit you the cash –
>
> I shall be happy to receive advts for you at any time if you will send a schedule or scale of prices and amount of Commission you allow –
>
> I also enclose you an Advt 'Housekeepers Receipt Book' this is on my own account – and you must consider whether you accept it or not –. *My offer is 5/- for 5 insertions*, if accepted & inserted I will remit cash at the end of the term or receipt of a/c – This offer is final – Yours &c J. W. Savill.[13]

The relative unimportance of provincial agents is not surprising. The original London agents had acted as a link between the large businesses of the capital and the country newspapers which provided their main means of reaching provincial customers. With the growth in the number of national papers, the London agent became handily situated for contact with media as well as clients. Then, as the number of agents in the capital increased and competition between them grew more intense, they turned their attention to important firms in the provinces. Thomas Smith, for example, recounts that his early search for business took him to see Campbell and Company in Glasgow, and Stewart Dawson and Company in Liverpool, while Louis Collins mentions that he had a client in Darlington. The result was that the agents outside London – if indeed they were agents in the true sense – seem to have dealt mainly with small advertisers using local media.

Throughout the second half of the century, a growing variety of firms was making use of the services which agents offered. Thomas Smith wrote in 1885, 'Our own list of articles advertised ranges from a £500 greenhouse to a cinder sifter, or from a marine engine of some five hundred horse-power to a toy spirit lamp warranted to boil water in five minutes.'

A few years later, Deacon's agency quoted major companies using agencies as including Mellins Food, Player's Tobacco, Colman's Mustard, Cadbury's Cocoa, Fry's Cocoa, Wright's Coal Tar soap, Pears, and Strange's Crystal Oil. By the turn of the century, agencies seem to have been acting for most of the leading consumer-goods companies. 'An Advertiser', writing in the twenty-first edition of *Successful Advertising* (1889), named companies using agents as including Cadbury's, Rowntree's, Suchard, van Houten, Bovril and Liebig, while S. H. Benson in 1901 gave a list of his agency's clients, among them such household names as Bovril, Rowntree's Elect Cocoa, Edward's dessiccated soups, Colman's starch, Lazenby's sauce and Ivory soap.

In *OBM 125 Years*, Stanley Piggott lists some of the major advertisers using the Mather and Crowther agency between 1884 and 1904. These include Mellins Food, Ivy soap, Venus Soap, Bond's soap, Player's Gold Leaf Tobacco, Fry's Pure Concentrated Cocoa, Clark's Carlton Tobacco, van Houten's Cocoa, Bushmill's Irish Pure Malt Whiskey, Dewar's White Label Whisky, Whiteway's Cider, Stower's Lime Juice, The Octopus Anti-Incrustator, Robert Brown's Four Crown Scotch Whisky, John Noble Knock-About Frocks, Wolsey Pure Wool Underwear, Royal Worcester American Corsets, Clarke's Ammonia, Yorkshire Relish, Mackintosh's 'Extra' Cream Toffee, H. Samuel's World Famed Watches, The 'Ever-Ready' Portable Electric Torch, Mother Siegel's Syrup, Dr Roberts' Alternative Pills, Phosferine, Ewbank Carpet Sweepers and Rudge-Whitworth Bicycles. It is interesting to note Piggott's comment that 'new business came less from clients leaving other agencies than from entirely new advertisers'.

As well as handling advertising for consumer products, agents were also working for the Government. According to Henry Sell, 'the Government Departments have always recognised the services of Agents, and nearly all of them pass their Advertisements through one or other of the leading agencies'.

Some types of business – particularly retailers, publishers, theatres, charities and educational establishments – traditionally placed their advertising directly with the media. In terms of turnover, however, they do not seem to have been of great importance. In Wareham Smith's view in 1907,

> About nine-tenths of the total business is done through advertising agents. The agents handle nearly all the business that is placed with daily newspapers. The monthly magazines accept a small amount of business from the advertiser direct. Of the advertising in the illustrated weeklies, about 25 per cent is arranged without the intervention of an agent.[14]

There are some indications as to the size of individual agencies to be gained from turnover figures, the number of clients on their books, and the number of staff employed. Financial information is scant. Mather and Crowther, one of the most successful agencies, increased its turnover from £20,000 in 1888 to £201,000 in 1903. In 1896, the firm changed from a partnership to a limited company with a capital of £20,000, most of the shares being held personally by Messrs. Mather and Crowther. Thomas Smith's turnover, according to an advertisement in the 1886 edition of *Successful Advertising*, was 'nearly £48,000'. By the time his agency reached its twenty-first anniversary in 1899, Smith was rather more reticent, an article in *Successful Advertising* that year stating:

'Probably Smith's Advertising Agency place advertising during a year's work to the tune of one multiple of six figures – say fifty or a hundred times as much business as the average advertiser has to give out.' It may be assumed that the agency's operation was highly profitable since when Smith died in 1904 he left nearly £109,000, and this after having begun his working life as a railway porter and at one point losing his life savings.

The number of an agency's clients can be grossly misleading. It might be assumed in Smith's case, for instance, that if the agency's turnover were fifty to one hundred times greater than the average advertiser, it would have between fifty and one hundred clients on its books. Yet according to a letter from Joseph Coote, Smith's cashier and accountant, included in *21 Years in Fleet Street*, the agency's client list contained 620 names, many of which must have been no longer 'active', while others were probably extremely small. The same is no doubt true of Horncastle's Central Advertisement Offices, which proclaimed ten years before Smith set up in business: 'References offered to nearly 1,000 clients distributed over all parts of the United Kingdom, all of whom advertise regularly through this agency.' Space brokers, who worked for a very low rate of commission, would obviously need more clients than bona fide advertising agents working for 15 per cent. Hence Percy Burton, a well known broker, was stated in 1912 to have 2,700 clients, while two years later the *Circulation Manager* magazine estimated that the top twelve or fifteen agents had 'as many as a hundred advertisers'.

In terms of people employed, Mather and Crowther had a staff of 100 in 1894. Five years later, Smith's staff were stated to number 43, while a photograph of S. H. Benson's employees in 1901 shows some 55 people who appear to be office staff, plus twelve messengers smartly attired in tunics and caps bearing the company's name. These were among the largest agencies, and offered a range of services. At the other extreme, Eric Field recalls that when he joined the Spottiswoode Agency in 1905, the staff consisted of three canvassers, a space-buyer, a book-keeper, two typists and two office-boys. When he later moved to the Caxton Publishing Company, that firm had set up its own agency consisting of two principals and a typist.[15]

It was in some ways a logical step from advising companies about press advertising to the active selling of space in particular journals – a practice known as 'farming'. Wareham Smith described how a farming agency operated:

> It takes over the whole of the advertising space in a journal. This is known as 'farming', and the financial arrangement is either a commission paid to the agency on the advertising revenue it earns for the publisher, or the payment of a fixed sum by the agency for a fixed amount of space.

It is important to put farming into perspective, since it is often assumed that all agents at this period ran their businesses in this way.

The case in favour was summarised by one of its more notable exponents, Henry Sell:

> The more important agents rent large spaces and prominent positions in various media, at lower or wholesale rates, which is alike profitable and convenient to the proprietors of papers, magazines & c., and to the Advertiser; for while it takes off the hazard of letting spaces, and gives a fixed sum without trouble to the former, the latter has the benefit of reduced prices.
>
> Thus it will be found that nearly all the best places in newspapers and magazines are in the hands of Agents.[16]

Farming could undoubtedly be beneficial to the publisher in that it relieved him of the responsibility of selling space. The young Alfred Harmsworth, for example, owed his successful beginning in publishing at least in part to T. B. Browne, a well-known agent who farmed space in *Answers* on commission. The practice also had advantages for the farmer-agent in the form of the large discounts he was able to obtain. (According to opponents, he generally retained these rather than passing them on to his clients.) For the advertiser, however, it seems that farming was something of a mixed blessing, since it gave the agent a reason for pressing the claims of particular publications which might be wholly unsuitable for the task in hand. The objective advice, on which earlier agents had prided themselves, could not be present in the case of the farmer. The point was not lost upon contemporaries. In 1875 'An Adept' wrote that 'The farming out to professional touters of advertising space by publishers of periodical and other works is a plan to be deprecated.' Ten years later Louis Collins declared 'The best agents hardly ever canvass. Such are consulted.' Considering the agent's position, he continued, 'He should not farm any publication, for, when it is to his direct interest to recommend a particular publication, that moment he ceases to be above suspicion . . . He must fill these spaces or he would lose money by renting them.'

In some cases, agents had a financial interest in, or even owned, the publications they were recommending to their clients. They saw nothing wrong in this, and even made a point of publicising the fact. The Walter Judd agency, for example, in a booklet published in 1912, proudly proclaimed the 'exceptional facilities' they were able to offer, 'as their Principal is the chief proprietor in eight of the leading trade papers, besides being a director of the two leading Weekly Illustrated Papers.'[17] Louis Collins, however, had argued over thirty years earlier that no one could work on this basis and still consider himself an agent:

> Human nature is alike all the world over, and if a man has a pecuniary interest in anything, he is sure to regard it with a favourable eye, and be blind to many of its imperfections.
>
> Therefore in the true interests of his clients, the agent should neither be part proprietor of any newspaper or periodical, nor should he be interested in it through what is termed 'farming' its advertising columns.

If he farms, according to Collins, he does so to make a profit on the transaction. He is then a contractor or a dealer, not an agent.

The range of services offered by agencies expanded in response to pressures put upon them by advertisers. They had always been involved in buying space, and to some extent in writing copy. As newspapers yielded to commercial pressures, however, and began admitting display advertisements to their columns, the mainstream of agency development divided. One direction was taken by the 'service agents', who kept the commission in full, and provided the creative work and technical expertise which became so important when illustrations were also permitted. Thomas Smith, writing in the twenty-first edition of *Successful Advertising* (1889), stressed the way that the responsibility for creating advertisements had moved away from the advertiser to his agency: 'Many firms who have had advertising departments of their own have relinquished them in whole or part because it was found in practice that the experience gained of advertising, and of the changing conditions ruling it, in an advertiser's own office are too partial and limited.'

Smith at this time already had what he called the 'Ad-writing and Designing Department'. By the turn of the century, leading agents were offering all the services which might be required in the preparation and execution of a campaign. Mather and Crowther, when they moved to new premises in 1894, were able to offer a media department handling newspaper and outdoor advertising, and advertisement checking; a production department in which the agency carried out its own type-setting, process engraving, and printing; an art department supervised by an art director; and an editorial department. A few years later, S. H. Benson was advising his clients regarding expenditure, media selection, and the geographical disposition of advertising, in addition to which his agency would prepare copy and designs, negotiate rates, buy printed material, and check that all advertisements had appeared when and where booked.

The second stream of agency development includes those agents whose sole function was to buy space on behalf of their clients, keeping only a small part of the commission – sometimes as little as one per cent – and rebating the remainder. It seems often to have been smaller agents, without the facilities to provide a full service, who operated in this way, though before World War I the R. F. White agency handled government advertising for a 2½ per cent commission. In addition, partial rebating seems to have been quite common, with the size of the rebate related to the services required, or the promptness with which the advertiser settled his account. Thomas Smith, for example, rebated almost £1,800 to his clients in 1886.

While there was little objection to rebating from advertisers, the larger of whom stood to save thousands of pounds, it was a matter which excited considerable controversy in other quarters. In particular, the system worked indirectly against the interests of newspapers in that it tended to make the position of agents less stable. In 1904, a group of fifteen London papers headed by *The Times* actually tried to stop commission-splitting by refusing to accept orders from agents unless they signed an agreement to retain the commission in full. Their effort was a failure, and Moran, writing the following year, commented that 'Most journalists have, however, withdrawn from this arrangement, finding the rule disregarded.'

As competition between agents grew more intense, the question of rebating became intertwined with that of the rates actually being charged for advertising space. Certain agents went touting for business, making it appear that to book advertisements through them would represent a saving. This they could do either by returning a higher-than-normal proportion of the commission, or by quoting lower rates for space than their competitors – sometimes lower even than the rates quoted by the newspapers themselves – or a combination of both. Cheap rates could be offered by farming agents with long-term contracts at advantageous rates with particular papers. Alternatively they could give a slightly smaller reduction on farmed papers, using their saving to offset an apparent rate cut on some major national publication, or simply quote a blanket rate for a long list of publications, many of which would be of little use to the advertiser, without giving individual rates for any of them. Other agents would quote cut rates for a list, but would rely on some of the publishers not inserting the advertisement as per contract – for example on the wrong page or in the wrong position – in which case the agent would refuse to pay the publisher but would still charge his client at the normal rate. As a variation he might cut out a page from the copy of the publication sent to his client so that the advertisement would appear to be facing editorial matter instead of another advertisement, and as such would be chargeable at a higher rate. Should none of these methods be possible, the agent could quote apparently low rates for space and offset this by high charges for blocks, or simply book less space than his client actually paid for.

To make matters more complicated, some papers were prepared to offer special deals and discounts to agents, so that the advertiser often did not know what his agent had paid for a particular insertion. The commission allowed to agents also varied widely, being as high as 30 per cent in the case of some weak and desperate publications. Should an agent undertake to rebate a percentage of his commission, there was in addition a subtle distinction between keeping say 5 per cent and returning the balance (which might include extra discounts), and rebating 5 per cent and keeping the balance for himself.

Sometimes practices such as these could cross the thin line which divides sharp practice from illegality. Deacon's agency in their *Handbook* cautioned readers against '. . . persons in London who send out from obscure alleys of Fleet Street or the West End long lists of newspapers, in all of which they offer to insert an advertisement at a most tempting price, sometimes as low as 2d or 3d per insertion . . . this list of country newspapers is in reality one and the same paper, an alteration being made in title only, to give the necessary number of country names.'

In a letter to *The Times* in 1870, 'Veritas' warned readers to check agents' invoices:

> Having detected an overcharge in one particular item, I demanded to see vouchers for the previous charges and, after considerable delay and trouble, they were produced, the result being that in about two months very limited advertising to

about £50, there was an overcharge of nearly £7, some made up by advertisements charged for but never sent to the paper; in one instance four insertions were charged on specified dates, but only one sent to the paper.

The following day, there was a reply from Street Bros., advertising agents, pointing out that advertisers ought in their own interests to inspect agents' files, and ask for accounts to be verified. Admitting there were black sheep, Streets stated: 'We have often been asked to examine accounts and give evidence with reference to the "gentry" who call themselves "advertising agents".'

In 1903 Albert Edward Gibson, describing himself as an advertising agent, appeared at the County of London Sessions on several charges of obtaining money by false pretences from the Guardians of the Poor of the Wandsworth and Clapham Union. Gibson had inserted advertisements on their behalf, but when submitting invoices had altered some of the figures so as to obtain more than he had actually spent. It was argued in his defence that this was common custom in the trade, though the day after *The Times* reported the case, it carried a paragraph stating: 'We have received a number of letters from leading advertising agents strongly denying the truth of this contention, and we have no doubt that in the case of firms of standing and repute the suggestion is entirely groundless.'

Far from trying to swindle their clients, the responsible full-service agents saw themselves as members of a profession, and were trying to run their businesses along professional lines. They even refused to act for companies who were competitors. As Louis Collins wrote in 1885, 'It would be absurd for one of the large cocoa advertisers to go to the same agent who worked for a rival. I have always declined business from firms running in direct competition to my clients . . .' Thomas Smith declared in similar vein: 'It frequently happens that new advertisers are sent to us, whose business we cannot handle from the fact that we are already doing similar business on a large scale for other clients.' What is particularly surprising in Smith's case is that his client list at that time (1899) numbered 620.

By the beginning of the twentieth century, there was a growing pressure for some kind of professional organisation to which bona fide agents could belong, membership of which would be an indication of competence and reliability. A writer in the *Magazine of Commerce* in 1907 not only backed such a proposal, but called in addition for the setting up of an organisation to administer some kind of test of ability, commenting 'The very fact of there being no such institution as I advocate . . . makes it possible for almost anyone to call oneself an advertising agent, particularly as the profession requires little or no outlay beyond that involved in the rent of a room and the purchase of a name plate.' The article was stimulated by the setting up of the Incorporated Society of Advertising Agents, whose existence seems to have been short-lived, apparently because of continued disagreement on the old question of rebating. The society represented the views of the service agents led by S. H. Benson, who tried to insist that commissions should be retained in full. This in turn led to disagreements as to who should be admitted to membership, and whether commission should be granted to non-member agents or to advertisers placing their advertisements direct with the press. Even the publishers, who had previously tried to institute similar provisions themselves, were by no means in favour of the new body, whose demise was therefore probably inevitable.

Before leaving the subject of advertising agents, some mention must be made of their near relative, the advertising consultant. According to Thomas Russell, he was the first person to use the title, when he set up on his own after leaving *The Times* in 1908. He also claimed that no one previously had offered a general consulting service. Working either for the advertiser or the advertising agency, the consultant undertook the writing and designing of advertising material, and provided general advice on broader aspects of a company's business. Payment was usually by means of a fee for work carried out or per consultation, though in some cases the consultant might be retained on an annual contract basis. Because they did not take commission from the media, consultants regarded themselves as being above the wrangles which surrounded rebating and rate-cutting, Thomas Russell saying that he functioned 'exactly as a consulting physician', and Goodall describing them as 'the Harley Street element of the advertising profession'.

Though Russell may have been the first person to use the title, he was certainly not the first to perform the functions of the consultant. In 1892 A. L. Teele, an American, was writing of how he had introduced to London 'a new sort of business, the writing of advertisements, and with it everything which pertains to the preparation of advertising matter'. He was emphatic that he was not an agent or a contractor, and did not take commissions – 'I believe I am the only professional advertising expert in England with an office distinct and separate from an advertising agency.'[18]

Consultants were later to form themselves into a society, membership of which was intended to designate someone who was not paid by commission, and even organised their own examinations. Their efforts were thwarted, however, by advertising agents who appropriated the title to give themselves an added respectability. As Thomas Russell wrote sadly in 1926: 'This calling is not yet sufficiently populous to give it the general importance which the independent services offered by it deserve: but it is slowly developing. It is practised by a number of persons who do not adopt the designation, and the designation is adopted by many more who do not practice the avocation in any strict sense.'

Ethical standards among agencies and consultants clearly varied considerably. The larger service agents seem generally to have been of good reputation, with undesirable practices occurring mainly on the fringes, and among small firms desperate for business. While it may seem strange at first sight that many of these practices were tolerated by advertisers, two points should be remembered. Firstly, many companies were becoming involved in advertising for the first time and, lacking professional knowledge, fell an easy prey to anyone calling himself an advertising agent and offering what appeared to be highly competitive terms. Secondly, there was a lack of information on the extent to which media rates were negotiable, this being one of the main reasons for employing an agency. The complex tangle of reductions, rebates, discounts and commissions made it exceedingly difficult for the advertiser to determine what kind of deal had been struck between agency and media, especially when some disreputable operators would even falsify invoices.

Criticism and Control in the Nineteenth Century

IT SEEMS TO have been inevitable that the nineteenth century should see abuses in the use of advertising. It was fast developing into a commercial weapon of awesome power. Limits obviously needed to be set, but because it was still in a state of evolution and was assuming so many new forms, there was no body of experience to which its practitioners could turn. Lines were therefore drawn empirically as the need arose, with advertisers and their agents exploring the limits of public tolerance by trial and error. At the same time there were forces at work which limited their freedom to a considerable degree. A number of advertising activities were brought within the scope of the common law, legislation was introduced to curb some of the worst excesses, and particularly in the later years of the century, efforts were made by people working in advertising to ensure reasonable standards of conduct.

This chapter deals firstly with criticisms which were voiced against advertising, secondly with the efforts made to reform the business from within, and thirdly with the legal constraints under which advertisers worked.

Criticism

The first half of the century saw a growing public reaction against advertising. Protest was sporadic, and in some instances was directed against things which today would not be considered as advertising at all. It does, however, provide an interesting indication of what were felt to be desirable standards of commercial behaviour, and reveals trends which can be followed through to the twentieth century.

The attack on advertising was originally directed not so much against its visible manifestations as the need for such an undesirable activity to take place at all. The most forceful statement of the case is probably that given by Macaulay in the *Edinburgh Review*, in the context of book advertising:

> The puffing of books is now so shamefully and so successfully practised, that it is the duty of all who are anxious for the purity of national taste, or for the honour of the literary character, to join in discountenancing it. All the pens that were ever employed in magnifying Bish's lucky office, Romanis's fleecy hosiery, Packwood's razor strops, and Rowland's Kalydor, – all the placard-bearers of Dr. Eady, – all the wallchalkers of Day and Martin, – seem to have taken service with the poets and novelists of this generation. Devices which in the lowest trades are considered as disreputable, are adopted without scruple, and improved upon with a despicable ingenuity by people engaged in a pursuit which never was, and never will be, considered as a mere trade by any man of honour and virtue. A butcher of the higher class disdains to ticket his meat. A mercer of the higher class would be ashamed to hang up papers in his window inviting passers-by to look at the stock of a bankrupt, all of the first quality, and going for half the value. We expect some reserve, some decent pride, in our hatter and bootmaker. But no artifice by which notoriety can be obtained is thought too abject for a man of letters.

It is clear that Macaulay sees advertising as a matter of taste and class, something which really ought not to be necessary. An article in the *Athenaeum* took the argument a stage further, pointing to the necessity for protecting some people from advertisements and from their own folly:

> There can be little doubt that the stupidest cluster of trashy papers, the most insignificant articles, may by dint of eternal paragraph be forced into sale. It could not otherwise happen that Day and Martin, Rowland, Colburn and Bentley, Eady, Warren and those after their kind could lavish so much money in the praises of their oils, their books, their pills and their polish if there did not exist a class of human beings who are greedy of belief. It is the duty of an independent journal to protect as far as possible the credulous, confiding, and unwary from the wily arts of the insidious advertiser.

Similar sentiments are to be found in an article in the *Illustrated London News*, supporting the London Hackney Carriage Bill. Protection is conceived here as something necessary, particularly in the case of the lower classes:

> It is in fact a palpable loss to the revenue to permit railways, cabs, and omnibuses to trade in advertisements, and to pay no duty upon them. But, independently of this consideration, neither the interior nor the exterior of public vehicles ought to be used for such a purpose. Railway directors and officials seem aware of the fact that first-class passengers would not approve of such a practice in first-class carriages. The impertinence is, therefore, confined to second and third-class travellers, who are presumed to be too poor to be indulged in the amenities of life, though wealthy enough to purchase the quack medicines or slop garments of pertinacious advertisers.

Carlyle also deplored the use of advertising, writing in *Past and Present* (1843) that 'There is not a man or hat-maker born into the world but feels, or has felt, that he is degrading himself if he speak of his excellences and prowesses, and supremacy in his craft.' Perhaps the most blistering attack, however, was to come from *Fraser's Magazine* in 1869, in an article entitled 'The Great Force'. The writer castigated advertising for its effect on commercial standards and on the interests of the public. It allowed shoddy and defective goods to be sold as perfect, and cheap products as expensive. It allowed quack doctors to foist their medicines upon perfectly healthy people. It facilitated adulteration, was a boon to promoters of shady companies and to moneylenders, enabled worthless plays and publications to prolong their existence, and enabled worthless products to be presented as necessities of life. '. . . The wholesome food, the common wants, the comforts and the health and very lives of the British people appear to depend on their guess, at what may be true or (more likely, less) false in the super-superlative appeals offered for their decision.'

A piece of advertising which Carlyle would surely have deplored.
(By courtesy of the Robert Opie Collection)

Attacks on the desirability of advertising were doomed to failure, because it was filling an obvious need and because it brought results. Ironically, there is no better proof of this than the way that Macaulay and the writer of the *Athenaeum* article are able to quote the names of nationally known companies who have reached that position by using the very method which is being condemned.

A second line of attack, which proved to be far more effective, concentrated on specific types of advertiser. One of the main targets, particularly in the second half of the century, was the medical quack, whose activities prompted the following outburst fom the *Pall Mall Gazette* in 1867:

> Foul advertisements, filling a considerable space and entering into details carefully arranged to excite alarm and prurient curiosity, are inserted at great expense in the columns of newspapers, many of which profess the highest principles, and claim to be the representatives of every form of progress and civilization. This loathsome and shameful source of gain is of great importance in a money point of view, and is no doubt found highly advantageous by several of our contemporaries.

Many patent medicines were perfectly harmless, were often useful for treating minor complaints, and probably had some value as a placebo. If their advertising caused annoyance, this was the result not of the claims being made, but of the frequency with which they were repeated – Gilbert's

> Advertising quack who wearies
> With tales of countless cures.

In other cases, the exaggerated and untruthful claims employed showed a cynical disregard for sufferers from serious diseases. Dr Collis Brown's Chlorodyne, for example, was promoted in the nineties as a treatment for a bewildering range of complaints, which included consumption, diphtheria, cholera, epilepsy, cancer and meningitis, while Leo's Microbe Pills were claimed to kill the microbes of consumption, nervous debility, cancer, worms and fever.

There is a distinction to be drawn between advertisements of this type, and those used to further an unlawful purpose. At the Central Criminal Court in 1864, John Ray (or Wray) and William Anderson were charged with demanding money with menaces. Wray had advertised as 'Dr Henery', and had been consulted by Captain Montague Augustus Clark concerning a complaint for which medicine was prescribed. Following this, Captain Clark received a bill for £150 and various letters, one of which stated that the bill was for advice for 'spermatorrhea brought on by self-pollution', and threatened to make this known to the War Office and to his father's neighbours in Scotland. Captain Clark, who had already paid £86, brought the matter to the attention of the police, and as a result of ensuing prosecution both defendants received terms of imprisonment.

The day after *The Times* reported the case, it carried a long editorial describing in detail the methods employed by quacks of this type:

> Their system is as simple as it is infamous. A person imagines himself to be suffering from some illness, about which, from motives of false delicacy, he is unwilling to consult a regular medical practitioner. He sees one of the advertisements of these quacks, which, to the disgrace of our Press, are scattered broadcast over the country, and is induced to apply to him. From that moment on, he ceases to be a free human being, and if he cannot summon up the courage and determination displayed by the prosecutor in this case, he is a slave under the lash of the quack he has applied to until he compounds with this tyrant for some monstrous ransom . . .
>
> It is notorious to medical men that hundreds – nay, thousands of pounds are constantly being extorted in this way. Persons in a good position will pay almost anything to avoid the exposure they are threatened with.

Among the correspondents who wrote congratulating the paper on its stand were a number of medical men, one of whom estimated that in twenty years he had helped force quacks to disgorge some £17,000.

The potential for blackmail was also exploited by some purveyors of abortifacients. A scheme organised by the three Chrimes brothers was uncovered by the police in 1898, and ripples of alarm ran through the ranks of the Newspaper Society as prosecuting counsel in the case warned newspapers of the risks they ran by publishing advertisements of this kind.[1] Worried members wrote to the Society asking if this applied to all advertisements for female complaints, and sending the examples. The Society showed them to its solicitor, whose response was as follows:

> In my opinion, advertisements of this description are most objectionable and improper. Anyone not a child must know their object, and that is a felonious one, and, in my view, if it could be proved that a woman obtained the medicine with a view to procure abortion in consequence of reading the advertisement of it in a particular paper, the publisher of that paper would run the serious risk of finding himself indicted for inciting the commission of a felony, or for being accessory to the commission of one, and I believe the judge would find his way to a conviction. Further, I am not sure that these advertisements are not obscene publications, for which a prosecution could be successfully maintained.[2]

Advertising was quickly exploited by the confidence trickster, to whom it offered the prospect of reaching a far wider audience than ever before, while at the same time preserving his anonymity behind a box number or pseudonym. One particular type of swindler is described by an officer of the law in Smeeton's *Doings in London*:

> He with his arm in a sling is an advertising swindler, and belongs to a gang, who live upon robbing people by advertising to borrow or lend money, or procure situations. If they borrow, they have sham deeds, and make false conveyances of estates; if they lend, they artfully inveigle the borrower out of his security, which they take up money upon, and convert to their own use, without the poor deluded person's knowledge . . . It is the greatest folly to pay attention to advertisements in the papers, offering assistance of the above nature.

The 'situations wanted' columns of newspapers provided a convenient means for girls wanting posts as governesses to attract the attention of potential employers, though it left them vulnerable to men whose intentions lay in other directions. One would-be seducer was exposed by *The Times* in 1843, in a splendid outburst of righteous indignation. The paper reminded readers that it had already published

> . . . An intimation that a brutal fellow was exercising his prurient ingenuity in entrapping governesses who solicited employment through the means of the public press. We then announced our intention in case his cowardice did not quench his lust, of exposing him to public infamy. It appears that his temerity is equal to his villainy. We learn from indubitable testimony that, instead of burying himself in proper obscurity, he still courts exposure by improper machinations against the

Hassall's famous Skegness poster – a simple way of conveying the concept of a bracing climate. (By courtesy of Skegness)

Dudley Hardy's work for the Albion Lamp Co contains characteristic figures, and also illustrates how an effective visual idea can be ruined by too much confusing copy.

Advertisers sometimes made use of public figures without their consent: neither the Queen nor Princess Alexandra would have allowed themselves to be exploited for these commercial purposes. (By courtesy of the John Johnson Collection)

Two of the most famous appeals used by the Government to stimulate recruitment during World War I: the charisma of the leader, Kitchener; and the moral pressure to fight for one's life and family. (By courtesy of the Imperial War Museum)

honour and innocence of fatherless friendless women. We can keep no terms with one who is at once so foolish and so wicked. We will keep no terms with him. We therefore tell the world that he lives in Marlborough-square, Chelsea. We also tell him to profit as best he may by this notoriety, and not to provoke further castigations at the hands of brave and honourable men.

Several correspondents took up the subject, and in a later article the paper described how Manchester girls advertising for posts received replies from a neighbouring town, stating that as the writer was only in Manchester once a week they should attend for an interview at his lodging, which generally turned out to be a brothel.

Ladies wishing to do some form of work at home also seem to have proved an easy target for tricksters. Advertisements asking for help in copying out sermons for ministers, doing needlework for churches, and other equally innocuous-sounding tasks, always carried some stipulation that money should be sent in advance to cover the cost of postage or materials, and this was usually the end of the story.

The pages of the Newspaper Society *Circular* contain numerous examples of the way that criminals exploited advertising. Bogus traders with addresses near Smithfield duped country readers into sending their produce for sale by promises of high prices. Loans offered on advantageous terms failed to materialise after the applicant had been persuaded to part with fees for registration, enquiries, travel, and so on. One enterprising criminal took advertisements in over 200 papers to offer non-existent Christmas hampers at two guineas each. In another instance, a youth named Thomas Cook placed advertisements offering cheap travel to Paris, even obtaining credit from a number of leading papers which failed to ascertain that he had no connection with the more celebrated firm of the same name. Bogus competitions could also show the criminal a good return if the public could be persuaded to send off money for a 'special sample' to qualify for a non-existent prize, or even to send stamps with their entries in sufficient numbers.

The medium *par excellence* for illegal communications was undoubtedly the penny post, since they need be seen by no one except the recipient. In a section of *London Labour and the London Poor* (1861) called 'Advertising Begging-Letter Writers' Andrew Halliday outlined some of the methods employed in fraudulent appeals for charity:

Sometimes they are printers whose premises have been destroyed by fire; at others, young women who have been ruined by noblemen and are anxious to retrieve themselves; or widows of naval officers who have perished in action or by sickness. There was a long run upon 'aged clergymen, whose sands of life are running out', but the fraud became so common that it was soon 'blown'.

From about the middle of the century, complaints begin to arise about the use of advertising to sell obscene articles and publications. The post was again the ideal medium, since circulars could be sent to selected members of the public without risk, unless the recipient chose to complain to the police. The author of *The Language of the Walls* (1855) was offered 'a new and choice assortment of voluptuous facetiae', in the form of twelve sets of engravings at prices from £1.1s.0d. to £21.0s.0d., and it seems probable that a considerable trade was carried on, the details of which will never be known. Under section 4 of the Post Office (Protection) Act (1882) any person sending by post 'Any indecent or obscene print, painting, photograph, lithograph, engraving, book, or card, or any indecent or obscene article' was guilty of a misdemeanour, though the Post Office's legal advisers were of the opinion that these were matters in which the postal authorities ought not to become involved. In 1897 a request from the Home Secretary to prosecute a dealer in obscene books was refused on the grounds that the Post Office were not guardians of public morals, any such action being the responsibility of the Home Office itself.

Obscene material was also offered through the columns of the press. In 1910 a member of the Advertisers Protection Society drew the attention of readers of the *Circular* to the advertisements being carried by *Reynolds News*. An editorial comment endorsed his view, drawing particular attention to the book publisher who claimed 'This remarkable book has been twice seized and prosecuted by the police during the last fifteen years.' Other papers seem to have been equally at fault, since when Walter Wilkins appeared before Lambeth Magistrates in 1901 to face a charge of selling obscene photographs, the prosecution produced in evidence a large number of advertisements, some of which were said to have appeared in newspapers of the highest respectability.[3]

In addition to criticism of particular types of advertiser, the second half of the century saw a growing attack on abuses which were related to specific media. The enthusiasm with which billposters went about their work had been the subject of adverse comment in earlier years, and was to reach a crescendo in the last quarter of the century, resulting in several acts of Parliament whose effect was to curb their activities. *The Times* in 1874 was concerned at what it called 'placarding the streets'. On 26 March a reader complained 'Was the magnificent thoroughfare of Queen Victoria Street intended for a huge advertising medium?' The paper took up the point on 20 April, in an article tracing the history of legislation aimed at curbing advertising in the streets. The writer commented acidly:

> It is sad enough to endure the exhibition of goods on the pavements and the thrusting forward of every kind of projection to attract the attention of passengers and induce them to become purchasers, but that only shows the bad taste of the dealer. The case is different when, besides, his house or warehouse is let to indiscriminate placarding for the benefit of 'railway companies, theatrical managers, auctioneers, and advertisers of every description, bill-posters, and others.

By 1892, *The Times* was adopting a more conciliatory tone towards the use of posters in towns – 'They cause a great deal of pleasure to a great many persons who live very dull lives, and in a very large number of instances their surroundings are already so hideous that they cannot be made worse' – though it still objected to placing hoardings in areas of rural beauty – 'There at least we must cry "hands off" to the advertiser.'

In fact, two of the most notable instances of public outrage against the activities of advertisers resulted from the erection of signs or hoardings within the jurisdiction of urban authorities. In 1897 the Bovril Company obtained an option on property in Edinburgh overlooking Princes Street and the Mound, announcing that it proposed to adorn the exterior with illuminated signs. Such was the outcry that the company announced it was deferring its plans until the wishes of the public could be ascertained, and subsequently abandoned them altogether. Four years later, a similar outcry greeted the erection of an advertising sign for Quaker Oats in a prominent position on Dover cliffs. Feelings ran so high that Dover Corporation successfully promoted a local Act of Parliament to enable it to deal with such abuses. In this instance, the furore seems to have owed something at least to the fact that the advertiser was an American company, since amid the indignation expressed at England being defiled as a result of policy decided in the United States, there is no reference to another sign, clearly visible in photographs of the site, advertising Pextons, a firm of clothiers and drapers in Dover.

The erection of signs and hoardings was, in fact, the only kind of advertising activity to provoke an organised public reaction, which came in the form of the National Society for Controlling the Abuses of Public Advertising, popularly known as SCAPA. Its first membership list, published in 1893, contains a number of notable names, including Robert Bridges, Sydney Courtauld, three members of the Fry family, Holman Hunt, A. V. Dicey, Millais, Quiller-Couch, and William Morris, while three years later, the Society's council could also boast the talents of Sir Walter Besant, Walter Crane and Rudyard Kipling. It was, however, essentially a minority upper middle-class movement, consisting mainly of members of the professions – academics, doctors, lawyers and churchmen – with a leavening of peers, painters and members of Parliament. The widespread publicity it received was out of all proportion to its support, and was due almost entirely to the unceasing efforts of Richardson Evans, its Honorary Secretary from 1893 until 1923. By lobbying for support among friends and acquaintances, writing a prodigious number of letters to the press, addressing meetings, and issuing occasional publications when the Society's finances allowed, Evans succeeded in keeping public attention focussed on SCAPA and its work. He originally believed there to be a reservoir of goodwill among members of the public, even though their inertia would preclude their ever becoming members. He soon seems to have realised, however, that the mass of the population was essentially apathetic. When he turned an article he had written for the *National Review* into what he called 'an overgrown pamphlet of 112 pages', the result was that 'it was commended by the reviewers, but, out of an edition of 500 copies, only 30 were sold to that undiscerning body, the general public'.

In 1907, after fourteen years' pressure, Parliament eventually passed the Advertisements Regulation Act, which empowered local authorities to make bye-laws for the regulation of hoardings and the protection of certain amenities. After this, the focus of SCAPA's activities changed to one of surveillance, pressing authorities to exercise the powers granted them by Parliament, and trying to ensure that those powers were as wide in scope as Parliament had allowed. By the end of 1914, some 30 counties and 34 boroughs had made byelaws under the 1907 Act, and for this the Society must take much of the credit.

Another advertising method to attract widespread – though not organised – criticism was the practice of clothing sandwich-men in something approximating to British army uniform. As a reader of *The Times* complained in 1892, 'Not the least hateful form of advertisement is that of sending board men and waifs to march up and down busy streets in grotesque costume, and especially in miserable travesties of the Queen's uniform.' This particular abuse was ended by the passing of the Uniforms Act (1894), though since the legislation only related to British uniforms, it was still possible in 1906 to promote a new novel, *The Enemy in our Midst*, by parading sandwich-men decked out as German soldiers.

Stunts and promotions did not always achieve the effects intended by their organisers. An early scheme devised by Thomas Lipton involved the issue of 'Lipton pounds', which looked like Scottish banknotes but carried advertising slogans and the message: 'I promise to give on demand in any of my establishments HAM, BUTTER and EGGS as given elsewhere to the value of one pound for fifteen shillings.' Unfortunately for Lipton, some illiterates could not distinguish his pounds from genuine notes, and a labourer received twenty days' imprisonment for trying to pass one in an eating house. Even worse, a man who received one in change at a bookstall brought an action against Lipton in the Small Debts Court, which although unsuccessful, led to Lipton's being censured by the sheriff as 'most impudent and reprehensible'.

Thomas Barratt of Pears Soap went a stage further, making use of actual coins. In the early 1880s, French ten-centime pieces were still in circulation, being accepted as the equivalent of an English penny. Barratt imported 250,000 of them, stamped them with the word 'Pears', and put them into circulation. The result was that Parliament had to pass a special act, setting a date after which French coins would no longer be accepted, and the Government was put to the trouble of collecting up and melting down all those which had been defaced.

Considerable annoyance was caused by the use of multiple-address telegrams for advertising. In a letter to *The Times* in 1896, 'A Nervous Old Lady' described how she had been awakened by her maid standing at the bedside holding a candle and a telegram. Having found her spectacles, she was able to read the message: 'Peter Robinson's sale now proceeding'. The method continued to be used even after the outbreak of war in 1914, and provoked a flood of complaints to the Post Office, especially from people with relatives in France. Public reaction was summed up by the *Daily Chronicle*: 'Few of us are without the anxiety as to some relative or friend "somewhere". It is unfair to give us the telegraphic start which may be the War Office, and turns out to be a music-hall advertisement!' The writer was probably referring to Percy Honri, an entertainer who made considerable use of telegrams, and who actually sent off 1,297 in one day in 1915. Far from intervening, the Post Office found the method so profitable that it was considering advertising it to advertisers.

It is difficult to say how widespread criticism became during the nineteenth century. The instances given above suggest that it was very much an upper-middle-class phenomenon. Advertising was not a political issue, and seems not to have worried the working classes, whose welfare was of such concern to the critics. The prevailing mood, as far as the mass of the public were concerned, is probably best summed up in the music-hall songs of the period, which give a quite different picture from the columns of *The Times* and the Reviews. For example, *Advertisements* with words by H. J. Whymark, which dates from 1865, displays amusement rather than concern:

> In this enlightened age, sensation's all the rage,
> And daily folks are some fresh scheme devising
> We scarcely pass a street, but what we're sure to meet,
> The novel ways they've now of advertising,
> The eye is sure to fall, on six-foot posters tall,
> Each hoarding, post or dead wall adorning,
> But in an hour or more they're by others plastered o'er
> And something new we witness ev'ry morning.
> (*Chorus*)
> If you doub't [sic] what I say, when out you wend your way
> Go large and small advertisements perusing
> You'll laugh and grow fat, and what's more besides that
> You'll find them both instructing and amusing.

Another song also called *Advertisements*, but this time by Herbert Tucker, was published in 1890. Making use of advertising slogans, it provides an interesting indication of how well known they were, and also of the disbelief with which most of them were regarded. It tells the story of an uncle who read only advertisements:

> He skipped the leading articles and scorned the latest news
> But every bold advertisement with rapture he'd peruse.
> He read, he talked of nothing else; the thing became a bore.
> You got quite sick of Eno's Salt and Rowland's Kalydor.

Disaster struck, however, when the old man was involved in a railway accident, and his mind became confused:

> He bade his wife use Reckitt's Blue to dye her grizzly locks,
> And he told her Beechams Safety Pills struck only on the box.

The chemist wondered what on earth the worthy man could mean
When he asked for Epps's Extract of Bronchial Chlorodyne.
He rubbed his horse with Worcester sauce to heal a sprain or scratch,
And he tried to take out grease spots with a Waterbury watch.
(*Chorus*)
There are fifty cures for every ill, and each one is the best,
You can drink them down, or rub them in, or nail them on your chest.
You can make hair grow on an ostrich egg, if you try the proper stuff:
You can make toes sprout on a timber leg, if you only use enough.

The reason for the apparent lack of concern must surely be that advertising was merely reflecting the trading standards of the time, statements which might seem startling to us being perfectly acceptable to a public used to dealing with the huckster and the horse-trader. In any case, the vast majority of advertisements were probably unexceptionable even by present-day standards – such anyway is the impression of the writer after reading many thousands of examples.

Control from within

During the first half of the century, there is clear evidence that some newspaper publishers were extremely concerned about advertising standards. Cobbett (though hardly typical) refused to accept medical advertising in the *Porcupine*, writing in the prospectus: 'While all other Advertisements will be gratefully received and carefully inserted, the *obscene* and *filthy* boastings of quackery will, on no consideration whatsoever, be admitted.' He took this stand despite being told that it would cost him £500 per annum in lost revenue. *The Times*, too, was exceedingly careful about the kind of advertisements it would allow to appear in its columns. The paper's manager, Mowbray Morris, refused to accept 'the name of another person by way of commendation of the advertiser's invention', and when offered an advertisement for the *Times Life Assurance Company*, he was sufficiently worried about possible confusion in the public mind to take legal advice on whether to accept it. Confirmation that these were not isolated examples comes from the *Periodical Press of Great Britain and Ireland* (1824) which commented: 'Every day there are advertisements offered to English newspapers, that are refused for the personal allusions they make, or the object they wish to accomplish.'

The second half of the century saw a mounting debate on all sides of the business about the extent to which advertisements were – or ought to be – truthful, and the practicability of excluding those which fell short of the desired standard. Advertisers, in the form of the Advertisers Protection Society, expressed concern to certain newspapers about some of the advertisements they were carrying. The response was hardly encouraging. One member was told by 'a very large newspaper' in 1906 that it could not put intelligence into the heads of its readers, and that they must look out for themselves because publishers could not act as their guardians. Other papers laid the blame for misleading advertising squarely on the agents, or argued that there was already enough protection under existing law. The Society's *Circular* attacked this apparent lack of concern, pointing out that one of the worst offenders was the *News of the World*, for whom there could be no possible excuse on financial grounds, since every week the paper attracted more advertisements than it could publish. In 1910 the Society wrote to the Association of Advertisement Managers (i.e. those responsible for selling space on behalf of publications) suggesting a meeting. The reply from the Association was that 'the matter having been thoroughly debated, it was decided that the ills are not so prevalent as was suggested in your letter, and that no good could come from a conference on the subject'.

It would be wrong to infer from these instances a total lack of concern on the part of publishers. What is apparent is an enormous discrepancy in standards between different publications, and an almost total inability to take any kind of concerted action. The first surviving copy of the Provincial Newspaper Society's *Circular* (1873) contains the following comment by a reader:

> We know which are, and which are not, swindling advertisements, and when for the sake of a few shillings we permit the infamous things to appear in our columns, we cannot deny that we are in a sense assisting to rob to a certainty a number of needy people among our customers. There is always a certain percentage of folks ready to be duped, but I think it is not the place of a newspaper to offer facilities for such a kind of robbery.

According to Thomas Russell, late of *The Times*, publishers argued it was impracticable for them to interfere since they could not examine every advertisement submitted, and if the public knew that some were being rejected, they would tend to put more trust in the others. It was therefore best to leave readers to question everything which appeared.

On the other hand, readers of some publications were able to benefit from elaborate safeguards introduced by the publishers. *London Opinion*, for example, guaranteed a refund in the case of any article advertised in its columns which turned out to have been misrepresented. Other journals required mail order advertisers to allow a representative to inspect the goods being offered. *The Times*, as we have seen, had always taken a strict line, and was to continue to do so into the twentieth century in spite of mounting financial difficulties. During December 1913, it carried the following statement on its front page:

> Whilst *The Times* cannot guarantee the bona fides of every single advertisement that appears in its columns, the greatest possible care is taken to ensure that all advertisements inserted are trustworthy, and readers may with an unusual degree of confidence, accept statements made by any firm whose advertisements appear in these pages. The Management invites correspondence with respect to advertisements which do not fulfil the spirit of the above assurance, and if upon investigation any reasonable complaint that reaches us is found to be justified, such advertisements will not be allowed to appear in future. Moneylenders' advertisements are rigorously excluded.

The difference in attitude between various publishers made it extremely difficult for G. W. Goodall, trying to describe the situation which existed on the eve of World War I:

> It is to be noted that the newspaper, recognising the close connection between its editorial and advertisement sides, is inclined to establish something in the nature of an advertisement censorship. Naturally, all papers of standing draw a more or less hard and fast line with a view to excluding obviously questionable and undesirable advertisements, the point at which the line is drawn varying according to the philosophy of life which the journal adopts.

The second half of the century also saw the poster trade coming under tighter control from within. To some extent the impetus came from site owners, who were able to impose conditions as to the kind of posters they would accept. In 1855, for example, W. H. Smith signed an agreement with the Chester and Holyhead Railway Company, under which he was to act as sole contractor for all the advertisements displayed on its stations. In appointing Smith, the company insisted on the following provision:

> And in case any of the said Advertisements shall be deemed by the said Company or the Board of Directors thereof to be of an objectionable character the said 'W. H. Smith and Son' shall within forty-eight hours of a request or complaint in writing by the Secretary of the said Company cause the Advertisements so objected to, to be removed or in default of their so doing the same may be removed by the said Company or their Officers.[4]

Posters were in fact the first advertising medium to have a formalised system of self-regulation. Towards the end of the century, the organisations representing billposters became particularly sensitive to public criticism and threats of legislation, realising that they tended to be blamed for any objectionable poster which found its way on to the hoardings. Such was their concern that in 1890 the two leading bodies – the United Bill-Posters Association and the London Bill-Posters Association – set up a Joint Censorship Committee. The scheme as originally conceived was entirely voluntary. Posters were not examined prior to distribution, but any member who received one which he felt to be questionable could submit it to the committee, which could order it to be amended or withdrawn.

Where matters of taste were concerned, the worst offenders were probably the touring theatrical companies, of which there were estimated to be between 700 and 800. They made considerable use of stock posters, which consisted of standardised designs run off by a printer in large quantities, and overprinted as required with the name of a play, a theatre, and a company. If a particular design was banned, it could therefore result in a serious loss to a printer who happened to have large quantities in his storeroom. Printers and theatre managers accordingly made representations to the Censorship Committee, complaining that they had no knowledge of how its decisions were arrived at, and claiming representation for themselves. In January 1901, a meeting was held between representatives of the three sides, resulting in a Joint Stock Committee being formed to review posters currently being held in quantity by printers. Some 113 were considered, of which 54 were passed, 23 amended and 36 condemned, following which most advertisers seem to have adopted the far more sensible course of submitting a sketch in advance.

In 1902 the United Bill-Posters Association proposed that the theatrical and printing interests be admitted to the Censorship Committee itself – a move violently opposed by the London bill-posters. As a result, a new censorship committee was set up, consisting of representatives of the United Bill-Posters and the printers and theatrical managers, with the London Association opting for a committee of its own.

The aim of the censorship system as stated was to exclude anything which was impure in suggestion, ultra-sensational, or offensive to religious susceptibilities. While major abuses falling into these categories were certainly avoided, bill-posters were hardly the best arbiters in aesthetic matters. So anxious were they to avoid trouble that they indulged in visual bowdlerisation, rejecting a partly clad female figure in classical style advertising the Rome International Exhibition of 1911 (the design having been accepted by every other country to which it had been offered), and insisting on suitably decorous modifications to a nude athlete on the poster for the 1912 Olympic Games in Stockholm.

In general terms, these efforts at control were appreciated by the more responsible advertisers, the Chairman of the Advertisers Protection Society commenting that 'The censorship of posters which has been established under the guiding hand of Mr Walter Hill of bill-posting fame, has worked well, and our hoardings are now fit to give pleasure and information to all, and offence to none.' Unfortunately, objectionable posters had not been entirely eliminated, since those rejected by the Censorship Committee could be posted by the theatrical companies themselves, or sent to a small fly poster who was not a member of one of the major organisations. In such circumstances, the only sanction left was to oppose the renewal of a theatre's licence.

Some of the most flagrantly dishonest advertising material of any description was sent through the post, as is apparent from evidence in the Post Office Records. The Post Office itself, however, remained reluctant to take action, on the ground that it was not empowered to do so. In spite of a number of complaints, nothing was done to curb the activities of I. H. Bos and Company of Amsterdam, describing themselves as cotton dealers, who invited recipients of their circular to subscribe towards the purchase of a quantity of American cotton, offering a return of £25 on each £5 invested. Complaints about money-lenders and bogus investment companies went similarly unheeded, even when coming from the police.

It may be that while adopting this apparently uncompromising attitude, the authorities were prepared to take action unofficially. This certainly happened in one instance, when the Postmaster General of the United States appealed for

Walter McIntosh of London to be prevented from selling nude pictures by post to American customers. While the request was refused, it is clear that someone at St Martins Le Grand had given instructions to sabotage McIntosh's business by cutting off his source of supply, since included in the records are four letters from him to a dealer in Budapest, requesting catalogues and asking why his orders had not been met.[5]

In two areas of advertising, the Post Office exercised remarkably tight control. The first was on postal envelopes themselves, where advertising was permitted in principle provided it did not include an excess of printing or the use of coloured backgrounds, which it was feared might prove harmful to the eyesight of sorters. The second was advertising in stamp books, with the agreement appointing Henry Sell as official contractor in 1911 stipulating that:

> No order shall be accepted or entertained for the insertion of any advertisement which shall in the opinion of the Postmaster General
> relate to alcoholic liquors, lotteries, betting or gaming or
> be contrary to public policy or
> relate to any illegal or immoral business or matter or
> be in any way unsuitable for insertion in Government publications.[6]

The authorities seem to have been conscious of the effect a misleading advertisement might have on the reputation of the Post Office, and conversely of how official approval might seem to have been given to a shady advertiser by allowing him in the stamp book. It is particularly fascinating to see the criterion applied by the Postmaster General in 1914 in rejecting an advertisement for Baudon's Tonic Wine, the copy for which read as follows:

> Invaluable in Medico-Chirurgical Maladies and most potent Remedy for CONSUMPTION and all Chest Affections, ASTHMA and BRONCHITIS, NERVOUS and GENERAL DEBILITY, SCROFULOUS & STRUMOUS Disorders, ANAEMIA and LYMPHATISM, RACHATISM (RICKETTS), CONSTITUTIONAL WEAKNESS, And in all Wasting and Exhausting Diseases, and Convalescences following Accouchments, etc.

The reason for its rejection was that the product contained alcohol.[7]

Considerable credit for the raising of standards in advertising must go to the more respectable and responsible advertising agents, who were able to exert a measure of control in three ways. Firstly, they refused to act for companies whose activities or products were open to question. Secondly, they were taking increasing care to ensure the truthfulness of the advertisements they created. And thirdly, they were beginning to avoid using media which accepted objectionable advertising. Agency proprietors around the turn of the century included men such as Thomas Smith, devout Christian and lifelong teetotaller, and S. H. Benson, fifteen years a naval officer, who was described by Thomas Russell as 'The finest and most upright man whom advertising has produced.' Russell also mentioned some years later that 'There are advertising men today who will not handle the account of a distiller or any producer of alcohol', while *The Times* in 1909 declared:

> The best modern advertising has the publication of facts for its basis. The day of successful claptrap and vulgarity, still more the day of exaggerated and deceptive misrepresentation, is quickly passing away. So far from these being fostered by advertising agents, the whole tendency of the best and most successful agents is to repress them. Even apparently trivial inaccuracies are on principle, excluded from advertising.

Obviously this was not the whole picture. Those advertisers whose deliberate objective was to mislead or defraud the public would deal directly with the media rather than using an agency, while those whose business might be questionable though not unlawful might go to one of the small firms on the fringes of advertising, for whom the term 'agent' was merely a flag of convenience. The Newspaper Society *Circular* contains many warnings against shady operators of this kind, the following being a typical example: 'Mr. James Frazer, of the Advertising, Literary, and Commission Agency, 61, Clarence Road, Kentish Town, is incorrigible, but his efforts meet with little success. His advertisements are of the 'cheap and nasty' kind and ought not to be inserted in any reputable newspaper.' Fortunately, the standards set by the more respectable agencies became accepted as the norm, and Frazer and his kind were driven out of the business.

Though advertisers may have imposed high standards as far as their individual advertisements were concerned, there is no evidence of any concerted pressure for controls. The Advertisers Protection Society made a few inconclusive moves, but was more concerned with safeguarding advertisers in their dealings with media. Truth seems to have been a matter of profit rather than ethics, with the Society's *Circular* commenting: 'Imagine your own advertisement appearing side by side with one of those "catch-penny" announcements, and meeting the eyes of people who have been swindled by the latter! Would they be likely to place much faith in your arguments, or to write for your catalogue?' Truth was also relative, since as a writer in the *Magazine of Commerce* observed: 'To exaggerate a little may, in view of the unscrupulous exaggerations of one's competitors, be absolutely necessary if one wish [sic] to remain in business.'

By the turn of the century, a powerful new influence for truth was beginning to make itself felt. The major growth area in advertising expenditure seems to have been in repeat-purchase consumer goods, where a single sale was of little value to the manufacturer. He needed regular purchasers, and these by definition needed to be satisfied with the product they had bought. A large-scale manufacturer could only build a successful business on the basis of continued patronage, but a consumer who found that a product did not perform as promised in the advertisement would not return a second time.

What brought this problem to the fore was probably the growing intensity of competition, which meant that in advertising terms, the simple reiteration of a company or product name was no longer sufficient. As well as ensuring that his products performed properly and offered value for money, the advertiser now also had to give the potential purchaser a reason for buying. As Thomas Russell wrote,

> He will ask in what way they differ from competing products, if any. He will seek out what are called the selling points . . . the selling points explained in the advertisements indicate the reason for preferring one product, or one particular brand before others.

In this situation, it was always possible that the over-enthusiastic advertiser or his agent might claim more for the product than it actually merited, which could mean a disappointed customer, and a sale for a competitor on the next occasion. Market forces were therefore helping to intensify the pressure for control from within. As *The Times* observed in 1904, in a feature on 'Commercial Advertising' (probably written by Thomas Russell): 'To spend time and money in advertising inferior goods, or wares that do not give the purchaser satisfactory value for his money, is one of the few processes in advertisement of which the result can be predicted with absolute certainty. It fails.'

Legal control

The widely held view of the nineteenth century as a time when advertisers could do virtually as they pleased is a long way from the truth. Controls of a kind existed from the early years, and gradually increased in scope and severity as the century advanced.

One of the first problems to be tackled was that of obscene advertisements. Under section 4 of the Vagrancy Act of 1824, 'Every person wilfully exposing to view, in any street, road, highway, or public place, any obscene print, picture, or other indecent exhibition . . . shall be deemed a rogue and a vagabond, within the true intent and meaning of this Act.' Such an offender was liable to three months' imprisonment with hard labour. Under the terms of a further Vagrancy Act passed in 1838, the earlier provisions were extended to cover material exhibited in windows.

Street advertisers in general had been restricted by the Metropolitan Paving Act of 1817, which empowered parishes to appoint Surveyors of Pavements whose duties included issuing licences for the erection of hoardings, removing boards from the pavements, and regulating and removing projecting signs. Under section 54 of the Metropolitan Police Act of 1839, many further advertising activities were specified as offences punishable by a fine of up to 40 shillings. Sandwich-men, and billposters carrying the tools of their trade, would have been affected by the restriction on 'Every person who shall roll or carry any cask, tub, hoop, or wheel, or any ladder, plank, pole, showboard, or placard, upon any footway, except for the purpose of loading or unloading any cart or carriage, or of crossing any footway' (S54(8)). Billposters and wallchalkers also found themselves caught by the prohibition against 'Every person who, without the consent of the owner or occupier, shall affix any posting bill or other paper against or upon any wall, fence, or pole, or write upon, soil, deface, or mark any such building, wall, fence, or pole with chalk or paint, or in any other way whatsoever . . .' (S54(10)). Judging from old engravings and the comments of contemporaries, it seems that this provision was impossible to enforce efficiently.

The Act also tackled the problem of noise, embracing 'Every person . . . who shall blow any horn or use any noisy instrument, for the purposes of calling persons together, or of announcing any show or entertainment or for the purpose of hawking, selling, distributing or collecting any article whatsoever, or of obtaining money or alms . . .' (S54(14)). Whatever the other effects of this subsection, it resulted in a member of the Salvation Army being convicted in 1890 for banging a drum.

Provisions similar to those in the Metropolitan Police Act were contained in the Town Police Clauses Act of 1847, which enabled them to apply to urban areas throughout the country.

The use of omnibuses for advertising provided some specific problems which were dealt with by legislation. The Metropolitan Police Act, for example, extended the provisions of the Vagrancy Acts to cover obscene exhibition to the annoyance of passengers, while the London Hackney Carriage Act of 1853 made it unlawful to display advertisements in such a way as to affect the light or ventilation, or to cause annoyance to the passengers.

The 1853 Act also dealt with obstruction of the highway by sandwich-men and advertising carts:

> It shall not be lawful for any person to carry about on any carriage or on horseback or on foot, in any thoroughfare or public place within the limits of this Act, to the obstruction or annoyance of the inhabitants or passengers, any picture, placard, notice, or advertisement, whether written, printed, or painted upon or posted, or attached to any part of such carriage, or any board, or otherwise. (S16.)

Vehicles now seem to have been permitted to carry advertisements so long as they also carried goods or passengers. If they were on a journey for some other purpose than to display advertising, and any display was incidental to the main purpose, then they could not be guilty of obstruction.

Towards the end of the period, a number of Acts of Parliament were prompted by the mounting criticism of outdoor advertising, which was concentrated in particular on the erection of unsightly signs. The Advertisements Regulation Act of 1907, for which the SCAPA Society had fought so long, empowered a local authority to make byelaws for regulating and controlling hoardings and similar structures exceeding twelve feet in height, and 'For regulating, restricting or preventing the exhibition of advertisements in such places and in such manner, or by such means, as to affect injuriously the amenities of a public park or pleasure promenade, or to disfigure the natural beauty of a landscape' (S2). In urban areas, local Acts of Parliament often laid down conditions for the erection and maintenance of hoardings around building sites, while the Public Health Act Amendment Act of 1907 laid down that 'A person shall not use any hoarding or similar structure, which is in, or abuts on, or adjoins the street, for any purpose, unless it is securely fixed to the satisfaction of the local authority' (S32(i)). This Act also extended the ban on sky signs (solid letters fixed to a frame, and visible as a silhouette against the sky) in force in London since 1891, to cover the whole country.

Flashing lights and other illuminated signs were a particular problem in London, where they were blamed for a number of traffic accidents. In 1900 the London County Council therefore introduced byelaws prohibiting the exhibition of flashing lights or searchlights so as to be visible from the street, or in such a manner as to cause danger to traffic, and prohibiting any owner or occupier from exhibiting them from his premises.

The Indecent Advertisements Act of 1889 was aimed at curbing the activities of the medical quacks. It provided for summary proceedings against persons affixing or inscribing 'any picture or printed or written matter which is of an indecent or obscene nature' so as to be visible to the public, or delivering, throwing down, or exhibiting it, or sending another person to do any of those acts. Matter of an indecent nature was defined as being 'Any advertisement relating to syphilis, gonorrhoea, nervous debility, or other complaint or infirmity arising from or relating to sexual intercourse . . .'

The distribution of bills and the use of sandwich-men was regulated in London by the Metropolitan Streets Act of 1867, which laid down that 'No picture, print, board, or placard, or notice, except in such form or manner as may be approved of by the Commissioner of Police, shall, by way of advertisement, be carried or distributed in any street within the general limits of this Act by any person riding in any vehicle, or on horseback or being on foot . . .' The Commissioner seems not to have used these powers, apparently on the grounds that it would deprive some poor people of the chance of earning a living, and in consequence there is an increasing volume of complaints in the early years of the twentieth century. Eventually in 1912, *The Times* noted a 'sudden cessation of the practice of distributing handbills to passers-by' as a result of the Commissioner announcing his intention to enforce the Act, and in particular to require police permission for the distribution of bills.

The parliamentary desire to stop off-course betting led to Acts being passed in 1853 and 1874 which drove English bookmakers first to Scotland and subsequently to Belgium and Holland, though English newspapers could still generally publish their advertisements. A particularly vicious aspect was singled out for special attention, however, in the Betting and Loans (Infants) Act of 1892 which made it an offence to send an infant a document inciting to betting, or inviting him to borrow money. The onus was put on the person whose name or address appeared on the communication to prove that he had no knowledge of it or that it was being sent, or to show that he had reasonable grounds for believing that the addressee was 'of full age'.

At the same time as Parliament was legislating to deal with particular advertising abuses, the judges were being asked to interpret the common law in the light of new situations which were arising. The increasing scale of newspaper circulations was giving tradesmen and businessmen the opportunity not only of bringing their own goods to the notice of the public, but also of destroying the reputation of their rivals in a manner hitherto unprecedented. As early as 1731, in the case of *Harman v. Delany*, the judge had issued a stern warning to advertisers: '. . . The law has always been very tender of the reputation of tradesmen, and therefore words spoken of them in the way of their trade will bear an action, that will not be actionable in the case of another person; and if bare words are so, it will be stronger in the case of a libel in a publick newspaper, which is so diffusive.'

The problem was bound to become more acute as advertisers began comparing their products with those of competitors, and several cases involve newspapers, as the fight for circulation and advertising revenue became more acute. In *Latimer v. Western Morning News* [1871] it was held to be libellous to say that columns of advertisements were copied from other papers, since this was an imputation against the character of those persons conducting the newspaper in question. A similar verdict was reached in *Russell v. Webster* [1874] concerning a statement that a paper had a column for quack doctors and usurers.

If an advertisement contained disparaging remarks only about the goods, rather than the maker, it was necessary for the plaintiff to show that actual damage had resulted. In *Evans v. Harlow* [1844] the defendant had published an advertisement warning the public that the plaintiff's self-acting tallow syphons and lubricators wasted the tallow. This was held only to be a reflection on the goods, which of itself was not actionable unless it could be shown that it had prevented the plaintiff from selling his goods to a particular person. In the second half of the century, the courts were prepared to allow advertisers to include comparisons in their advertisements, provided that there was no false representation about the quality of the rival product. In *Young v. Macrae* [1862], a case involving two suppliers of paraffin oil, Macrae published a report by a Dr Muspratt who compared the products to Macrae's advantage. Young thereupon sued, but Chief Justice Cockburn held that a comparison showing the defendant's product to be better than the plaintiff's was still compatible with the plaintiff's product being a very good one. 'If this is libel,' he declared, 'the effect would be to put down ninety-nine out of every hundred advertisements of articles that we see.'

Similarly, in *Hubbuck v. Wilkinson, Heywood and Clarke* [1899] it was stated that the defendants had published a circular comparing their zinc paint with that of the plaintiffs and claiming:

Exactly nine pounds of paint were used in each case, and each coat took the same quantity of paint. Judging from the finished work, it is evident that W. H. & Co's zinc had a slight advantage over Hubbuck's, but for all practical purposes they can be regarded as being in every respect equal.

Lord Lindley, Master of the Rolls, declared that this was a mere puff, and that 'If the only false statement complained of is that the defendant's goods are better than the plaintiff's, such a statement is not actionable, even if the plaintiff is damnified by it.'

Although advertisers enjoyed considerable freedom as far as comparisons were concerned, an instance of where the courts drew the line is provided by *The Western Counties Manure Company v. The Lawes Chemical Manure Company* [1874]. The defendants had circulated an analysis of their respective products, in which it was stated that the plaintiff's guano 'appeared to contain a considerable quantity of coprolites, and was altogether an article of low quality'. This was held by the court to be sufficient grounds for an action to be maintained.

Throughout the nineteenth century and well into the twentieth the names of well-known public figures are to be found in advertisements for a wide range of products, particularly patent medicines and similar preparations. (See illustration on p. 131) Often, it would seem, this was done without the consent of the persons concerned, and might even be promoting products of which they disapproved. In *Lord Byron v. Johnston* [1816] a publisher who had advertised poems as being the work of Byron was restrained by injunction from publishing those poems, or any part of them, in the poet's name. However, when Sir James Clarke, Physician in Ordinary to the Queen, sought an injunction in 1848 to stop a patent medicine vendor from selling 'Sir James Clarke's Consumption Pills', he was notably unsuccessful.

Freeman, the defendant, had issued advertisements couched in the following terms:

BY HER MAJESTY THE QUEEN'S PERMISSION.
SIR JAMES CLARKE'S CONSUMPTION PILLS.
A certain cure for consumption, and an unfailing remedy for coughs, asthma, difficulty of breathing &c. In the long list of maladies which affect mankind, none can be regarded with more terror than consumption; so stealthily (sic) is it in its approach and so insidious and fatal in its effects, that many, merely labouring under a temporary cough or shortness of breathing, are already within the fatal grasp of this powerful enemy, whose terrible inflictions have rendered desolate so many thousands of happy homes, and blighted the hopes of so many anxious and doting parents. When we reflect upon the prevalence of pulmonary consumption, and the fatal termination which in almost every instance follows, under the ordinary mode of treatment, we cannot but regard the discovery as an invaluable boon to society, for averting so deadly a scourge. Such is the unfailing nature of the medicine now offered to the public, that the numbers who have been pronounced past recovery are now in the enjoyment of perfect health, and can scarcely imagine, that at one time, they were suffering from that hitherto fatal disease, consumption.

Advertisers were keen to promote their products using famous personalities – sometimes without permission of the people concerned. (By courtesy of Bovril Ltd)

In addition, Freeman had produced handbills and advertisements with the following words purporting to have been written by Sir James: I am fully aware that by introducing my cure for consumption as a Patent Medicine, it will create some astonishment in the minds of the profession; but it is only by having recourse to such means, that the knowledge of this discovery can be disseminated amongst these unfortunate persons whom it has been my aim to relieve.' The pills actually contained mercury and antimony, both of which could be harmful in cases of consumption.

The judgement of Lord Langdale, Master of the Rolls, must have opened the way for many rogues trying to lull their victims into a sense of security by the use of impressive names:

> I do not go along with the notion, that this physician, eminent as he is, and an honour to any country, has been seriously injured in his reputation by any such false statements as have been published by the defendant. It is one of the taxes to which persons in his station become subjected, by the very eminence they have acquired in the world. Other persons try to avail themselves of their names and reputations for the purpose of making a profit for themselves: that unfortunately continually happens.

In *Dockrell v. Dougall* [1899] a London physician failed in his action against a mineral water company which had used his name without permission, though Lord Vaughan Williams in the Court of Appeal was at pains to point out that this did not mean that any person could say a physician had recommended a quack medicine when it was not true. 'He did not mean anything of the sort, and in such a case the jury would properly award considerable damages, in addition to any remedy to which the plaintiff might be entitled.'

Company promoters were also given to parading an array of impressive names in their advertisements. Sometimes the injured parties would write letters to the press indicating that they were not connected with the company concerned. Others had recourse to the courts. In *Routh v. Webster* [1847] the plaintiff sought an injunction to stop his name being used in a prospectus for the Economic Conveyance Company, which showed him to be a trustee. In his judgement, the Master of the Rolls declared:

> I am of opinion that the plaintiff is entitled to the injunction; and if it subjects the defendants to expense, let it be a warning to them as well as to others not to use the names of other persons without authority. What! Are they to be allowed to use the name of any person they please, representing him as responsible for their speculations, and to involve him in all sorts of liabilities, and are they to be allowed to escape the consequences by saying they have done it by inadvertence? Certainly not!

The increasing promotion of branded products led to a growing emphasis being placed on the use of trading names, and a number of cases coming before the courts concern attempts by an advertiser to benefit from another firm's advertising by making use of its name. In *Croft v. Day* [1844] it was stated that both the founders of the famous blacking manufacturers, Day and Martin, were dead. A nephew of the original Day, together with a friend named Martin, had set up in business as Day and Martin in the same street as the older firm, selling blacking with an almost identical label. The Master of the Rolls condemned such practices in forthright terms:

> It has been very correctly said, that the principle, in these cases, is this:– that no man has the right to sell his own goods as those of another. You may express the same principle in a different form, and say that no man has the right to dress himself in the colours, or adopt or bear symbols to which he has no peculiar or exclusive right, and thereby personate another person, for the purpose of inducing the public to suppose, either that he is that other person, or that he is connected with and selling the manufacture of such other person, while he is really selling his own. It is perfectly manifest that to do such things is to commit a very gross fraud.

In *Holloway v. Holloway* [1850] 'Professor' Thomas Holloway, the patent medicine manufacturer, brought an action against his brother Henry, who had set up in business a few doors from Thomas's premises in the Strand, and was offering 'H. Holloway's pills and ointments' in boxes and wrappers deliberately copied from those which Thomas had spent £150,000 in advertising. It was held by Lord Langdale that though the defendant had the right to sell pills and ointments, '. . . he has not the right to do so with such additions to his own name as to deceive the public and make them believe he is selling the plaintiff's pills and ointments . . .'

Protection could also be granted by the courts in respect of a fancy name which had become associated with the goods of a particular firm. In *Reddaway v. Banham* [1896] it was held that the term 'camel hair belting', though originally signifying just that, had come to denote belting produced by the plaintiffs. In addition, Parliament passed a series of Trade Marks Acts in 1875, 1883, 1888 and 1905, though the difficulties of framing a satisfactory definition of a trade mark were such that considerable litigation ensued, and the main beneficiaries seem to have been the legal profession.

As the use of competitions and promotions increased towards the end of the century, a number of them were brought before the courts as constituting lotteries. The position in law was broadly that the organising and advertising of any lottery was unlawful, though numerous Acts had been passed between 1699 and 1846, fourteen of which were still on the statute book by the turn of the century. In the leading cases of the period, judges were asked to decide whether various promotional schemes relied on chance for the distribution of prizes, which would bring them within the accepted definition of a lottery. Usually they are not concerned directly with advertising, but relate to the distribution of gifts by travelling salesmen, small retailers, and entertainers, and the validity of competitions aimed at boosting newspaper circulations. Probably the most interesting instance, however, is one which did not reach the courts. Thomas Lipton was in the habit of ordering monster cheeses from America, which were towed through the streets by traction engines to the delight of cheering crowds. For increased sales appeal, a quantity of sovereigns and half sovereigns was added to the cheeses, on the Christmas pudding principle. Since it was a matter of chance whether a purchaser received a coin, and what its value might be, this brought the scheme within the definition of a lottery as being 'a scheme for the distribution of prizes by lot or chance', and Lipton received a formal warning from the police. His reply was to publish advertisements warning the public that anyone finding money in a piece of cheese should return it to the shop. Needless to say, no one did.

As a postscript to this episode, the police issued a further warning to Lipton that the coins in the cheese were likely to be swallowed by the public, and were therefore a danger to health. Again, his riposte was masterly. Large advertisements were published with the headline 'Police Warning', telling all purchasers of cheese from Lipton's to take care in case they should choke to death on gold sovereigns.

One of the most important cases to come before the courts during this period was *Carlill v. The Carbolic Smoke Ball Company* [1892], the result of which was to curb the use of financial guarantees in advertising by establishing that an offer made in an advertisement could constitute part of a contract. The company had advertised its smoke ball as a cure for a wide range of ailments, including influenza, this being a strong selling point during the epidemic of 1889–92. An advertisement in the *Pall Mall Gazette* listed various complaints, together with the time in which they could be cured by using the smoke ball. Influenza, it was claimed, would disappear within 24 hours. In addition, the copy contained the following statement:

> £100 REWARD
> will be paid by the
> CARBOLIC SMOKE BALL CO.
> to any person who contracts the Increasing Epidemic
> INFLUENZA
> Colds, or any Diseases caused by taking cold, after having
> used the CARBOLIC SMOKE BALL according to the printed
> directions supplied with each ball.
> £1,000 IS DEPOSITED
> with the ALLIANCE BANK, Regent Street, showing our sincerity
> in the matter.

The plaintiff, Mrs Carlill, bought a smoke ball for ten shillings, used it as directed, subsequently contracted influenza, and so applied to the company for the £100 reward mentioned in the advertisement. The company refused to pay so a writ was issued, the ensuing case being heard in the High Court.

The company's main defence was that no contract existed between the parties. It was argued that the wide terms in which the offer was framed showed there was no intention to be bound. Moreover, Mrs Carlill could not have become entitled to the money by her own efforts since it became payable not

CARBOLIC SMOKE BALL

WILL POSITIVELY CURE

COUGHS Cured in 1 week	**CATARRH** Cured in 1 to 3 months.	**HOARSENESS** Cured in 12 hours.	**THROAT DEAFNESS** Cured in 1 to 3 months.	**INFLUENZA** Cured in 24 hours.	**CROUP** Relieved in 5 minutes.
COLD IN THE HEAD Cured in 12 hours.	**ASTHMA** Relieved in 10 minutes.	**LOSS OF VOICE** Fully restored.	**SNORING** Cured in 1 week.	**HAY FEVER** Cured in every case.	**WHOOPING COUGH** Relieved the first application.
COLD ON THE CHEST Cured in 12 hours.	**BRONCHITIS** Cured in every case.	**SORE THROAT** Cured in 12 hours.	**SORE EYES** Cured in 2 weeks.	**HEADACHE** Cured in 10 minutes.	**NEURALGIA** Cured in 10 minutes.

As all the Diseases mentioned above proceed from one cause, they can be Cured by this Remedy.

£100 REWARD

WILL BE PAID BY THE

CARBOLIC SMOKE BALL CO.

to any Person who contracts the Increasing Epidemic,

INFLUENZA,

Colds, or any Diseases caused by taking Cold, after having used the **CARBOLIC SMOKE BALL** according to the printed directions supplied with each Ball.

£1000 IS DEPOSITED

with the ALLIANCE BANK, Regent Street, showing our sincerity in the matter.

During the last epidemic of **INFLUENZA** many thousand **CARBOLIC SMOKE BALLS** were sold as preventives against this disease, and in no ascertained case was the disease contracted by those using the **CARBOLIC SMOKE BALL.**

THE CARBOLIC SMOKE BALL,

TESTIMONIALS.

The DUKE OF PORTLAND writes: "I am much obliged for the Carbolic Smoke Ball which you have sent me and which I find most efficacious."

SIR FREDERICK MILNER, Bart., M.P., writes from Nice, March 7, 1890: "Lady Milner and my children have derived much benefit from the Carbolic Smoke Ball."

Lady MOSTYN writes from Carshalton, Cary Crescent, Torquay, Jan. 10, 1890: "Lady Mostyn believes the Carbolic Smoke Ball to be a certain check and a cure for a cold, and will have great pleasure in recommending it to her friends. Lady Mostyn hopes the Carbolic Smoke Ball will have all the success its merits deserve."

Lady ERSKINE writes from Spratton Hall, Northampton, Jan. 1, 1890: "Lady Erskine is pleased to say that the Carbolic Smoke Ball has given every satisfaction; she considers it a very good invention."

MRS GLADSTONE writes: "She finds the Carbolic Smoke Ball has done her a great deal of good."

Madame ADELINA PATTI writes: "Madame Patti has found the Carbolic Smoke Ball very beneficial, and the only thing that would enable her to rest well at night when having a severe cold."

AS PRESCRIBED BY

SIR MORELL MACKENZIE, M.D.,

HAS BEEN SUPPLIED TO

H.I.M. THE GERMAN EMPRESS.

H R H. The Duke of Edinburgh, K G.
H R H. The Duke of Connaught, K G.
The Duke of Fife, K T.
The Marquis of Salisbury, K G.
The Duke of Argyll, K.T.
The Duke of Westminster, K G.
The Duke of Richmond and Gordon, K G.
The Duke of Manchester.
The Duke of Newcastle.
The Duke of Norfolk.
The Duke of Rutland, K.G.
The Duke of Wellington.
The Marquis of Ripon, K.G.
The Earl of Derby, K.G.
Earl Spencer, K.G.
The Lord Chancellor.
The Lord Chief Justice.
Lord Tennyson.

TESTIMONIALS.

The BISHOP OF LONDON writes: "The Carbolic Smoke Ball has benefited me greatly."

The MARCHIONESS DE SAIN writes from Padworth House, Reading, Jan. 13, 1890: "The Marchioness de Sain has daily used the Smoke Ball since the commencement of the epidemic of Influenza, and has not taken the Influenza, although surrounded by those suffering from it."

Dr. J. RUSSELL HARRIS, M.D., writes from 6, Adam Street, Adelphi, Sept. 24, 1891: "Many obstinate cases of post-nasal catarrh, which have resisted other treatment, have yielded to your Carbolic Smoke Ball."

A. GIBBONS, Esq., Editor of the *Lady's Pictorial*, writes from 172, Strand, W.C., Feb. 14, 1890: "During a recent sharp attack of the prevailing epidemic I had none of the unpleasant and dangerous catarrh and bronchial symptoms. I attribute this entirely to the use of the Carbolic Smoke Ball."

The Rev. Dr. CHICHESTER A. W. READE, LL.D., D.C.L., writes from Banstead Downs, Surrey, May 1890: "My duties in a large public institution have brought me daily, during the recent epidemic of influenza, in close contact with the disease. I have been perfectly free from any symptom by having the Smoke Ball always handy. It has also wonderfully improved my voice for speaking and singing."

The Originals of these Testimonials may be seen at our Consulting Rooms, with hundreds of others.

One CARBOLIC SMOKE BALL will last a family several months, making it the cheapest remedy in the world at the price—10s., post free.

The CARBOLIC SMOKE BALL can be refilled, when empty, at a cost of 5s., post free. Address:

CARBOLIC SMOKE BALL CO., 27, PRINCES ST., HANOVER SQ., LONDON, W.

after using the ball but after contracting influenza, which was something over which she had no control.

The judge was quite clear, however, that the offer in the advertisement, taken together with Mrs Carlill's performance of the conditions set out in the advertisement, constituted a legally binding contract, and that the mention of a deposit of £1,000 was clearly intended to make readers believe that the company was serious in its offer. This decision was upheld on appeal.

The case has a two-fold importance in the history of advertising. Firstly, it showed that an advertisement could constitute a general offer capable of acceptance, and was not simply an offer to receive offers from others – an 'invitation to chaffer'. Secondly, it was a warning to advertisers and agencies to exercise greater care in the writing of copy, not only where financial guarantees were concerned, but also in the wider context of advertising claims generally.

Our attention has tended to be focused on the higher courts and on leading cases. It must be remembered, however, that throughout the period the lower courts were dealing with a considerable number of cases covering the whole range of advertising activities. Advertisers were apt to fall foul of the law because of the extreme lengths to which they would go to attract publicity – a point clearly illustrated by the following two bizarre cases. The first was preceded by a letter to *The Times* in October 1910 complaining that the name of a certain newspaper had been stencilled at twenty-yard intervals along the pavements of the Strand and Arundel Street. Three days later, the paper reported that Charles Wallace, a labourer, had been charged at Marylebone with 'wilfully depositing a quantity of paint upon the footpath at Marble Arch to the danger of foot passengers'. Since the alleged offence had taken place at 4.15 a.m. on a Sunday morning, the magistrate acquitted Wallace with a warning as to his future conduct, and a comment that a prosecution for obstruction might have been more suitable.[8]

In 1913 James Wilson of the Covent Garden Opera House appeared before the City Summons Court, summoned for carrying a certain placard by way of advertisement. It was stated in evidence that he had been dressed in armour, riding a grey horse, and carrying a banner with the words 'The Miracle', and a shield emblazoned with 'Covent Garden 3 and 6–30'. It was argued by the defence that there were advertisements on omnibuses and other vehicles in the City, but the clerk pointed out that these were carrying on an ordinary business, while the defendant was there 'particularly for the business of advertisement'. He was fined five shilling with costs.[9]

Conclusion

It is often assumed that advertisers in the nineteenth century were virtually free from any sort of control, and were totally irresponsible in the kind of claims they made. This misconception has probably arisen in three ways. Firstly, published collections of advertisements from the nineteenth century tend to concentrate on the more bizarre products and claims because they are more likely to prove interesting to the present-day reader. Secondly, there is always a tendency to apply the consumerist standards of the twentieth century to the products and promotional methods of the nineteenth, with the result that we reject in outrage things which contemporaries were quite happy to accept. Thirdly, advertising people of today are inclined to blacken the reputation of their predecessors in order to present current conditions in their most favourable light to anyone considering the introduction of tougher legal controls. Many abuses certainly occurred in the last century. In some cases legislation was not yet forthcoming, as for example with some of the scandalous claims being made for certain patent medicines. In others, existing legislation was not being strictly enforced, as with the Metropolitan Streets Act, and the Indecent Advertisements Act which was described in the House of Lords in 1907 as 'a dead letter'.

From this survey, however, it is clear that advertisers were far from enjoying complete freedom in terms of what they could say and how they could say it. There were common law restrictions on the kind of claims which could be made, particularly as regards rival products, and a further limitation came with the decision that a general offer in an advertisement could constitute part of an enforceable contract. The common law protection afforded to traders' names was also extended to cover fancy names associated with their goods, and the Trade Marks Acts attempted to bring greater order to the area of branded competition. In addition, specific statutory controls were introduced to deal with such problems as advertisements for bookmakers and pox-doctors, and various aspects of outdoor advertising.

It is of course true that, had all advertisers acted responsibly, such measures would not have been necessary. Advertising, however, was still in a state of evolution. Even by the end of the period, new teachniques and methods of attracting the public attention were still the subject of constant experimentation, and as they progressed, fresh limits had to be set. This increasing power was exercised responsibly enough by the vast mass of advertisers, with questionable advertisements, as was emphasised earlier, constituting a relatively small proportion of the total. The need for control should therefore be seen as a symptom, not of the low standard of advertising, but of the need to protect the respectable majority. As John Braun remarks in *Advertisements in Court*, 'What is surprising, considering the millions of advertisements which have appeared in all conceivable media, is not that there have been so many advertisements in court, but that there have been so few.'

The First World War

ON 6 AUGUST 1914 Sell's advertising agency issued the following communication to its staff:

> Important Notice
>
> In consequence of the unprecedented state of affairs in Europe and especially the Declaration of War between Great Britain and Germany resulting in the almost complete stoppage of business and stringency of money, the Board have decided, after the fullest consideration, to adopt the half time principle from Monday next for the whole of the staff without exception during the continuance of the War.
>
> Each member of the staff will only be called upon to give the half of each week to his duties, such time to be arranged by mutual consent, and for the time only half salary will be paid. This reduction in salary will come into force on Monday the 17th inst.
>
> The Board greatly regret the necessity for this action, but the future of the business, no less than the necessities of the whole nation, call for sacrifices in every direction.
>
> The Directors have full confidence in the staff fulfilling their part, however trying the conditions may be.
>
> Any member of staff wishing to join the Territorial Forces will be guaranteed a post of equal value on the cessation of the War.
>
> Alfred Sell
> Managing Director.[1]

After the immediate shock, the mood of the advertising industry seems to have become quite buoyant. Many companies, having stopped advertising completely when war was declared, resumed their activities after a few weeks, tempted perhaps by the soaring newspaper circulation figures. Some London dailies were printing up to three times the normal quantity without being able to satisfy the demand, and many provincial dailies reported a similar situation. Such was the public desire for news that the only limitations on newspaper sales were those of materials and production capacity. By the summer of 1915 the circulations of the leading dailies had settled down at around 50% above their pre-war level. Even so, some advertisers were unhappy with the situation. Arguing that under wartime conditions advertising space was worth less than in peace-time, they pressed unsuccessfully for a general reduction in rates of 25%.

The effects of the war became gradually more noticeable. Even by the end of 1914, many companies had full order books, either because of an abnormal demand for their products, or because they were engaged on government contracts. Their reaction was often to stop advertising completely, closing down their advertising departments, dismissing staff, and terminating their agreements with advertising agencies. Billposters and poster printers were particularly hard hit by this cutback, with costly machinery standing idle, contracts cancelled, and hoardings blanked out.

By the end of 1915 it became clear that newspapers had also suffered a large drop in the volume of advertising they carried. (See Table VIII.) In their case, however, this was not so much the result of cutbacks by advertisers as of a shortage of newsprint, which was forcing them to run smaller issues, with the column inches available for advertising correspondingly reduced. The shortage of space was in fact sufficient to send rates soaring. In one sense, this situation was to mark the end of a battle which had been waged for some decades between advertisers and agents on the one hand, and publishers on the other. Particularly in the case of the 'quality' papers, it was now impossible to keep to the traditional format, and advertisements had to appear in positions in which they had never before been permitted. The old tradition of the 'clean' page had to go, with even that most conservative of papers, the *Morning Post* being obliged to give way by 1916.

TABLE VIII

The reduction in Press Advertising during World War I.
August 1914–November 1915 compared with a similar period 1913–14.

Type of Publication	*Average loss* (%)	
	Display advertising	Classified advertising
London penny mornings	28	23
London halfpenny mornings	37	35
London penny evenings	24	37
London halfpenny evenings	7	28
	Display and local display advertising	Classified advertising
Provincial penny mornings	18	21
Provincial halfpenny mornings	22	16
Provincial halfpenny evenings	28	16
Sundays	21	25
Monthly magazines	—	38

Source: *Advertising World*, December 1915

The paper shortage eventually became so serious that in 1917 the Government was forced to introduce the Paper Restriction Order. After 10 March nobody was permitted to distribute by any means any catalogue, price list, or advertising circular, unless he or someone acting on his behalf had previously submitted a request in writing. This measure was followed up by the Paper Restriction Consolidation Order of 22 October, which virtually banned all circular distribution after the end of January 1918. One small relaxation granted to advertisers came with the statement that year by the Paper Commission that printing would be permitted on the backs of posters already held in stock.

Other sectors of advertising were also feeling the strain. Electric signs were switched off along with street lights because of the fear of Zeppelin attacks. Some of the more bizarre media of prewar years disappeared. A number of smaller and less secure agencies went out of business as their clients stopped advertising. At the same time, wartime conditions brought unexpected opportunities in some quarters. The manpower needs of the armed forces left vacancies, particularly in agencies, which were filled by women. Local and provincial papers benefited from advertising which the nationals were unable to accommodate, as well as turning the war itself to grisly advantage by carrying an increasing amount of *In Memoriam* advertising. The first anniversary of the Somme Advance saw many of them run special memorial advertising features, consisting in some cases of up to 15 columns of notices.

The period of the war saw a marked change in the types of companies which were advertising, and in the kinds of appeals used. German goods and manufacturers, of course, disappeared from the market. Advertisements for luxury items were rarely to be seen, and railway companies were largely absent from the newspapers and hoardings, since unnecessary travel was discouraged by the authorities. According to *Advertising World* in July 1917:

> It is chiefly owing to the department stores, military outfitters, vendors of branded tobacco and cigarettes, and manufacturers variously connected with the motor industry that advertising in the leading dailies and weeklies continues to make a brave show.
>
> But for the large amount of space occupied by them it would be clearly apparent, in spite of smaller papers, how many of the active advertisers of normal times have now reduced their advertising to the smallest minimum, if they have not retired from operations in the field of publicity altogether for the time being.

There was fierce competition in the cigarette field, as new brands selling at one shilling for twenty competed with existing brands selling at eightpence. Soap manufacturers also battled over prices and pack sizes. American cars were advertised, particularly before the United States's entry into the war, as British firms, committed to military production, were unable to meet the growing demand. British manufacturers retaliated by opening waiting lists, and urging potential purchasers to add their names as soon as possible, so as to ensure early delivery when conditions returned to normal. West End theatres took large spaces in the press offering a respite from the pressures of war, and there was an increase in advertising by the 'safe' holiday resorts of the south and west, the east coast being felt to be under the threat of invasion. Advertisements also appeared for products with special wartime relevance, such as Kohlo – 'halves your coal bill'.

Of particular importance was the large volume of advertising directly connected with the war, particularly that placed by the government. Before the introduction of conscription, the army recruitment campaigns produced some of the most famous posters of all time. Skilled labour was urged to move to areas of greatest need. In an effort to increase the acreage under cultivation, the Department of Agriculture ran 'tillage' campaigns in Dublin and Scotland. The small investor was tempted to buy loan-stock, war-bonds and savings stamps by means of a range of promotions using press, posters, and a display in Trafalgar Square reproducing a section of the battlefront complete with guns, which was so successful that it was sent on tour round the country. In addition there was considerable advertising by bodies such as the YMCA with its 'Huts in France' scheme, the Church Army, and various religious denominations and charitable organisations trying to raise money to provide help and comfort for British soldiers.

The patriotic appeals to be found in advertisements of this type were also employed to a considerable extent by commercial advertisers. In the months after the outbreak of war there was a notable concentration on 'Britishness', coupled with attempts to exploit the widespread anti-German feeling. The Maypole Dairy Company proudly proclaimed that its margarine was made from nuts captured from German ships, while Royal Worcester Corsets appealed for patronage in the following terms:

The Grand Assault on
Germany's Trade
NO German Capital
NO German Partners
NO German Hands
NO German Coutil
NO German Busks
NO German Steels
NO German Trimmings
NOTHING that is German
in
Royal Worcester Kidfitting Corsets.

The irony of this passionate declaration was that the company concerned was American, and therefore officially in a state of neutrality.

Sunlight soap used a drawing showing the trenches and a carton of soap, with the headline: 'The CLEANEST fighter in the World – the British Tommy', the copy beneath reading:

> The clean, chivalrous fighting instincts of our gallant soldiers reflect the ideals of our business life. The same characteristics which stamp the British Tommy as the

> CLEANEST FIGHTER IN THE WORLD have won equal repute for British Goods. SUNLIGHT SOAP is typically British. It is acknowledged by experts to represent the highest standard of Soap Quality and Efficiency. Tommy welcomes it in the trenches just as you welcome it at home.

Even the most patriotic of publics must have wearied of such an approach, and as the war progressed there was an increasing tendency to emphasise economy and value. This may be seen particularly in such areas as food, beverages, clothing and furniture. Considerable stress was also put on performance, with Lux for example – in contrast to the Sunlight copy – claiming simply: 'Lux won't shrink khaki'.

Perhaps the most notable feature of advertising during World War I was the extent to which its techniques and its men were used by the government in the national interest. In the absence of official expertise, the War Cabinet was forced to call in advertising experts. A committee was formed to advise on army recruitment advertising, its members being Hedley Le Bas (a well-known publisher and major advertiser), C. A. Kerman (Editor of *Advertiser's Weekly*), C. E. Higham (advertising agent), Thomas Russell (advertising consultant), H. Simonis (Advertising Director of the *Daily News*), and Wareham Smith (Advertising Director of the *Daily Mail* and *Evening News*). The efforts of the members were not confined to recruitment. Higham had been the first man to organise a regiment of volunteers at the outbreak of the War, and was much involved in other areas of government publicity such as the Victory Loan Campaign of 1917. Le Bas became Joint Honorary Secretary of the Prince of Wales National Relief Fund, helping to raise £13 millions, and is also credited with having rescued the Second War Loan from failure. Both men were awarded knighthoods for their efforts. When conscription was introduced, help was also sought from Paul Derrick, the American advertising agent long resident in London. Neville Chamberlain appointed him Comptroller of Publicity for the National Service Department, with Philip Benson of S. H. Benson's as his assistant.

Some disquiet appears to have emerged in agency circles regarding the basis on which such appointments were being made. Possibly there was an element of professional jealousy creeping in – this comes across from some of the bitchy comments in the trade press of the period concerning government campaigns. There was certainly a realisation that whereas most trades and professions had representative bodies from which the government could seek advice on matters of national importance, the advertising agents had none. It was this which seems to have been the motivating force behind the establishment in 1917 of the Association of British Advertising Agents, later to become the Institute of Incorporated Practitioners in Advertising.

By 1917 the government was appealing directly for free advertising space, advertisers being asked to help promote the sale of War Bonds. A scheme was set up on behalf of the National War Savings Committee by Horatio Bottomley, at that time editor of *John Bull.* He organised a 'boom week' in which many major advertisers prepared special War Bond copy, and many others mentioned the Bonds in their normal advertisements.

Although priority was given to the war effort, time was still found to introduce controls in one particular area of advertising. In 1914 the House of Commons Select Committee on Proprietary Medicines reported:

> British law is powerless to prevent any person from procuring any drug, or making any mixture, whether potent or without any therapeutical activity whatsoever (so long as it does not contain a scheduled poison), advertising it in any decent terms as a cure for any disease or ailment, recommending it by bogus testimonials and the invented opinions and facsimile signatures of fictitious physicians, and selling it under any name he chooses.

The immediate relevance of this report lay in the context of venereal disease. The authorities seem to have taken the rather curious view that since sexually transmitted diseases were on the increase, as usually happens when a large proportion of the population is under arms, the advertising of treatments for such diseases should be prohibited. Under the Venereal Diseases Act of 1917, it was forbidden to advertise in connection with 'any condition associated with sexual indulgence'. Section 2 laid down that a person might not treat or offer to treat anyone for venereal disease; or prescribe or offer to prescribe a remedy; or give or offer to give advice in connection with treatment. The penalty for a conviction on indictment was imprisonment for up to two years, while summary conviction could bring a fine not exceeding £100 and up to six months' imprisonment. This statute is still in force in 1981, and at a time when the incidence of such diseases is rising, continues to prevent the advertising of special clinics and treatment centres.

The sexual mores of the population also provoked the Advertisers Protection Society to act in unison, their collective ire being aroused by a certain cinema in the Strand where, as the Secretary of the Society wrote to the Home Office, 'the drop curtains and the programmes both exhibit advertisements of firms selling Malthusian appliances'. Again the logic is somewhat curious, the Society feeling these advertisements to be particularly undesirable since the cinema in question was frequented by soldiers and young girls. As a result of these representations the Home Office had the advertisements withdrawn.

By the end of the war, people working in advertising and related fields could at last feel, with some justification, that their activities had acquired respectability. The need for publicity in the broadest sense had been acknowledged at the highest levels, and its power demonstrated beyond doubt. The government had called in leading figures in the advertising industry to help with its campaigns, and had also brought in Beaverbrook, Northcliffe, and Robert Donald from the newspaper world to take charge of its propaganda. The enhanced status which advertising now enjoyed is well illustrated by the guest list of the Aldwych Club, an organisation of men working in the business. Among the prominent personalities it welcomed during 1918 were Lord Derby, Lord Jellicoe, Asquith and Bonar Law, while its President for the year was Sir Albert Stanley, President of the Board of Trade. The long struggle for acceptance had surely been won.

The Interwar Period

Advertising people

THE PERIOD BETWEEN the wars was in many ways the golden age of advertising. It was an era of powerful personalities, of exciting new media, of improved precision and effectiveness. It saw advertising people at last take steps to organise themselves along professional lines, and act formally to curb some of the worst abuses which for so long had been the despair of the respectable majority within the business. The 1920s were a time of expansion in advertising, with national expenditure rising from an estimated £31 millions in 1920 to £57 millions in 1928, though the economic depression of the 1930s meant that the total had only reached £59 millions by 1938.[1]

In the decade after World War I, the advertising scene was dominated by two agency heads, Charles Higham and William Crawford, both of whom were to receive knighthoods. Higham had come to prominence during the war through his involvement with various government advertising campaigns. During the 1918 election he was Director of Publicity for the Coalition, and subsequently became Member of Parliament for South Islington from 1918 to 1922. As a public figure and a brilliant speaker, he was constantly in demand for conferences, meetings and dinners, and few weeks seem to have passed without his addressing himself to some advertising topic of note. He was a self-made man, orphaned at eleven, an emigrant to America at thirteen, and by his own account unsuccessful at some sixty jobs before his eventual return penniless to London. It was through selling advertising space on theatre curtains that he eventually found his way into the agency business, where by hard work and sheer force of personality he managed to carve for himself a unique position. He could attract an audience of 500 on a December night in 1927, when he spoke to the Publicity Club of London about his life in advertising. He won new business for his agency by telling prospective clients that if their sales did not increase by one third, they need not pay for their advertising. (This offer was restricted to carefully-selected moribund companies.) He was always capable of the grand gesture. Arriving at his open-plan office one summer morning in the early 1930s, he decided it was too hot to work, and promptly sent all the staff home for the day.

TABLE IX

Estimated National Advertising Expenditure 1920–38.

Year	*Press*	*Posters & Transport*	*Cinema*	*Radio*	*Total*	*As % of GNP at factor cost*
	£m	£m	£m	£m	£m	
1920	28	3	—	—	31	n/a
1922	33	3.5	—	—	36.5	0.83
1924	39.5	4	(a)	—	43.5	1.02
1926	41.5	4.5	(a)	—	46	1.07
1928	52	5	(a)	—	57	1.26
1930	48	5	(a)	—	53	1.16
1932	40	5	0.4	0.1	45.5	1.13
1934	49.5	5.5	0.5	0.3	55.8	1.30
1935	51.5	5.5	0.6	0.4	58	1.29
1936	53	5.5	0.7	0.8	60	1.29
1937	53	6	0.8	1.3	61.1	1.16(b)
1938	51	5.5	0.6	1.7	58.8	1.14

Notes
(a) not measurable
(b) change in GNP measurement

Source: Based on David S. Dunbar, *Estimates of Total Advertising.*

Although Higham kept abreast of new trends in the sphere of advertising, especially by trips to the United States, he was by no means always in sympathy with them. He believed the growing emphasis by agencies on research was a nonsense, and said so when addressing a meeting of the Business Research Association. By the mid-1930s he no longer enjoyed his earlier dominance, perhaps because the new generation of advertising men and women, coming in increasing numbers from the universities, and sitting professional examinations, were looking for something more sophisticated than Higham's old-fashioned blend of salesmanship and advertising evangelism. Ill-health also seems to have sapped much of the essential dynamism in the years immediately before his death in 1938.

Higham's great rival, William Crawford, came from a totally different background. He was the son of Robert Crawford, D.L., LL.D., J.P., of Glasgow, was educated at Blair Lodge and at Frankfurt-am-Main, and married Marion, daughter of William Whitelaw, M.D., J.P., of Kirkintilloch. Like Higham, however, he worked as a space canvasser before setting up his own agency in 1914. He concentrated initially on retail advertisers, but his reputation was

WE ARE COMING IN THE CHRYSLER!

We shall not mind the rails and cobbles along the docks—(springs mounted in live rubber, shock absorbers, body built long and low—for steadiness!)

Out on to the great white road we shall shoot like a rocket—('Silver Dome' engine, six cylinders, seven crankshaft bearings!)

Up, up the mountain side a hundred miles ahead we shall flash (crankcase ventilation keeping the engine cool and clean!)

Down again into the valley beyond we shall sweep, like a bird, without fear—(brakes hydraulic, self proportioning!)

We shall not be tired when we reach you.

We shall not be late.

We are coming in the Chrysler!

Three great 6-cylinder ranges—Chrysler Imperial 80, Chrysler 75, Chrysler 65! The four-cylinder Plymouth—also by Chrysler! Chrysler cars of every type and price. See the models in the dealers' showrooms.

WRITE FOR CATALOGUES · CHRYSLER MOTORS LTD · KEW GARDENS · SURREY

A typical Crawford's advertisment, carrying the signature of Ashley Havinden, a director of the agency for many years. (By courtesy of W. S. Crawford Ltd.)

really built on his involvement with official campaigns, serving as a member of the Advisory Publicity Committee to the Ministry of Health in 1923, as a member of the Imperial Economic Committee from 1925 to 1926, of the Empire Marketing Board from 1926 to 1931, as adviser to the Ministry of Agriculture from 1929 onwards, and chairman of the Buy British Campaign in 1931. Later he was also to be involved with publicity for the Post Office and for National Savings. Like Higham, he was greatly respected by his staff. On one occasion he told an important client to take his business elsewhere, after hearing that the man had been rude to one of the agency's executives. Under his leadership, Crawford's became one of the leading agencies in London, and after Higham's death, Crawford himself became very much the *eminence grise* of advertising. He died in 1950 at the age of 72.

Crawford and Higham were business rivals, yet each had a high regard for the ability and integrity of the other. Hubert Oughton, who worked with Crawford for many years and succeeded him as the agency's chairman, remembers his old boss arguing at great length with a client over the agency's proposals for an advertising campaign. Finding he was getting nowhere, Sir William took the work and the client round the corner to Higham's office for him to act as arbiter.

In the 1920s advertising was a business which spawned remarkable characters. As well as Higham and Crawford, there were people such as Paul Derrick, the pioneer American agency owner who astonished the business world by introducing a five-day week for his staff; Sir Hedley Le Bas who had been one of the driving forces behind wartime publicity; and Horace Imber of the *Evening News*, of whom Northcliffe wrote, 'Getting out of his Rolls-Royce in Bond Street with eyeglass, stock and white spats, he looks more like a peer than most of my friends in the Lords and is, by the way, much better off than half of them.'

There were also notable people attracted into the business from other walks of life. In 1927 the Edward Hunter agency recruited Sir Cecil Beck, former Lord Commissioner of the Treasury, Parliamentary Secretary to the Ministry of National Service, Vice-Chamberlain to His Majesty's Household, and coalition whip. The Imperial Advertising Agency meanwhile hired Professor A. M. Low to help with the advertising of technical and engineering products. Even the names cropping up in trade journals of the period seem to set advertising men apart from ordinary mortals – names such as Ashley Havinden, C. Maxwell Tregurtha, A. Bede Harrower, Amos Stote, Barrington Bree, Dillon Damen, J. Bede Egerton, Aesop Glim, T. F. Aveling Ginever, and many more.

Nor were advertising's personalities solely men. It remained one of the few businesses which offered women the prospect of a responsible post and a high salary. As Viscountess Rhondda told an interviewer in 1924, 'It is just about the one profession in which women have equal chances with men. There is no difference in prospects and salaries, especially in the higher branches. At one time advertisers did not care to deal with women, but that prejudice has almost entirely disappeared.'

To some extent this was a reflection of the growing importance being attached to the housewife – both as custodian of the household budget and as buyer of a range of specialist products in her own right – and the feeling that suitable advertisements would probably be more likely to emanate from women writers and designers. At the same time, however, women had moved into managerial and executive positions during the war years, filling them with considerable distinction. Even in times of high unemployment, with the intense competition for jobs and complaints against working wives, they were still to be found in places of authority, the determination needed to attain them ensuring that those women who succeeded were indeed of formidable calibre.

By 1923 Mrs E. M. Wood, daughter of Quintin Hogg, was already a director of the Samson Clark agency. That year saw the founding of the Women's Advertising Society, whose president, Miss Marion Jean Lyon, was advertisement manager of *Punch*. A number of important agencies employed women as space-buyers, among them Crawford's – which has later to have a woman vice-chairman – Higham's and Pritchard Wood, and they were also to be found as account executives, production managers and company secretaries, as well as in considerable numbers in accounts departments. Sir William Crawford, one of the most notable employers of women, is reported as saying, 'I never think of men and women in separate categories – as far as I am concerned, whoever does the job best can have it.'

Taken overall, advertising between the wars was very much a 'people' business. Individual flair was still the most important factor in creating successful advertisements and making successful decisions, though this was probably true to a lesser degree during the later 1930s. Outstanding individuals were therefore prized by employers on all three sides of the business, and perhaps for that reason tended to change jobs with a frequency quite unusual at that time. This movement took place in particular between agencies and media, with a number of successful agency heads having worked as newspaper and magazine advertisement managers. The reason for this is probably that the agency's main function was still to a large extent the buying and filling of space, so that an agent with direct experience of the media side of the business would be at a distinct advantage. He would also have considerable personal contacts, not only among media people, but also more importantly among advertisers on whom he had called, who would now be potential clients.

On these sides of the business in particular, the financial rewards were considerable – sufficient, for example, to tempt the President of the Oxford Union to join the Mather and Crowther agency as an apprentice in 1937. Advertising, as we have seen, had long offered salaries far higher than those in other branches of commerce, and this trend was possibly even more pronounced in the 1920s and 1930s, to judge from a remark of Sir William Berry. Speaking at a dinner in 1924, he claimed to know of two people in the business earning £20,000 per annum, these not being the principals of companies. To avoid any misunderstanding among his audience, he added: 'I have never paid my brother that salary and he has never had the good judgement to pay it to me.'[2]

The advent of new techniques

People responsible for advertising decisions were often still making them on the basis of hunch and instinct rather than research, and carrying them out instantly without pausing for reflection. During World War I, Hedley Le Bas went to talk to Chancellor McKenna about War Bond advertising on a Thursday morning, and proceeded to organise a campaign which broke in the press on the following Saturday. The publicity manager of C. C. Wakefield, looking out of his office window one morning in 1930, saw the airship R100 making its first test flight over London. Although it was then 11.30, by 3 p.m. that same afternoon the *Evening News*, *Evening Standard* and *Star* were all carrying advertisements telling the public that the R100 used Wakefield's Oil. From the mid-1920s onwards, however, it is possible to see a gradually increasing emphasis being put on the careful planning of advertising campaigns, and in particular in undertaking some kind of market research before advertising was even considered. By the mid-1930s the age of the colourful personality was passing, and the age of the planner had arrived.

The idea that successful advertising could only result from detailed preparation and research was by no means new. S. H. Benson, writing at the turn of the century, had stressed the importance of ensuring an acceptable product readily available at a realistic price, before advertising was contemplated. In the United States before World War I, Professor Walter Dill Scott was writing on how psychology could be used to make advertisements more effective. In the 1920s, advertising men and sales managers began to look at how Britain's consumers could be divided into target groups so that the advertising and selling efforts could be deployed more effectively. Statistical studies were produced based on population censuses, with 1924 for example seeing the appearance of the *Survey of the British Market* published by the *Daily Sketch* and *Illustrated Sunday Herald*, and the *Population Handbook of Great Britain and Ireland* compiled by the J. Walter Thompson Advertising Agency. This period also saw the beginnings of research into the number and nature of the readers of a particular publication, as distinct from the number of copies sold.

Like any new technique, market research seems to have attracted a high degree of scepticism. In this case, however, attacks were aimed not only at the validity of the techniques employed, but also at the honesty of those working in the field. Researchers were claimed to have been seen in public libraries, filling in questionnaires that were supposed to have been completed by members of the public. A number of charlatans also seem to have appeared on the scene, in some cases coming over from the United States secure in the knowledge that the British businessman would always treat with reverence the man who calls himself an expert and uses jargon which no one else can understand. By the mid-1930s, however, market research had been purged of some of its wilder excesses, and its evolution could be summed up by *Advertiser's Weekly* in 1935 in the following terms:

> In the early days of research its reputation was unquestionably compromised by some puerile investigations, carried out by incompetent amateurs, by showy research departments hastily installed as window-dressing to impress clients, and by controversies which suggested they were not as impartial as those who used their information had a right to expect.
>
> Controversy died down, market research was left to find its own level. And, remarkably enough, it has survived not only the campaign of disparagement but several years of prolonged trade depression which might have been expected to be fatal to its chances.
>
> The reason for its survival is that its practitioners have vastly perfected their methods and have been gradually demonstrating the value of research in making methods more precise.

In the United States, meanwhile, research had moved a stage further. As well as using published data, and asking consumers about their purchases, attention was being focused on patterns of actual behaviour, with researchers watching the housewife in the process of making purchases, and investigating the contents of pantries and bathrooms to check on what products had been bought. By 1938 the Marketing Information and Research Agency had been set up in London to introduce those methods to Britain, and after World War II this line of enquiry was to lead naturally to the question of *why* people buy, focusing attention on the problem of consumer motivation.

Apart from its use as a tool in making advertising more effective, market research was also acting as a catalyst in business thinking. It seems gradually to have helped bring about the realisation among advertisers and agencies alike that the questions of what to make, where to sell, and how to advertise were in fact interrelated. In 1922, for example, the United Drug Company rationalised its product range, pruning some 9,000 items which had previously been regarded as essential, and finding in the process that its sales of soap were higher with twenty brands than they had been with fifty. Research also brought home the realisation that a company's success or otherwise could be determined by circumstances entirely outside its control, which must be taken into account when planning its policies. Sinclair Wood, director of a leading agency, wrote of a firm selling water-softeners which had achieved no success whatsoever in a certain area of the country, in spite of having fired a succession of salesmen. In desperation they called in a market research expert, who within three days had found the reason: this particular district had the softest water in England. *Advertiser's Weekly* in 1923 reported the sorry plight of Day and Martin, the blacking manufacturers founded in 1770, and one of the pioneers of advertising. 'There is no doubt,' the firm's manager was quoted as saying, 'that the business has been ruined because, when in 1896 the firm became a limited company, no definite policy regarding advertising was adopted.' A fortnight later he wrote an article pointing out that the company's troubles were also caused by the footwear industry's change to chrome-leather tanning, which required the use of wax polish. When Day and Martin were forced eventually to produce one, they gave it a different name, so that the consumer did not connect it with the old-established firm. They then proceeded to try to bolster their sagging turnover by introducing an ill-conceived assortment of extra lines – a move which only made matters worse.

To the larger process of which these various functions formed a part, thinking men began to apply the term 'marketing'. The marketing department was not to come into existence to any extent in Britain until after World War II, but the concept was certainly understood. As early as November 1923, E. E. Reinhold, late general sales and advertising manager of Sorbo Rubber Sponge Products Ltd, addressed the Portsmouth Manufacturers Association on the subject of marketing a product. 'It should take into account,' he said, 'investigation into the consumers' habits and tastes, and the kind of product needed, as well as the name, price, packaging, promotion and selling.'

Consumer goods manufacturers were coming to realise that the product they were selling was more than the sum of the ingredients plus performance. Although there was no talk yet of brand-images, care was being taken, for example, in the design of packaging, and researchers were concerning themselves with the psychological factors involved in a product's success. They began to look at how the consumer used the product, whether the package opened or closed easily, whether it was easy to pick up and grip firmly, whether it looked appropriate to the contents, and whether it fitted in with the consumer's concept of price and quality. A trade journal, *Shelf Appeal*, was founded to cater for the growing interest in package design and product presentation. Its founder and editor, Richard Lonsdale-Hands, set up a design consultancy in 1938 to work specifically in this area, where he felt advertising agencies in particular were sadly lacking. Twenty years later he was himself to be head of one of the largest agency groups in London.

The integrated approach implicit in marketing was bound to come eventually. Much though some of the diehards might object, advertising's days as a universal business panacea were numbered. During the coming years it was to become integrated firmly into the larger process and recognised as the communications arm of marketing.

The organisation of advertising

The period between the wars saw advertising organise itself along professional lines, with attention being focused particularly upon the agencies. Since the middle of the nineteenth century, as has been seen, the name 'advertising agent' had been adopted by a wide range of shady operators on the fringes of the business who were not in fact agents at all. As late as 1935, *Advertiser's Weekly* observed that every week it received press-cuttings showing that two or three so-called 'agents' had been sentenced to prison sentences ranging from three to twelve months for offences from petty larceny to fraud, adding, 'They are for the most part small-time canvassers of doubtful and insignificant guides. But they are advertising agents to the sub-editor, and he cannot be blamed for describing them as such.'

Two pressures were at work to improve the status and reputation of agents. First, in 1917, the larger service agents had formed themselves into the Association of British Advertising Agencies, which in 1927 became the Institute of Incorporated Practitioners in Advertising. The Association had originally petitioned the Privy Council with a view to obtaining a Royal Charter. This was not granted for several reasons – charters are only given to bodies of people of service to the public, never when members are limited companies, and the proposed scope was too restricted – but it does indicate a strong desire on the part of agents to be taken seriously as a profession. The name 'practitioner' represents a similar line of thought, with agents likening themselves to professional men such as architects and doctors. They could not use the term 'consultant' as this was already claimed by the organisation founded by Thomas Russell, whose members advised on advertising problems, but did not buy space, and who therefore wished to differentiate themselves from the agents. Various suggestions were put forward including such horrendous inventions as 'publicator' and 'advertecht', but 'practitioner' presumably had a more professional ring. Nevertheless, it failed to achieve common usage except on letterheads and nameplates, and the term 'agent' is still in use today.

The second pressure came indirectly from the agency side, but was applied by the newspaper publishers. The Institute of Incorporated Practitioners apparently suggested to the London Advertisement Committee of the Newspaper Proprietors Association that it would be in both their interests if much tougher conditions were to be introduced to govern the recognition of agencies – that is to say the granting of credit and payment of commission. The proposal would certainly have appealed to the NPA, whose own members were concerned at the growing number of failures among agencies, which was leaving some large space bills unpaid. Clearly, the problem could be overcome easily if recognition were restricted to soundly-based and financially secure firms, and withheld from shady traders operating from back-rooms, with only a plate on the door as testimony to their supposed competence. A move in this direction had in fact already been made in 1921 when *The Times* signed an agreement with some sixty members of the Association of British Advertising Agents allowing commission only to 'recognised' agents, prohibiting rebating, and stipulating that recognition would only be accorded to those of suitable knowledge, ability and financial standing. Although similar arrangements were also introduced by Odhams and Hultons, the publishers were forced to back down within a matter of months, abandoning their attempts to dictate the qualifications for recognition and to stop rate-cutting.

By December 1932, the time was considered ripe for another attempt. The NPA therefore produced an agreement form, which all new agencies had to sign as a condition of recognition and of the payment of commission. The new agreement required details of agents' training and experience, and of connections with other firms, including advertisers, printers and similar concerns. In the case of new accounts it banned the rebating of commission, including 'disguised' methods such as the provision of cut-price blocks or printing. It prohibited the recognised agency from employing directors or principals of an agency from which recognition had been withdrawn, or from taking over any of its business, without the consent of the Advertisement Committee. And agencies were made responsible for notifying the Committee should there be any changes of directors or key personnel, should any bad debts arise, or should the agency find itself in financial difficulties. Existing agents and existing arrangements for handling accounts were not affected. Nevertheless, as new agencies emerged and accounts moved from one to another, the grip of the new agreement soon tightened. Not every loophole had yet been plugged, and there still remained the problem of existing accounts where rebating could take place. When World War II brought another spate of agency failures, the newspaper publishers took advantage of a demand for advertising space much greater than they could meet, and formally banned rate-cutting. And that, at any rate in theory, was to remain the situation until 1979.

The newspaper publishers also used the recognition agreements to protect themselves against agencies in another respect. In 1935, a new clause was introduced, constituting an undertaking by the agent to indemnify the publishers in the case of an action for libel in respect of any advertisement which he supplied. This measure caused great consternation among agencies, a number of which at first refused to sign, though they were forced to do so when the NPA introduced a deadline for acceptances. The clause itself, which is still in operation, is of doubtful value in the sense that a major payment of damages would be more than many agencies could stand. It does have the advantage, however, of making them more careful about the advertisements they create, particularly as regards using identifiable people without their consent.

The interwar period witnessed several other organisational advances which are worthy of note. December 1925 saw the founding of the Advertising Association, which grew out of one district of a world-wide association of advertising clubs. Though its early history was somewhat stormy as it sought its proper role, the Association was to develop in time into the body representing the industry as a whole, promoting the concept of advertising, speaking for British advertising interests at governmental and international level, and playing an important part in raising and enforcing standards.

Another important move was taken by major advertisers in 1931, when the Incorporated Society of British Advertisers took steps to establish in Britain a body to be responsible for the verification of press circulation figures. Advertisers, it will be remembered, had been doing battle with publishers since the later years of the nineteenth century in an effort to make them produce reliable estimates of net sales, instead of quantities printed, exaggerations by space salesmen, or no figures at all. Some headway had been made, but Britain still lagged behind the United States, where an American Audit Bureau of Circulations had been established in 1914, as well as behind France and Switzerland, where similar organisations were set up in 1922 and 1925 respectively. Eventually in 1929 a conference organised by the Incorporated Society of British Advertisers unanimously adopted a resolution urging that:

> a British Audit Bureau of Circulations would result in considerable benefit to advertisers, to publishers of repute, and to British Advertising generally, and that its establishment is a matter of urgency.
>
> The Conference therefore, calls upon the advertisers of this country to take steps forthwith to establish such a Bureau in co-operation with the other interests concerned.

In the ensuing discussions, the Bureau was set up as a limited company in October 1931. The battle for accurate circulation figures was virtually won, though some pockets of resistance – notably among consumer magazines, and trade and technical journals – were still fighting obdurately against the general advance well into the sixties.

A trend evident between the wars is the banding together of advertisers for publicity purposes, financing their campaigns on a co-operative basis. Advertising appeared for a variety of products, likely and otherwise, with the public being exhorted to buy British cars, to eat more fish and fruit, to smoke imported Havana cigars, dress themselves in Harris tweed, warm themselves by coal fires, protect their woodwork with white lead, retreat behind British wire-netting, and send their friends British Christmas cards. Similar campaigns were mounted in many other fields, but in spite of their popularity, they seem to have achieved little, apart from often cushioning weaker and less efficient producers against the pressures of competition, and drawing attention away from deficiencies in other aspects of marketing. In one instance in January 1930, the British United Potato Marketing Board found itself left with a crop worth some £30 millions at market prices, which it was desperately trying to dispose of by means of advertising. In spite of the many advances which had been made, the misuse of advertising on a grand scale was to continue.

Advertising media

The interwar period saw a ferocious circulation battle waged among the major national newspapers. The publication of circulation figures meant that the success of one paper as against another was now clear for all to see, and the popular dailies struggled desperately to attract extra sales, preferably at the expense of their competitors. Between 1929 and 1939 every major national paper rebuilt its plant in the effort for faster printing speeds and better quality, while readers were tempted by offers of free insurance and free gifts, as well as by the more usual competitions and publicity stunts.

Although these efforts were intended ultimately to make a particular paper a more attractive proposition for advertisers, their effect in practice seems to have been somewhat different. *Advertiser's Weekly* carried out enquiries in 1933 which it claimed showed that most advertisers would welcome an end to gift-schemes, both because of the damage caused to advertised goods, and because a circulation inflated in this way was really not worth much, since purchasers of the paper would be collectors of coupons and gifts rather than 'readers' in the true sense.

Perhaps the most ridiculous episode in the whole circulation war occurred during that year, when the *Daily Herald* offered its readers a sixteen-volume set of the works of Dickens for only eleven shillings. Within a few days, the *News Chronicle*, *Daily Express* and *Daily Mail* were all offering sets to their readers for ten shillings.

John Cowley, chairman of Daily Mirror Newspapers, criticised the tactics employed by other papers when he addressed the firm's annual general meeting in 1938. Declaring that the *Mirror* did not canvass for readers or distribute free gifts, he continued, 'We have not frittered away our money on useless and abortive attempts to secure sales by pestering every householder in the country to become a reader, nor have we endeavoured to bribe them with an offer of a free gift.' Such methods, in his estimate, were costing the other dailies around £1 million per annum.[3] *Advertiser's Weekly* put the figure at nearer £1.45 millions, reckoning that the *Mail*, *Herald*, *Express* and *Chronicle* between them employed 3,850 canvassers, an increase of 300 within a year.[4] Little wonder that Lord Beaverbrook admitted the hundreds of thousands of readers he bought were costing 8s. 3d. each. Such tactics, however, produced the desired results, since the circulations of the *Express* and the *Herald* both increased to over two millions.

Radio

While the newspapers were locked in mortal combat, they were also becoming apprehensive about the new medium of radio, which was increasingly catching the public attention. Apart from a few sponsored transmissions in the early days of the British Broadcasting Company, there was as yet no commercial radio in Britain. Enterprising businessmen therefore entered into arrangements with conveniently sited foreign stations with transmitters powerful enough to ensure good reception for at least part of the British audience which was not finding Reith's idea of radio to its liking. First in the field was Captain Plugge, whose International Broadcasting Company began transmissions from Radio Normandy in 1930. During the following decade, listeners in various parts of Britain were able to receive programmes from Radio Luxembourg, Radio Lyons, Poste Parisien, Radio Méditerranée, Radio Juan-les-Pins, Radio Toulouse, Radio Madrid, Radio Hilversum and Radio Athlone. In 1938, Radio Normandy announced the construction of a new transmitter at Louvetot, designed specially to serve the south of England.

Commercial radio was certainly successful in terms of the audience it attracted, as is apparent from two surveys carried out quite independently of each other in 1935, one by the International Broadcasting Company and the other by the J. Walter Thompson Agency. The IBC survey covered 9,029 homes of which 77 per cent had radio sets, with 61 per cent of radio-owning homes claiming to listen to advertising programmes.[5] Thompsons, remarkably, arrived at identical percentages based on a separate survey of 25,000 homes.[6] A further report published by IBC in the following year claimed a morning audience of 400,000 families for Radio Normandy, and an evening audience approaching 750,000. Almost 900,000 families listened to Paris, and nearly one million to the powerful 150 kilowatt transmissions from Luxembourg.[7] A member of parliament complained to the Postmaster General that 50½ hours of sponsored programmes were being broadcast to Britain each week from continental stations, but the public, undeterred, continued listening to Normandy's programmes recorded live at the Union cinema, Kingston, and to Carroll Levis promoting the cause of Quaker Oats from the stage of the Odeon, Leicester Square.

Such popularity was not achieved without opposition. Newspaper publishers, after pretending at the outset that commercial radio did not exist, became convinced that it was robbing them of advertising revenue. Such fears seem to have been without foundation, since a survey among advertisers carried out by *Advertiser's Weekly* in 1935 indicated quite the reverse. Many firms had increased their press expenditure by more than the total amount spent on radio, and a number using radio had not previously advertised at all.[8] Hostility nevertheless persisted, with the Newspaper Proprietors Association instructing its members not to allow advertisers to give details of their radio programmes in newspaper advertisements, and expelling the *Sunday Referee* from membership when it failed to comply. This attitude must have seemed all the more absurd when major radio advertisers such at Ovaltine, Brown and Polson, and O.K. Sauce were able to include all the information they wanted on their posters.

Opposition to commercial broadcasting was also to be found in official circles, both at home and abroad. In 1935 the Post Office apparently discovered that the Lucerne Agreement, which allocated international wavelengths, also contained a clause stating that no country should allow stations on its soil to broadcast permanently in foreign languages. The Foreign Office was thereupon asked if the Agreement could be implemented to put an end to advertising programmes aimed at Britain. This was enough to bring about a hurried meeting of major radio advertisers to discuss what steps could be taken to fight the proposed ban. Any moves the Foreign Office may have made, however, seem to have met with little success, no doubt because of the valuable revenue the stations produced, and in 1937 it was reported that the cause had been abandoned. The following year panic broke out again when the French government announced that a bill was to be introduced with provisions to ban foreign-sponsored programmes. This was only one aspect of the measure, which was aimed chiefly at enabling France to counter the flood of radio propaganda to which it was being subjected, and seems to have owed little to Foreign Office machinations. The threat passed with a change of administration.

At about the same time, an official of Dr Goebbels' ministry let it be known that, in the event of France's withdrawal from commercial broadcasting, Germany would be quite prepared to take over the transmission of sponsored programmes to Britain, giving as reasons that it would cement the Anglo-German business relationship, promote Anglo-German trade, and attract British money into Germany. Fortunately, the implications of this ingenious proposal seem to have been realised at official level. Advertisers, for their part, began looking at the possibility of broadcasting from Iceland.

Such was the success of commercial radio that many businessmen had believed the BBC's Charter, due to expire in 1936, would not be renewed. As an indication of the general expectation, the Commercial Broadcasting Company of Great Britain, set up in 1935, prepared plans for three stations in London and was able to announce signed options for radio-time from 300 advertisers. The following year, however, such hopes were dashed when the Ullswater Committee recommended that the Charter should be continued. It was to be another forty years before commercial radio in Britain gained official approval.

Cinema

The interwar period also saw the emergence of the cinema as an important medium for advertising. The number of cinemas opened before 1914 is estimated at between 4,000 and 5,000, but many of these had been closed by

An advertising cart in use, and a simpler solution to the problem – encasing the horseman in a pair of boards. (By courtesy of K. C. Matthews)

An example of Aubrey Beardsley's commercial work, which often seems unrelated to its subject. (By courtesy of the Victoria & Albert Museum)

Frederick Walker's celebrated design for *The Woman in White*. (By courtesy of the Victoria & Albert Museum)

An instance of advertisers' obsessions with famous personalities.

A typical example of advertising for a hair restorer at the end of the nineteenth century – though outrageous by our standards, it probably accorded with medical opinion of the time.

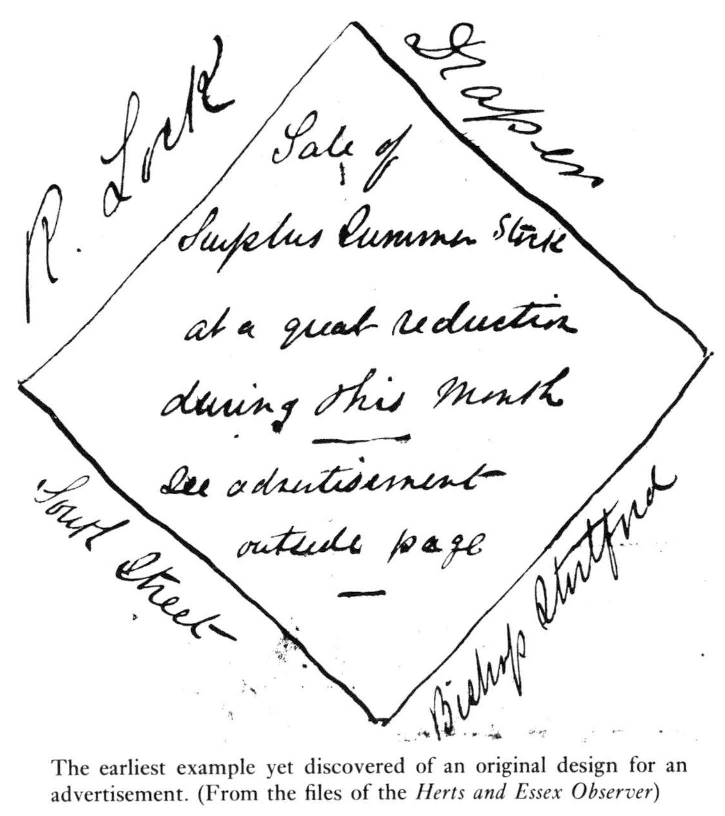

The earliest example yet discovered of an original design for an advertisement. (From the files of the *Herts and Essex Observer*)

(a) (b)
(c) (d)

(e)

Sir Richard Evans, Honorary Secretary of the SCAPA and resolute campaigner against advertising excess; seen here with his wife.

Opposite: Five men who contributed to the establishing of the advertising agent's position and respectability: (a) Samuel Deacon; (b) S. H. Benson; (c) Sir William Crawford; (d) Sir Charles Higham; (e) John Derrick. (By courtesy of the I.P.A.)

During World War II the Government employed advertising for a variety of purposes, including to exhort the population to save its money. This original campaign concept features a rodent-like creature called the 'Moneygrub', later metamorphosed into the 'Squanderbug' – complete with swastika markings.

World War I, and the wartime Amusements Tax which stayed in force until 1924 probably helped keep down audiences in those cinemas which remained. The lifting of the tax, followed shortly afterwards by the appearance of the 'talkies', ushered in a period of tremendous expansion, with almost 1,000 cinemas being built between 1924 and 1932, and many theatres and music halls being converted to show films.

Cinema proprietors originally objected to the showing of obvious advertisements, which were therefore generally incorporated into short story films – what was known as the 'powder in jam' method of advertising. Apart from being expensive in terms of production, this approach often provoked an adverse reaction because of poor technical quality and general lack of expertise. It seems to have been the advent of the cartoon which made the advertising film acceptable in its own right, by allowing the message to be incorporated into a humorous and entertaining setting. The Screen Advertising Association, founded in 1924, also helped to foster the use of the cinema for advertising, but even on the eve of World War II the proprietors remained far from convinced. In December 1938 the Associated British Picture Corporation announced that in future no advertising films were to be shown in any of its 500 or so cinemas. John Maxwell, Chairman and Managing Director of the Corporation, declared, 'I think it is unethical to take money from customers at the box office then, when they are inside, sell them products from the screen. People come to be entertained, not to be advertised at. The general public I am sure do not approve'. The public for its part, was happily choosing in ever growing numbers to be 'advertised at' by commercial radio stations.

Other media

These years also witnessed the appearance of a remarkable range of miscellaneous media. Advertisers could have their names towed through the sky on banners, emblazoned on the sides of cruising dirigibles, or written overhead in letters of smoke. At night these same names could be projected on to the clouds by powerful searchlights, or picked out in neon signs carried on the undersides of aircraft. Messages could be boomed from aloft by airborne loudspeakers, or recorded on unbreakable plastic records to find their way into the recipient's home. In the streets the new motor-vans often resembled the original advertising carts, as they carried on their roofs some enormous company emblem, such as the Mazawattee teapot. Moving models tapped shop windows to attract the attention of the passer-by, and continuous films made sure that the required selling-points were repeated *ad nauseam*. City centre walls, drab by day, came alive with scintillating neon by night. Some local authorities allowed advertising on pavements. The Treasury even permitted it on the backs of dog-licences.

Advertising promotions continued to feature famous personalities, used with – or still sometimes without – their consent. The 1934 F.A. Cup finalists, Manchester City and Portsmouth, were depicted wearing Sportown flannel trousers and using Harlequin Redrub Massage. The Manchester side trained on Shredded Wheat and Grips, while their rivals wore Swallow raincoats and their star player Jack Smith, cleaned his shoes with Cherry Blossom. When the cricketer Len Hutton scored his record 364 runs against Australia in 1938, his success was instantly attributed to his consumption of bread, milk, Seagers egg-flip, and Yorkshire Relish, in addition to which he became known as a smoker of de Reszke cigarettes and a user of BP petrol.

A new form of exploitation developed with the promotional use of Mickey Mouse. In 1934 George Kamen, managing director of Walt Disney-Mickey Mouse Ltd., told the Regent Advertising Club that Walt Disney was making £30,000 p.a. from manufacturers using Mickey in their promotions. The company laid down a rigid policy which licencees had to observe, including the maintenance of retail prices. Kamen quoted Sharps in Britain as selling 18 million pieces of toffee per year with the help of Mickey Mouse.

Criticism and control

Advertising was by now a far more disciplined process than it had been in Victorian times. Advertisers and their agents were approaching the planning of campaigns in a more scientific spirit, guided by the advances being made in marketing and research. Increasing emphasis was put on ensuring that the product satisfied the needs of the consumer, both in terms of what was claimed for it and how it performed. The general trend was therefore away from wild, irrelevent statements, and claims which could not be substantiated. Of course there were many exceptions, but there is no evidence of public disquiet regarding advertising as a whole. In fact, the growing audience for commercial radio seems to indicate that they rather enjoyed it.

Criticism, when it arose, came chiefly from two quarters. Firstly, there was an intellectual dislike of advertising which goes back to Macaulay, Carlyle and beyond. Macaulay, it will be remembered, had been particularly critical about the use of promotional methods in the literary world. Similar sentiments were echoed by A. A. Milne, writing in *Time and Tide* in 1935:

> Appeal-value is what the modern advertising expert supplies. The goods and the appeal-value come from separate buildings.
>
> Books are now being sold and advertised in just the way that other commodities are sold and advertised – by engaging a special shouter-down to shout down the other man.
>
> And why not, it may be asked? Because books are not like other commodities. That the sale of cheap cigarettes is in the hands of a few big firms does not matter; one cheap cigarette, I imagine, is very much like another, and if the big firms have killed the little firms by their clamour, well, the little firm's cigarette was no better

> and could hardly be cheaper. But the books of a little firm, with little money to spend in advertising, are not like the books of any other firm, whether big or little. They have a personality of their own and should be given a chance of survival.
>
> Nobody accuses a soap-advertiser of immorality because he praises a soap which he has never used. If he were so accused, he would answer: 'I trust to the assurances of the manufacturers. They know; they tell me; and I put it into a more appealing form.[9]

Another notable standard-bearer in the critical tradition was C. P. Snow. Speaking in a debate broadcast by the BBC in 1936, he declared:

> I have no objection to display in a shop window or to a catalogue – advertising of the kind which helps us to find our way about. But a form of advertising has grown up in the last fifty years which aims at something much more forceful than merely informing us. In that force there is a danger.
>
> I see modern advertising as an attempt to impel people to buy what, if it were not for the advertisement, they would never think of buying. Advertising begins by taking our money and ends by depriving us of our freedom. . . .
>
> Advertising degrades the people it appeals to; it deprives them of their will to choose. If the fear motive in advertising takes away our peace of mind, all advertising is an attempt to take away our minds themselves.[10]

Generally, however, criticism took a second and less extreme form, being directed against specific abuses. As in earlier years, one of the main targets of outraged public opinion was the outdoor advertiser whose activities – though limited by the attentions of the SCAPA Society and by legislation – were still likely to cause the occasional outcry. In 1927, for example, Shell announced that, because of widespread public opposition to advertising signs in the country, it was withdrawing all signs except those designating brand and price at filling stations.

Another target for specific criticism was advertising claims. In some cases the tactics employed by medical advertisers were adopted for use with different types of product. The medical quacks, for example, successfully persuaded the public that they were suffering from a wide range of non-existent maladies, invented in order to provide a reason for buying a 'cure'. This ploy was subsequently taken up by the makers of a number of seemingly innocuous products, which were offered to combat complaints unknown to medical science. Typical was Wright's Coal Tar soap, the perfect answer to the dire problems posed by 'skin constipation'. 'Your skin is unable to breathe', the reader was told, 'unable to give off those waste poisons which should be expelled through the pores every hour of the day and night. To keep fit and fresh all day you must use a soap that really frees the pores – that keeps them active.' Illustrations brought home the results of the fearful malady, a typist for instance being depicted working late, and lamenting to her friend, 'I can't get through my work like you do, I feel so drowsy and sluggish.' Another series of advertisements aimed at mothers explained how Wright's would prevent their children being stricken by skin constipation.

Disquiet was also being voiced at the apparent freedom with which advertisers could indulge in gross distortions of fact. The city analyst of Salford, in his report for 1927, was severely critical of the advertising for a certain brand of toffee. The copy described the ingredients as 'a delightful concord of pure cane sugar, full cream milk and fresh Irish butter – three fine body building foods.' In fact some 50 per cent of the fat content was coconut oil. Again, the advertisement claimed 'You can taste the butter in it,' although the actual butter content was only 5 per cent.

On all sides of the business there was a feeling that some action ought to be taken to rid advertising of its less desirable aspects. The Advertising Association accordingly set up a National Vigilance Committee, whose services were found to be so valuable that they were expanded and taken over in 1928 by the Association's newly formed Advertisement Investigation Department. The value of the Department's work over the years has probably been underestimated. Critics made much of the fact that it was set up and financed by those interests it was supposed to control, and it is true that its successor, the Advertising Standards Authority, with much greater resources and independence, has more to show for its efforts. There is no doubt, however, that the Department helped drive a number of shady operators out of the columns of the press, and did much to introduce a sense of responsibility in certain quarters with regard to claims. It circularised agencies in 1935, for example, drawing their attention to instances of fraudulent advertising, and reminding them that they must check the bona fides of any new client whom they might have reason to suspect. By October 1937 it had built up a total of 2,860 confidential dossiers, and had dealt with 1,169 enquiries during the previous twelve months.

As well as this action taken centrally, there were considerable efforts made to improve standards in individual sectors of the business. The Newspaper Society, representing the regional and local press, set up its own Advertisement Investigation Department in the late twenties, to advise members on problems specific to them – work it is still carrying on to excellent effect. The Newspaper Proprietors Association, representing the nationals, was also able to take action through its Advertisement Committee, as for example when it banned advertisements containing money-back guarantees, in the wake of a celebrated court case. Leading newspapers claimed to turn away a considerable volume of advertising for less reputable patent medicines, though looking at examples of what was admitted, we can only wonder what criteria were employed. Individually, there were some notable instances of standards being enforced. Northcliffe at the *Daily Mail* had been extremely particular as to the advertisements he would allow to appear, and though the main considerations seem sometimes to have been the personal likes and dislikes of Northcliffe or his lieutenants – Wareham Smith once having an advertisement rejected because a man illustrated in it was wearing a soft collar – he probably had the interest of his readers genuinely at heart. After his death, Horace Imber, advertisement director of the *Evening News* wrote:

> Lord Northcliffe had a true conception of a newspaper's obligations to the public who responded to its advertisements. 'The reliability of advertisers' announcements should be as much the concern of the proprietor and editor as that of the advertisement manager,' he wrote.
>
> The Chief made great endeavours to bar all misstatements and fraudulent advertisements from his papers. He maintained that advertisements should be as truthful and open to investigation as news in the Editorial columns.

This tradition was continued in forceful fashion. In 1924 the *Mail* printed a lengthy condemnation of Yadil, a preparation heavily advertised for the treatment of a wide range of complaints including consumption, cancer, bronchitis, pleurisy, pneumonia, malaria, scarlet fever, measles, diphtheria and pernicious anaemia. The article, written by Sir William Pope, Professor of Chemistry at Cambridge University, resulted in a widely reported court case, as the company which manufactured Yadil tried unsuccessfully to prevent the publication of yet more damaging facts. They failed, and the product had to be taken off the market.

Further evidence of the *Mail's* high standards comes from a speech made by Sir Charles Higham in 1937, in which he stated that the paper had rejected some 634 advertisements in the previous five years, either because it had no faith in the value of the goods, or because it believed that certain statements were misleading. The *Mail*, as might be expected, reported the speech at length, and later quoted Higham in its own advertisements.

Two further instances of individually enforced controls are worthy of note. Firstly, *John Bull* operated a guarantee scheme for food advertising, under the terms of which it analysed samples of all foods for which advertisements had been submitted, and compared the results with the claims made. This was said to cost the paper 'large sums' annually in analysts' fees and lost revenue. Secondly, the *Radio Times* introduced a scheme in 1932 whereby all its medical advertisements would be vetted by a panel of doctors. By this means the BBC no doubt hoped to avoid having its name linked with such products as the anti-rheumatic radio-active corset which had previously been promoted within the journal's pages.

In spite of these and many other individual instances of the enforcement of standards, the overall problem of patent medicines remained. Not all were objectionable, many of them being simple and trusted family remedies. Only too often, however, they did not perform what was claimed for them. And in the case of those put forward outrageously as panaceas, there were always media short of advertisement revenue which would be prepared to publish. Pangs of conscience were noticeably weaker when money was at stake.

The various advertising interests were unable to act together. Even worse, it was hotly denied in some quarters that action was necessary at all, on the time-honoured grounds that it was not the publisher's responsibility, that people could not be protected against themselves, that there was no harm in advertising what could lawfully be sold, and so on. Meanwhile, public concern continued to mount, particularly from the mid-1930s onwards. In 1934 a report by the Royal College of Surgeons to the Standing Committee of Scientific Research of the Economic Advisory Council declared that claims for patent remedies were 'always exaggerated and are, in general, purely fraudulent'. Some of them, it was said, contained injurious ingredients, but in general they were held to contain 'no substances of therapeutic value'. The report went on to make unfavourable comparisons with the regulations in force in a number of countries overseas. The following year the Chemistry Society joined the fray, urging the medical profession to educate the public as to which products and substances were good for them and which were not. In 1936 the Medicines and Surgical Appliances (Advertisement) Bill was introduced in Parliament. Its main purpose was to ban the advertising of 'cures' for a range of complaints including tuberculosis and cancer, and after some four years of negotiations, it had been drafted in consultation with the Pharmaceutical Society. Even some of the more responsible medical advertisers supported it. When it came before the Commons for its second reading, however, the bill was counted out. Worried advertisers were convinced they could detect powerful interests at work behind the scenes, who felt it did not go far enough. Cynics pointed out that it had come on to the floor of the House on Grand National day.

In the meantime, quackery continued to flourish. W. B. Robertson of Amalgamated Press told the Publicity Club of Birmingham of a 'professor' who advertised hair-lotions, claiming them to be individually prepared for each customer after the analysis of a lock of hair. He had submitted identical scientific reports in response to samples taken from a blonde, a brunette, a Persian cat, a dachshund, a bearskin rug and a feather pipe-cleaner, though he eventually became suspicious when confronted with a piece of coconut matting.

Publishers remained unable to agree. A product called Ephazone included in its advertisement copy the words 'ends asthma'. This the popular nationals happily published. The provincial press, however, rejected the wording, though they were ready to accept 'relieves'. Whether the public would, or even could, differentiate between ending, relieving and curing must be open to doubt.

Eventually it was the medical advertisers themselves who took action, perhaps hoping that a scheme of control introduced voluntarily would head off attempts at legislation. A body called the Proprietary Association of Great Britain had been set up in 1919 by fifty of the more reputable medical manufacturers to 'provide for the establishment of schemes for regulating the conduct of persons, firms or companies engaged in the industry and for precluding the use of inaccurate or misleading practices'. In 1936 the Association formalised its activities in the advertising field by introducing a code of standards, which although of limited value in the short term because it applied only to members, was of enormous value in the long term, in that a precedent had been set. At last a section of the industry had grasped the nettle, and had produced a set of rules to which members must adhere. In 1948 the principle was extended to cover all medical advertisers, with the introduction of the *British Code of Standards Relating to the Advertising of Medicines and Treatments,* and a quarter of a century after the Proprietary Association's initiative, the Advertising Association produced the *British Code of Advertising Practice* applying to every kind of commercial advertisement.

The interwar years saw advertisers brought under tighter legal control in several important respects. Firstly, a leading case in libel at last gave some hope to people whose names had been used in advertisements without their consent. Fry's, the chocolate manufacturers, ran a campaign in 1928 which included a caricature of Cyril Tolley, a well-known amateur golfer, captioned by the following stanza:

> The caddy to Tolley said, 'Oh, sir!
> Good shot, sir, that ball, see it go, sir.
> My word, how it flies
> Like a Cartet of Fry's –
> They're handy, they're good and priced low, sir.'

In the illustration, Tolley was shown playing an unlikely stroke, with a packet of Fry's chocolate projecting from his back pocket. His permission had not been sought, Fry's having told their agency that they considered such a procedure to be 'rather bad form'. The agency had, however, taken counsel's opinion, and on the basis of his reply felt sufficiently confident to go ahead. In the event, Tolley brought an action for libel, on the grounds that anyone seeing the advertisement would assume he had been paid for allowing his name to be used, and that this being so, he would automatically forfeit his amateur status. The case eventually came to court, Fry's having declined the opportunity of avoiding legal action by giving equal publicity to a statement that the advertisement had been published without Tolley's knowledge or approval, and that he had not been paid for it. His counsel called as witness Eustace Storey, a member of the Walker Cup team, who confirmed that an amateur golfer who appeared to have allowed himself to be used in advertising would damage his reputation and give the impression that he was surrendering his amateur status. Two golf club secretaries then stated that in such a situation, unless the golfer concerned could prove he had nothing to do with the advertisement in question, he would be asked to resign from the club. The jury thereupon found in Tolley's favour, awarding him £1,000 damages. The case went to appeal where Fry's were successful. The House of Lords, however, eventually decided for Tolley, and another milestone had been reached in advertising history. The days were gone when advertisers could make use of anyone they chose, and if the person concerned became really difficult, get away with an apology, probably printed long afterwards and in very small type.

FRY'S CARTETS

SUIT ALL POCKETS

The Caddy to Tolley said, "Oh, sir!
Good shot, sir! that ball, see it go, sir—
My word, how it flies,
Like a Cartet of Fry's—
They're handy, they're good and priced low, sir."

LEO CHENEY

5 KINDS

VALENCIA
Milk chocolate made even more delightful with fruity raisins and choicest almonds.

FRUIT & NUT
Delicious plain chocolate, mixed with juicy raisins and crisp almonds.

BELGRAVE
Perfectly plain, plainly perfect — a chocolate quite out of the ordinary

SOMERDALE
Milk chocolate made with fresh milk from English farms.

NUT MILK
A profusion of crisp fresh nuts embedded in the most delightful milk chocolate imaginable!

SUIT ALL TASTES TOO!

6D EACH

Try also the new 2d Cube Block Milk Bar.

FRY'S CUBE BLOCK

(By courtesy of Cadbury Schweppes Ltd.)

Aspro, only two years earlier, had run a campaign featuring drawings of Lloyd George, Baldwin, Ramsay MacDonald and Austen Chamberlain. (An old lady was said to have told an Aspro salesman, 'I'm glad to see you have such good men behind you.') Fry's own campaign had also included ex-King Tino of Greece, Michael Arlen, Gerald du Maurier, Asquith, Woodrow Wilson, and Sir Alfred Mond as well as Cyril Tolley. Now, although no general rule had been laid down, the possibility was always present that a person so used might be able to show in court that he had suffered damage to his reputation.

The lesson was not learnt at once. In 1935 a photograph of a perspiring policeman on point duty was used in an advertisement for Jeyes Fluid, the headline reading, 'Phew! I am going to get my feet into a Jeyes' Fluid footbath.' The photograph had actually appeared in a newspaper some six years previously, since when the officer concerned, P.C. Plumb, had retired from the force and joined the Post Office. His permission had not been sought by Jeyes, and would not have been given, since Civil Servants (as Post Office employees then were) are not allowed to appear in advertising. There was also the innuendo that, in the words used in the case, 'The publication meant that by reason of slovenly and uncleanly habits, or otherwise, the exudation and/or general condition of his feet was so unpleasant and noisome, that a bath or wash would be inadequate and a solution of Jeyes Sanitary Compound would be necessary to deodorise his feet.' He was awarded £100 damages and costs.

Although the cases of Plumb and Tolley concerned the advertiser, Miss Gitta Alpar, a celebrated soprano, adopted a different course in 1937 when, having been featured in an unauthorised advertisement for an alcoholic stimulant, she brought an acton against the *Tatler and Bystander* which had published it. She accepted they had done so in good faith, but insisted that the damage to her reputation could only be undone by an apology in open court, which was duly given.

If certain sectors of the advertising business seemed slow to appreciate the dangers of the unauthorised use of personalities, the same was also true of another kind of advertisement – the money guarantee. Mrs Carlile, it will be remembered, had been successful in extracting a £100 reward from the Carbolic Smoke Ball Company when she had caught influenza after using the appliance as directed. This was not enough to stop Letrick Ltd. from advertising in the following terms:

> New hair in 72 hours . . . Letrick Electric Comb. Great news for hair sufferers. What is your trouble? Is it grey hair? In 10 days not a grey hair left. £500 guarantee. Is it a bald patch? Covered with new hair in 72 hours. £500 guarantee . . . 661,000 Letrick Electric Combs are in daily use – All grades of society from Royalty downwards – not one has failed to do anything we claim for it.

A Mr Wood, having used the comb without result for 11 days, claimed the reward, and when the company refused to pay, pursued the matter successfully in court. Not only was this a sharp reminder to advertisers, particularly in the medical field, but it also brought home to others the effect which such advertisements were likely to have upon the reputation of advertising generally. The Newspaper Proprietors Association therefore took action to ban this type of advertisement from the national press.

As increased sums were being devoted to the promotion of branded products, there was always the temptation for the unscrupulous operator to produce a product packaged so as to resemble one being advertised. The advertiser's protection lay in an action for 'passing-off', as happened in 1927 when Cadbury's took strong exception to an imported chocolate bar which strongly resembled its own 'Bourneville', and which was offered for sale under the name 'Bournemouth'. Mr Justice Romer is reported to have compared the two bars, shaken his head, and remarked, 'This won't do at all.'[11]

Advertising was subjected to somewhat tighter statutory controls during the interwar years. Merchandise Marks Acts, passed in 1926 and 1938, laid down requirements for showing the country of origin, and made it clear that 'applying' a description also included its use in advertising. A new Trade Marks Act was passed in 1938. Legislation introduced in 1925 corrected certain anomalies in the 1907 Advertisements (Regulation) Act, but the Betting and Lotteries Act of 1934 did little to clarify the situation regarding competitions and promotions. Some of the damage wrought by the medical advertisers was repaired by the Cancer Act of 1939, which made it an offence to take part in the publication of any advertisement containing an offer to treat any person for cancer, or to prescribe any remedy for cancer, or give any advice calculated to lead to the use of any remedy.

By the end of the thirties, therefore, activities of the irresponsible few had been curbed considerably, both by legislation and by action taken voluntarily within the business itself. Respectability, even in the darkest corners, was now almost a reality.

Before the outbreak of World War II, the reputation of advertising was to suffer one more blow. In a book which appeared at the end of 1938, Wickham Steed, former editor of *The Times*, alleged that major advertisers had warned newspapers during the Munich crisis that should they play up the seriousness of the situation, this would be regarded as bad for trade, and advertisements would be withheld accordingly. There is no evidence to support Steed's claim, which was flatly rejected by the *Daily Telegraph*. Some agencies had sent out orders marked 'subject to cancellation in the event of war involving Great Britain', but the Newspaper Proprietors Association had pointed out bluntly that, war or not, their normal conditions still applied – i.e. no cancellation later than three days before the scheduled date of appearance. As a wit commented in the Christmas edition of *Advertiser's Weekly*:

> 'There'll be no war!'
> Beaverbrook's word was law,
> And only the cads
> Withdrew their ads.

The Second World War

DURING WORLD WAR II advertising fulfilled three important roles. Firstly, major advertisers endeavoured to keep their names before the public, even though their goods might not be available. Secondly, the government spent enormous sums on communicating essential information, trying to regulate public behaviour and sustain morale. And thirdly, classified advertising, especially births, marriages and deaths in the local press, helped to preserve community links.

Continued expenditure by major advertisers was encouraged by the Advertising Association which ran a campaign of its own, reminding those concerned that goodwill was a valuable asset needing to be sustained by advertising. No doubt older managers also remembered the difficulties encountered after World War I by firms which had stopped advertising completely during the war years. Reminder campaigns are accordingly to be found, for example, for various brands of biscuits, soap-flakes, soft drinks, cars, tyres and fireworks.

The general tone of consumer advertising was obviously much affected by the prevailing conditions. Customers were urged to use products sparingly, and advice was given on how to make them last longer. Economy and performance were constantly stressed – 'Viyella socks that do not shrink save more coupons than you think.' Flavourings were offered with recipes to brighten up the wartime diet, Milton disinfectant to kill germs in air-raid shelters. Glamour and sex-appeal had given way to 'utility', and since almost everything was rationed, there was a notable absence of hard-sell. In technical and industrial advertising, emphasis was often placed on maintenance and repairs. Some advertisers sought public approbation by donating spaces to worthy causes such as National Savings, and many announcements emanating from a variety of ministries bore the legend, 'Space presented by the Brewers Society'. In almost every kind of advertisement, patriotic symbolism abounded in forms ranging from idealised servicemen and gallant British housewives to caricatures of Hitler.

IMPORTANT NOTICE

..to the manufacturer

OF BRANDED PRODUCTS

Reduced opportunities for window displays underline the need for advertising during war-time. Indeed, the only satisfactory way of protecting your goodwill is by keeping your brand name before the public. Don't allow interest in your products to languish in war-time. Maintain regular contact with your public, and so keep alive the prestige and reputation built up for your products in past years.

..to the customer

WHO BUYS INTELLIGENTLY

Choose always, for preference, the branded product. It is invariably the best of its class. The value of a brand name as a guarantee of consistently good quality is inestimable. It is a guarantee of goodness. Branded goods have to be good, or the manufacturer would soon be out of business. Goods which are unidentifiable by either brand name or mark are difficult to trace to their source in the event of complaint. Buy branded goods, and be safe.

Issued by The Advertising Association

(By courtesy of the Advertising Association)

But the advertising scene was undoubtedly dominated by the Government. Between March 1940 and June 1945 its expenditure totalled some £9,500,000 with up to 34 different departments advertising in any given quarter. Most important were the National Savings Committee, which during this time spent some £2,250,000, and the Ministry of Food, with £2,000,000. These two placed their advertising direct, but in the case of other departments it was co-ordinated by the Ministry of Information, (whose staff included two admirals and the Director of the Victoria and Albert Museum) largely to help newspapers establish an order of priorities for official bookings. The public were told about ration books, gas-masks, identity cards and air-raid shelters. They were asked to walk more, eat less, save more, spend less, and say nothing. Shanks's pony

BUT MOTORING MUST GO ON!

War cuts a rift across the lives of all of us. Habits change—almost overnight. New conditions swirl up—settle down upon us.

But *motoring* must go on. The Government wishes that. The nation's business demands it.

So Ford—ever marching on—brings to you the new wartime car—the "Anglia," the latest triumph of Ford engineering.

It is built to give exceptional mileage on 'pool' petrol. It has the all-round economy and modest tax of an efficient 8 h.p. car. It meets the needs of everybody these days.

Yet—see what brilliant Ford engineering has combined with these! Impressive appearance. Lively performance. Spacious interior. The large outside luggage compartment and generous equipment.

. . .

A car produced for wartime—and a car which would make its mark in the easy days of peace! . . .

From the great Ford factory at Dagenham by the Thames large numbers of the "Anglia" are now streaming forth. The Ford dealer in your neighbourhood has one to show you.

See it. Try the "Anglia"! You *need* this new car for the new times. Britain asks for such a car.

SO . . . FORD MARCHES ON . . .

Advertising during World War II frequently incorporated visual symbols of the conflict into designs, as well as suiting its tone to wartime conditions.
(By courtesy of Ford Motor Company Ltd.)

appeared on poster hoardings, the squander-bug leered from the pages of newspapers. Salvage was to be conserved, fornication avoided.

In addition to its enormous spending power, the Government enjoyed two other advantages over ordinary advertisers. Firstly for the duration of the war it received from the press a special discount of 2½ per cent on all space orders. Secondly, it was able to obtain bigger spaces, often using 8″ × 2 columns,

11″ × 2 columns, or even 11″ × 3 columns at a time when the limit for other advertisers was usually 4″ or 5½″ × 2 columns.

As well as dominating the national press, Government announcements also figured strongly at local level. In the local press over 30 per cent of the advertising carried was classified – that is to say, set in solid lines of type in columns under classified headings. Apart from Government announcements, much of this was births, marriages and deaths, and it was felt to have an important role to play in sustaining public morale. Small ads are one of the main means by which members of a community can keep in touch with strictly local happenings, and constitute a legitimate channel of local news. The preservation of a sense of identity in face of the pressures of war was felt to be particularly important, since as well as being read locally, papers were frequently mailed to friends and relatives on essential work in other parts of the country, and to servicemen overseas.

The reason why advertisements were restricted to small sizes was the shortage of newsprint. Before the outbreak of war, the British press had consumed 21,000–23,000 long tons per week. Difficulties in obtaining supplies from Canada, together with the stoppage of imports from the Baltic after Hitler's invasion of Norway, brought about a reduction in consumption to 4,320 tons per week during 1942 and 1943. To achieve a fair distribution, the Newsprint Supply Company allocated supplies to different sectors of the press, working to overall targets set by the Paper Control Department of the Ministry of Supply.

A great many measures were used to reduce consumption. Standard-reel and a lighter weight paper were introduced, and the standard size of a roll reduced by 1 per cent. Narrower margins, condensed types, and an increase in the number of columns meant that more material could be accommodated on each page. A ban was put on circulation promotions, and even on competing newsbills. No new journals were allowed to be printed without special authority. Sale or return as a method of distribution was abolished. More important from an advertising point of view, the number of pages in a newspaper was drastically cut, with most dailies coming down to four pages, Sundays to six or eight pages on alternate weeks, and local weeklies to 156 pages per 13 weeks to allow for seasonal variations.

Until March 1942, the allocation of the space available between advertising and editorial was the concern of individual newspapers. A Paper Control Order (No. 48) then set limits for various types of publication, which meant in essence that advertising was not to exceed 40 per cent of the space in morning or Sunday papers, 45 per cent in evenings, and 55 per cent in any others. The limit in the case of magazines and periodicals was to be the average for the year ending 31 August 1939. In practice those proportions seem rarely to have been reached, not because there was any shortage of advertising, but because rates had increased to such a high level.

The gains which had been made in the thirties in terms of a planned approach to advertising were largely lost during the war years. Staff from agencies and advertising departments were away in the services. There were few new products to be launched. The availability of most media was curtailed, with some disappearing altogether, which meant that buying was done on the basis of what could be obtained rather than what was most suitable. Newspaper advertisement rates soared, the rate per inch in the *Daily Express* for example rising from £6.10s.0d. in 1939 to £12.0s.0d. in 1945. Circulation figures meant little, being the result of newsprint management, rather than a reflection of popularity. The public demand for newspapers often went unsatisfied, with newsagents having waiting lists of people wishing to place regular orders. Papers even encouraged the sharing and passing on of copies, so that the number of readers per copy was far higher than during peacetime.

Newspapers were the main advertising medium throughout the war, gaining in prestige through their relative scarcity and their association with important news. In other areas of the press, magazines such as *Picture Post* enjoyed enormous popularity, partly because of the newspaper shortage, but also because of their photographic coverage of the war, as in Robert Capa's famous shots of the Normandy landings.

Technical and industrial journals, printed on lighter paper and often pocket size, found the standard of advertising they carried was generally improving as the larger agencies, with fewer consumer goods campaigns to handle, began to pay more attention to technical advertisers. Some types of publication, however, such as sporting papers, disappeared for the duration of the war.

The shortage of paper hit direct mail and led to special permission being required for the production of catalogues and brochures. On the other hand, it brought increased business to the cinema, where audiences were flocking for a few hours' respite from the harsh realities outside. Commercial radio programmes from the European continent had disapeared, to be replaced by broadcasts of a more sinister kind by the Nazi propaganda machine.

In theory, the advertising campaigns of the war should have provided some useful lessons for advertisers and agencies, in that economy and brevity of style were essential. The constraints of small spaces ought to have brought a discipline of their own, particularly when the advertiser might be in competition with a larger space and a more important message from the Government. In practice, however, these wartime campaigns – public service advertising excluded – had no objective other than keeping a name before the public. They were holding operations, not normally subjected to any kind of evaluation. The products they were promoting were usually rationed, in short supply, or nonexistent, and as a result probably some millions of pounds were wasted in limp phraseology, misplaced humour or total irrelevance. In fairness to the agencies, it must be said that they often faced considerable problems with regard to staff, losing many of their younger men and women to the armed forces, the Ministry of

Information, and such mysterious fields as photo-intelligence. George Begley, in *Keep Mum*, describes the situation thus:

> Some of them had gone into the Army as Territorials, the Navy as Reservists, and the Air Force from the RAFVR. Others had been called up, and a fair number had put themselves in baulk by joining the Ministry of Information. A remnant were being congratulated on having flat feet, astigmatism or murmuring hearts. A friend of mine so moved the doctors at his medical that they apologised for calling him and sent him home in a taxi. With such a qualification and a great deal of ability he was a valuable man, and became art director of one of England's biggest agencies. At one agency the creative staff – to use the Miltonic expression for those who supply words, pictures and TV scripts – consisted of an art director with a weak heart, a one-armed Marathon runner of about 50 who was also a devout nudist, and a short-sighted young man with a weak chest, who had been assistant editor of *Health and Strength*. Between them they produced brilliant work . . .
>
> While the reserves of fit advertising men were dwindling, there remained plenty of women. Some of these were Communists who exerted themselves against the war effort during the time of the Russo-German pact but hurled themselves into battle when Russia became an ally. At any rate the flat-footed, short-sighted, elderly men plus some women produced the advertising . . .[1]

The war years and those which immediately followed were to have a serious effect on the future of British agencies, leaving them, as will be seen later, creatively, financially and mentally unprepared for the struggle which they were to face in the fifties.

British advertising was becoming generally less accountable in terms of justifying the effectiveness of the money expended. In the United States at this time, enormous strides were being made as regards integrating advertising into the marketing programme. British companies had no marketing programme. It was unnecessary because Britain was a sellers' rather than a buyers' market. In the 1950s, when British manufacturers and their agencies found themselves subjected once more to the test of competition, they were in no position to withstand the onslaught from across the Atlantic of advertising and marketing shock-troops, who had been training and drilling and improving their techniques while Britain had been fighting for survival. During the war, rather than competing, firms helped each other when stocks or supplies were affected by enemy action – highly commendable as part of the war effort, but disastrous in the long term because it killed the competitive spirit. British business grew soft. The habits acquired in the war years – cosy co-operation, allocation rather than selling, treating competitors like school chums – had no place in the marketing-orientated 1950s and 1960s, and the desire of British management to preserve the system which worked while nobody rocked the boat does much to account for what was to follow.

The shortage of advertising space had one beneficial side-effect, in that it enabled publishers to exercise a tighter control over the kind of advertising they accepted. The demand from 'legitimate' advertisers was such that undesirable advertisements could be excluded without suffering any loss of revenue. The

Advertising Association's Advertisement Investigation Department was nevertheless active during the war years, concerning itself particularly with aspects of advertising related to the war effort. It warned members, for example, against accepting advertisements for air-raid devices and shelters not approved by the Ministry of Home Security. Medical advertisements were condemned for their defeatist character, and their tendency to stress the low standard of public health. A special communication under secret cover also drew the attention of members to the possibility of advertisements giving information to enemy agents.

From 1943 the situation for advertising gradually began to improve. In September of that year there was actually an increase of 11½ per cent in the newsprint supply, though this was to be for increased circulation only and not for more pages. Supplies were further relaxed after D Day, again in April 1945 in anticipation of the end of the war, and in June 1945 for the period of the General Election, in each case the stipulation being made that they must be used for extra copies only and not to increase the number of pages. National expenditure also grew by some 11.5 per cent between 1942 and 1944, though much of this increase was probably due to rising advertisement rates.[2]

The advertising business therefore faced the advent of peace in a mood of growing optimism, ready for what was expected to be the great postwar expansion.

The Latest Phase

IN RECENT YEARS the whole area of marketing has become increasingly sophisticated, with universities awarding masters' degrees and postgraduate diplomas, and a new breed of business academic producing a proliferation of books and articles pursuing particular aspects to ever higher levels of abstraction. Within the advertising business, job-titles, people and agencies have come and gone, while fashionable practitioners have evolved new theories to explain consumer behaviour and the workings of advertising, only to see them consigned to the intellectual dustbin along with phlogiston and the philosopher's stone. Such changes as have occurred are concerned for the most part with technique rather than principle. They are simply overlays upon a business which in essence remains much as it was in the 1930s.

The latest phase has witnessed a considerable growth in expenditure, as may be seen from Table X (p. 177). It is also apparent, however, that especially since 1970 this has resulted from rising media rates in a period of high inflation rather than any notable increase in the actual volume of advertising.

After the war

The expansion in advertising did not begin with the return of peace. Wartime controls were to remain in force for some years. Britain, seriously weakened as a result of the war, required a period of economic convalescence, and after the public had celebrated victory with a short burst of spending the Treasury watchword became 'austerity'. Hugh Dalton, Chancellor of the Exchequer, wishing to restrain demand, produced a plan under which only 50 per cent of a firm's advertising expenditure would be allowable against profits for taxation purposes. His successor, Sir Stafford Cripps, accepted instead a proposal from the Federation of British Industries for a voluntary limitation on advertising

TABLE X

Estimated National Advertising Expenditure 1947–1980

Year	*Total Expenditure (£ million)*	*Expenditure in 1970 Prices* (1) *(£ million)*
1947	76	n/a
1948	78.5	n/a
1949	91.5	n/a
1950	102	n/a
1951	111	n/a
1952	120	n/a
1953	134.5	n/a
1954	152	n/a
1955	170	n/a
1956	190.5	n/a
1960	323	n/a
1961	338	436
1962	348	436
1963	371	465
1964	416	500
1965	435	514
1966	477	516
1967	451	507
1968	503	520
1969	544	563
1970	554	554
1971	591	544
1972	708	608
1973	874	716
1974	900	667
1975	967	565
1976	1188	556
1977	1499	602
1978	1834	645
1979	2137	652
1980	2562	628

(1) Figures in this column are obtained by deflating the current price figures by the combined index of media rates.

Source: 1947–56, Dunbar *op. cit.*; 1960–80, Advertising Association

expenditure. As from 1 March 1948 there was a reduction of 15 per cent by all firms spending over £2,500 per annum in certain specified categories: consumer and household goods covered by ration-books, coupons and dockets; liquid and solid fuels; alcohol and tobacco products; and goods attracting a purchase tax rate of 66⅔ per cent or more. Firms whose expenditure in these areas was less than £2,500 undertook not to increase it.

Cripps's strategy was to cut back home demand in order to stimulate exports, and the limitation was to run until the end of February 1949. In October 1948 he asked the Federation to extend it for another year, but eventually accepted a compromise whereby advertisers were freed from their general obligation to reduce spending by 15 per cent, but agreed not to undertake heavy advertising of products in short supply as this might lead to an increase in inflation.

The controls which had been imposed in wartime were dismantled only slowly. The Order regulating the specifications, brand names and prices of soft drinks was revoked in November 1947, but food rationing was not finally abolished until 1954. From an advertising point of view, the long-awaited expansion really came during the years 1952–4, which saw the end of controls not only on food, but also on coffee, tea, biscuits, sugar, confectionery products, eggs and petrol. In addition, the lifting of restrictions on hire purchase agreements in July 1954 gave an impetus to the sales of such products as radios, televisions, refrigerators and washing machines. Growth in one area stimulated demand in others, with the increase in house building, for example, bringing a greater demand for fittings and furnishings.

The country was by now in a mood of general economic prosperity sustained by full employment. For virtually the first time since before the war, British manufacturers found themselves in competition. As branded foods reappeared, company competed with company, and as the consumer was tempted by an increasing choice of products, industry found itself competing with industry for public patronage.

Meanwhile, developments were beginning to take place in manufacturing and distribution which were to have a profound effect upon advertising and the job it was asked to do. The small independent retailer was giving way to larger-scale operations in the shape of multiples, supermarkets and, later, discount stores. As his importance declined so did that of the wholesaler, since the large-scale retailers dealt directly with the supplier instead of through middle-men, being able to obtain advantageous terms by virtue of the size of their orders. The emphasis was now on heavy promotion of individual brands, something the prewar wholesaler had often strongly resisted. At the same time there was an increasing trend towards self-service in retail outlets. Coming first into food retailing, it soon spread into non-foods, made attractive by rising wage levels and a general shortage of labour. Advertising in many fields was now being asked to perform something rather different from its traditional function. When a customer made a purchase in prewar days, he or she would be served personally by the retailer, who would give help and advice as required and was often involved in preparing the product for sale, as for example in cutting cheese or weighing and packing rice. Now many products were offered in pre-packaged form, with the customer serving herself from a display. The manufacturer, therefore, could no longer use his advertising simply to awaken the consumer's interest and get her into the shop, leaving the retailer to clinch the sale. Instead, advertising was being called on to act as the complete communications link, putting across information which in years past would have come from the retailer. At the same time, considerable attention was being paid to the design of the product itself and its packaging, since particularly in the case of supermarket products, 'shelf appeal' was becoming a vital factor in securing a sale.

As controls were lifted and the tempo of marketing increased, new brands were introduced in the consumer goods field at an ever faster rate. While some of these represented genuine innovations, many of them had no obvious advantage over their competitors, which meant that they offered no greater benefit to the consumer. In such a situation, advertisers and agencies struggled to find some claim to uniqueness which would set their product apart from the rest. Such a claim might be factual but irrelevant. (Did anyone really want a pen which wrote under water?) The advertiser might be the first to base a claim on a feature common to all products of that type – a tactic known as pre-empting a claim. Or the claim might be pure invention, as with the beer which reaches parts of the body that other beers cannot reach. The process of distinguishing a brand from its competitors by claiming a unique feature, real or invented, became formalised into the doctrine of the USP (unique selling proposition) expounded by American agency man Rosser Reeves, whose book *Reality in Advertising* was eagerly read on the British side of the Atlantic.

Another approach to the problem of too many similar brands was to give each one its own personality or 'image', the theory being that the consumer would choose a brand which complemented his or her own personality. As advertisers struggled to find memorable images, friendly tigers were used to symbolise the power of petrol, green giants proffered vegetable produce for public consumption, caped crusaders brought household cleaners to the aid of overworked housewives, and lovely girls with flowing tresses floated ethereally in slow motion through idyllic meadows to the accompaniment of sweeping chords from glutinous violins.

The pattern of advertising was also influenced by social changes which were taking place. The increased number of women in paid employment meant a demand for convenience foods, and a movement towards one-stop shopping and bulk buying. The extra income provided by the working wife helped to pay for a car – possibly a second car – in which to transport her purchases, and a refrigerator and deep-freeze in which to keep them. Labour-saving devices in the home became all important. The advent of television brought changes to the diet, the pattern of social life, and to popular tastes in entertainment.

The movement in manufacturing and retailing alike was towards economies of scale. The country entered an era of mergers and takeovers. 'Big is beautiful' became the business battle cry, as British products suffered at the hands of competitors having the economic advantage of much larger home markets. International companies, many of them American-based, moved into Britain, often as a springboard for future expansion into continental Europe. They brought with them more sophisticated techniques of marketing, which British companies had to try and match, initially by turning for help to their advertising

getupangogas

Fast gas, flame gas, instant-heat-on-tap gas!
Heat you can see, heat that obeys you,
only comes from clean, quick gas. Speeds up cooking, cuts out
waiting, instant heat for modern living.
Glorious gas heat, flame heat, fast heat,
world's quickest heating comes from **HIGH SPEED GAS!**

HIGH SPEED GAS IS NEWS – and so are all the latest HSG cooking and heating appliances. Go see them at your gas showroom.

Today advertising is used to create or reinforce company and product images. This campaign was created by the London Press Exchange when the Gas Board decided to face the challenge of cooking with electricity. (By courtesy of the British Gas Corporation)

Full flame heat at the flick of a wrist!
That's the miracle of instant gas.
Heat you can see, heat that obeys you, only comes with clean, quick gas. Meals come faster, homes are warmer, brighter lives are lived by gas! Only heat that's right for today—the instant heat of ***HIGH SPEED GAS!***

HIGH SPEED GAS IS NEWS and so are all the latest HSG cooking and heating appliances. Go see them at your Gas Showrooms.

FRED GIVES IT THE THUMBS DOWN.

'NO' TO DALGETY.

* Spillers shareholders have now received the formal offer document.
* Our prospects and asset strengths make this offer derisory.
* This bid is bad for Spillers shareholders, bad for employees and bad for customers.
* We will be writing to you fully in a few days.
* Do not sign the acceptance form.

"The Directors of Spillers Limited have taken all reasonable care to ensure that the facts stated and opinions expressed herein are fair and accurate and they jointly and severally accept responsibility accordingly."

Examples of advertising to appeal to a company's shareholders during a takeover battle. Spillers's flour-graders had already achieved widespread recognition through heavy television advertising; but Dalgety eventually carried the day.
(By courtesy of Spillers Ltd. and Dalgety Ltd.)

Before you back one, study their track records.

Let's start with the financial year ending in 1975.

Since then Dalgety's dividend for each Ordinary Share has increased by 63% (after adjusting for inflation).*

On the same basis, even allowing for their latest forecast, Spillers' dividends per share have failed to keep pace with inflation.

Over the same period, Dalgety's total profits before tax have gone up by 363%. Spillers' by less than 110%.

How has Dalgety become such a thriving and prosperous family of companies? There are two main reasons:

A wide spread of risk.

Some 49% of our turnover is in this country, 26% in North America, 25% in Australia and New Zealand.

We have the same protection in our spread of markets: cereals, malt, animal feed, timber, wool, frozen vegetables, chemicals and meat.

Thus we can ride out a storm in any one continent or product group, secure in our profits from the others.

A strong management team.

The second main reason for Dalgety's successful track record is our management philosophy. We believe in a high degree of decentralisation. In other words, we allow our managers to manage – within of course, sound commercial disciplines. This is precisely how we would approach our task with Spillers.

Together a formidable force.

We consider that together the two companies would be a formidable force in food and agriculture.

The combined group would be substantial in the UK in grain, animal feed, malt, petfoods and flour, certainly able to handle competition from anywhere in the world.

Why not get an unbiased opinion?

We naturally hope that all of this will help you view our offer favourably.

But if you are still in two minds why not go to someone who will give you impartial and professional investment advice?

Take all the documents and ask him or her two questions:

1. Is your investment likely to show better growth with Dalgety, or with Spillers?

2. What will happen to the price of Spillers' shares if our offer is unsuccessful?

We think we know what his advice will be, and we look forward to a long and fruitful association with you.

Post your acceptance today.

DALGETY

THE DIRECTORS OF DALGETY LIMITED HAVE TAKEN ALL REASONABLE CARE TO ENSURE THAT THE FACTS STATED AND OPINIONS EXPRESSED HEREIN ARE FAIR AND ACCURATE AND THEY JOINTLY AND SEVERALLY ACCEPT RESPONSIBILITY ACCORDINGLY.

*As measured by the Retail Price Index.

agencies, and later by developing expertise of their own. The larger agencies in particular found themselves dealing with different types of client, discussing marketing policy with the marketing manager of an international corporation, involving themselves in research and planning of considerable sophistication, and quite possibly operating on an international rather than a purely British basis. No longer could advertising be handled as something independent of all other considerations. The late 1950s and early 1960s therefore witnessed the culmination of changes which, as we have seen, first began forty years previously.

At the same time, company managers were looking to advertising to justify itself in terms of cost. An increasing number of accountants were finding their way into senior managerial positions, while business schools were turning out graduates who, as well as being articulate and literate, were also numerate. These new managers were not prepared to see advertising expenditure steadily increasing with no obvious benefit to the company other than a putative reservoir of goodwill, and began to press for research to back up the claims which agencies had long been making about the necessity of advertising.

Agencies seem firmly to have believed that spending would remain unaffected because of the effect a reduction would have on sales, but their naive optimism was shattered when their clients were faced with economic problems in the sixties. To the manager taking an overall view of the company's affairs, the cancellation of some planned advertising might be far less harmful in the long term than other alternatives open to him, such as redundancies or cancelling capital projects. Advertising was becoming integrated into company planning and policy, to be used as a means of helping achieve corporate objectives, and to be modified in the light of broader economic and business trends.

The position of advertising was also affected by the abolition of resale price maintenance in 1964. So long as the selling price to the consumer remained fixed, the advertising industry was bound to benefit, in that competition had to take place to a large extent in terms of advertising in the mass media. When RPM disappeared, the marketing manager had another call on his resources, and an extra tactical weapon which he could deploy. The importance of advertising as part of the marketing process had suffered a still further blow.

Advertising media

The Press

In the decade after World War II, the position of the press as the leading medium was unchallenged. Although newsprint remained rationed until December 1956, newpapers were actually freed from the wartime restrictions on sales as early as September 1946, when a number of sporting papers reappeared for the start of the football season. There was no resumption of the prewar circulation battle, however, since the Newsprint Supply Company made it clear that, in such an eventuality, sales restrictions would be reimposed.

The crisis of 1947 saw newsprint supplies lower than they had been the previous year. Faced with a directive from the Chancellor of the Exchequer that imports must be cut, the Supply Company rationed papers on a tonnage basis, allowing them the option of reducing the number of pages or cutting down their circulation. The popular dailies opted for the former course, *The Times* and the *Daily Telegraph* for the latter. A number of factors contributed to the difficulities being experienced by the press. They include the dollar crisis and a drought in Scandinavia both of which affected the supply of newsprint, and the fuel shortage which led the Government to close down all publications except newspapers for two weeks during February. It was not until January 1949 that restrictions could again be eased.

By 1952 there was a noticeable increase in the number of pages in both newspapers and magazines, though a limit on the number which a publication could publish during any quarter was still fixed by Government orders. In practice, the allocation of pages seems in most cases not to have been used, the reason apparently being that insufficient advertising was attracted to cover the cost of bigger issues, even though advertisers were once again being offered large spaces such as full and half pages. A few of the popular dailies constituted an exception to this trend, claiming not to be able to meet the demand for space, but even in 1953, only 74 out of 968 provincial weeklies took up their permitted number of pages.

The mood of prosperity in 1954, with a wider choice of goods than at any time since the war, and promotional battles being waged among heavily advertised brands in such areas as margarine, petrol, detergents and cigarettes, meant a shortage of press space for major advertisers wishing to mount national campaigns. With newsprint still rationed, the popular dailies were only appearing in 8-page editions, while the provincial press was an extremely expensive alternative in terms of the cost per thousand readers if used on a national basis. At this time, therefore, there was a shortage of an effective and freely available national advertising medium – something which does much to explain the rapid success of commercial television, which was launched in September 1955.

The abolition of newsprint rationing did not mark the end of the problem of shortage. In 1973 it reappeared in a different form, as Britain felt the effects of excess world demand, caused particularly by the growing newsprint consumption of the United States and Japan. There was no official action to limit supplies, but in what was a boom year for advertising, the regional press found itself particularly hard hit. Supplies to newsagents were cut, the number of editions and pages was reduced, and the situation became sufficiently serious for the Newspaper Society, the Newspaper Publishers Association, and the American Newspaper Publishers Association to pledge themselves jointly to come to the rescue of any paper which was in danger.

In the decade after the war, in spite of the limitations imposed by the shortage of newsprint, the national newspaper constituted a remarkably effective advertising medium. When sales were freed in September 1946, demand was often double what had been expected, with the *News of the World* reaching a world record sale of 7,400,000 copies a week, the *Evening News* providing the world's biggest evening sale at 1,500,000 and the *Daily Express* Britain's biggest daily sale at 3,700,000. Two years later the *News of the World* had reached over 8,000,000, and the *Daily Mirror* over 4,000,000. Though purists might lament how this reflected the lack of public taste, such matters are not the concern of advertisers. From their viewpoint, all that counted was that over half the households of the country took the *News of the World*, and over a quarter the *Mirror*, this making them excellent vehicles for advertising messages.

A setback occurred in 1951, when rising costs forced newspapers to take a number of measures, including raising their cover prices, which went up from 1d to 1½d for the popular dailies, and 2d to 2½d for the Sundays. This brought about a reduction in the sales of both newspapers and periodicals. Some smaller provincial papers merged or ceased publication. People wishing to economise on newsagents' bills were reported to be cancelling periodicals rather than newspapers. The mass circulation magazines seem to have been particularly vulnerable, since their success, as Harry Henry has pointed out, was probably due only to a shortage of other reading material, and circulations of such titles as *Picture Post*, *Illustrated*, *Everybody's* and *John Bull* were in any case falling as the supply of newsprint increased.

It was mid-1954 before newspaper circulations regained something like their 1951 levels, and by this time the picture was changing. Papers found themselves competing for advertising revenue, prize competitions were reintroduced in an effort to increase sales, the *Daily Graphic* was relaunched as the *Daily Sketch*, and two new newspaper proprietors made their appearance. One of these, W. J. Brittain, launched a short-lived daily called the *Recorder*. The other, a middle-aged Canadian with a background in newspaper publishing and commercial radio, bought Scotsman Publications Limited. This was Roy Thomson, later to become Lord Thomson of Fleet.

Thomson's rise was rapid. By 1959 he was not only Chairman of Scottish Television, but had bought the Kemsley family's holding of one million shares in Kemsley Newspapers Ltd for £5 million, and changed its name to Thomson Newspapers. Two years later he tried unsuccessfully to arrange a merger with Odhams Press, and in 1966 obtained control of *The Times*. At a time when provincial newspapers were closing, Thomson opened new ones, offering the reader a high standard of journalism allied to colour printing. He launched the *Sunday Times Magazine*, maintained his belief in it even when it failed to attract advertising support, and saw it become one of the great publishing successes of postwar years. He foresaw the potential offered by the Post Office telephone directories as a means of advertising, and introduced the Yellow Pages to

The dramatic comparison of the gleaming white Persil garment with an anonymous grey one was first used in consumer advertising in the mid-1930s, and is a classic long-running campaign. (By courtesy of Unilever Ltd)

The Bisto Kids go back to the period before World War I, though their faces have been somewhat simplified since that time.

The Guinness animals provided a theme which could be adapted to special occasions – in this case, the 1953 Coronation. Guinness also produced an imaginative 'one-off' advertisement to celebrate the nine hundredth anniversary of the Battle of Hastings. (By courtesy of A. Guinness & Son Ltd)

World War II saw advertising used to promote a variety of causes; this dramatic design by Abram Games demonstrated the dangers of careless talk. (By courtesy of the Imperial War Museum)

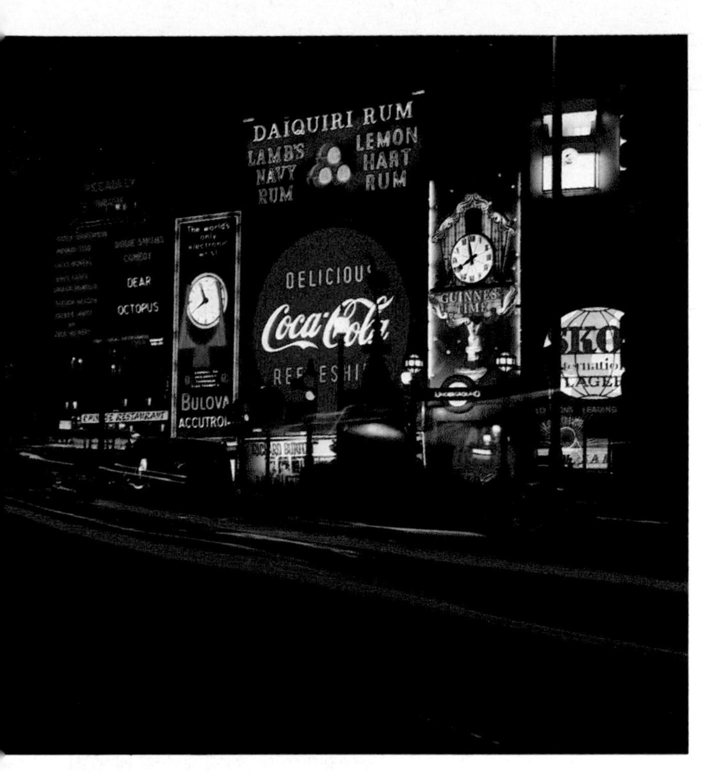

The end of rationing and the consumer boom of the 1950s and 1960s saw new and extravagant forms of advertising. Illustrated signs, such as those on display in Piccadilly Circus, grew ever more resplendent; and London Transport offered to advertisers buses specially painted to their requirements. (By courtesy of the London Tourist Board and the London Transport Executive)

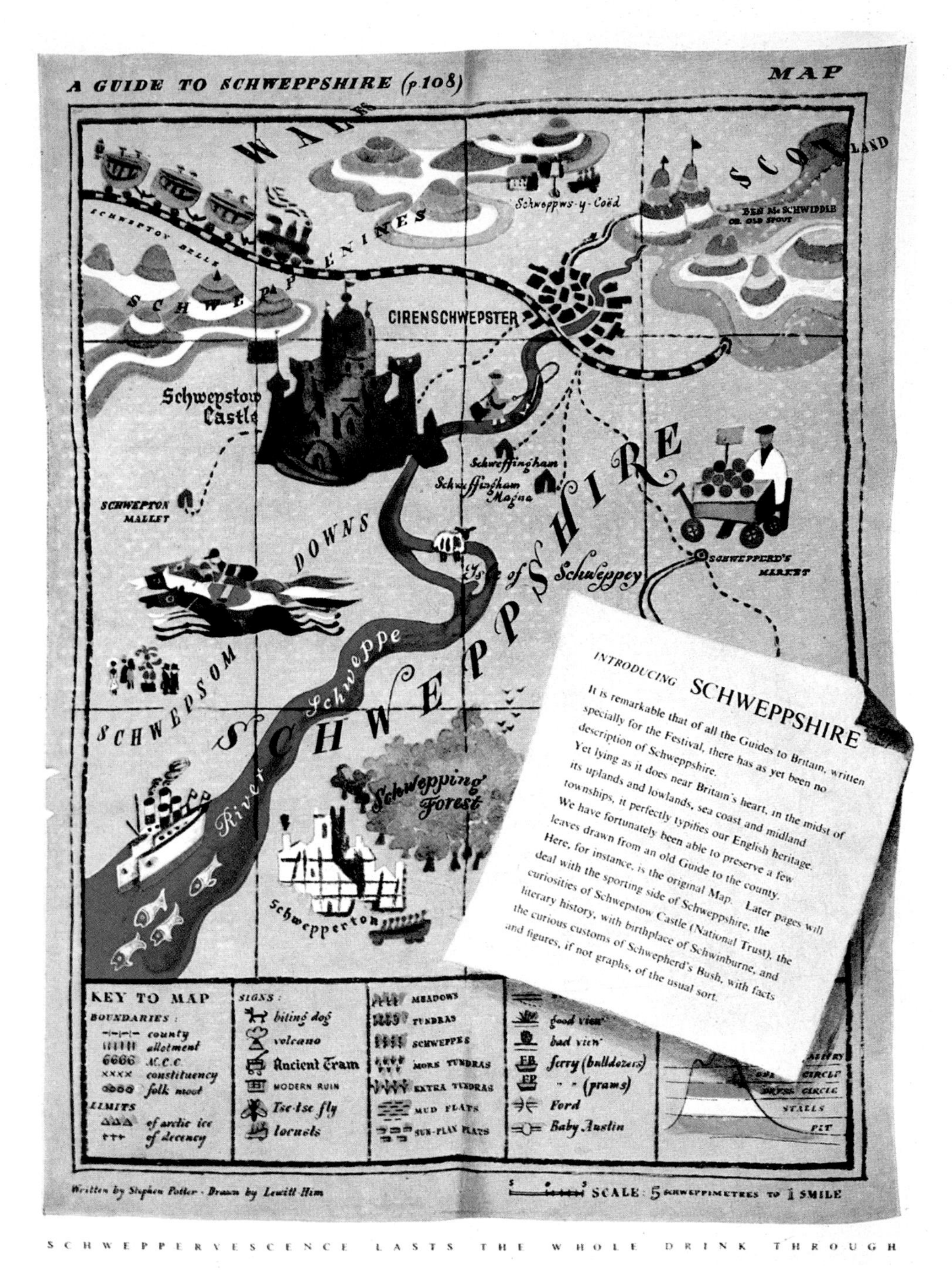

An example of the classic 'Schweppeshire' advertisement series by Stephen Potter – the best of the English whimsical style of campaign. (By courtesy of Schweppes Ltd)

Two of the most outstanding campaigns of recent years: the phonetic spelling of 'Beanz Meanz Heinz' has kept its product in a leading position; and the Esso tiger is used to symbolise power in many parts of the world. (By courtesy of H. J. Heinz Co Ltd and Esso Petroleum Co Ltd)

Television is now the spearhead for most mass consumer campaigns; but even greater impact can be gained if the music track can be exploited separately as was the case with this Coca-Cola commercial. (By courtesy of the Coca-Cola Export Corporation)

Britain. He diversified into growth areas away from the world of advertising media, taking his organisation into holidays and North Sea Oil. He also sometimes made mistakes, as in the case of newscasters.

By the beginning of the 1960s, newspapers and popular magazines alike were affected by higher production costs, continuing labour troubles, and the effects of television, while many were faced in addition with falling circulations. Reorganisation and rationalisation became inevitable. The decade opened with the disappearance of the *Sunday Graphic*, the *Empire News*, the *Star* (London's third evening paper), the *News Chronicle* and a number of locals and provincials. The future of the *Daily Herald* was in doubt. The *New Daily* appeared for a brief spell. With *Picture Post*, *Illustrated* and *Everybody's* having closed between 1957 and 1959, an effort was made to save *John Bull* by relaunching it in 1960 as *Today*, though this only gave it a stay of execution until 1964. In 1962, *Reynolds News* was re-presented in tabloid form as the *Sunday Citizen*, only to go under in 1967. The Labour Party 'Reith Commission' reported in 1966 that only three national papers were operating profitably, and that one of these was on a downward trend. The *Daily Herald* began a new life uncertainly as the *Sun* and was subsequently sold to a thrusting Australian publisher, Rupert Murdoch. He at once reversed the decline, and a concern which had lost £12.7 millon in eight years startled Fleet Street by adding one million to its circulation in twelve months. At the time of writing he has recently bought *The Times* from the Thomson Organization, which in spite of a lengthy and expensive strike had been unable to secure the agreement of its workforce to the introduction of new technology. Fleet Street, meanwhile, is beset with rumours about a possible replacement for the *Evening News* (now merged with the *Evening Standard* to form the *New Standard*), a new Sunday paper, and the impending demise of several dailies.

The recent development of the press has also been considerably affected by changes in social habits and spending patterns. There has been a growth of specialist magazines catering for a more affluent public with increased leisure time in which to pursue its hobbies and interests. Escalating labour costs have forced many householders to undertake tasks which forty years ago would probably have been performed by local tradesmen, and this in turn has led to the appearance of magazines covering the do-it-yourself field. The changing status and earning power of women has been reflected in journals dealing with such areas as the career girl and her sex life. Children's tastes altered markedly during the war years, leading to the appearance of publications such as *Eagle* (1950), and the demise of such old favourites as *Chips* and *Comic Cuts* (established 1890) and the wholesome *Boy's Own Paper*. And the changing pattern of the British weekend led London's *Evening News* and *Evening Standard* to stop producing Saturday editions. It remains to be seen whether the rising number of people unemployed will significantly affect the pattern of media development.

Television

Certainly the most important happening in advertising since 1945 has been the advent of commercial television. The Television Act of 1954 set up a strong central body, the Independent Television Authority, supervising a network of fourteen regions, each of which had its own contractor responsible for programmes and the sale of advertising time. Unlike their counterparts in the United States, British advertisers had – and still have – no influence over the content of programmes, and could not sponsor them. Under the terms of the Act:

> Nothing shall be included in any programmes broadcast by the Authority, whether in an advertisement or not, which states, suggests or implies, or could reasonably be taken to state, suggest or imply, that any part of any programme broadcast by the Authority which is not an advertisement has been supplied or suggested by any advertiser.

The Croydon transmitter, covering the London area, was brought into service in September 1955, followed by Lichfield (Midlands) in February 1956, Winter Hill (Lancashire) in May, and Emley Moor (Yorkshire) in November. These four between them covered some 60 per cent of the population, with coverage of the remaining areas being completed by 1962.

Although the advertising world was surprised by the speed with which the new medium established itself, the reasons for its success are not difficult to find. In 1955, when commercial transmissions began, national newspapers were still affected by newsprint rationing, and unable to meet the demand for advertising space. The cinema, the other audio-visual medium, was already in decline, apparently as a result of competition from BBC television. At the same time, there was a great expansion in set ownership, the number of licences issued rising from 3 million in 1954 to 8 million in 1958, 13 million in 1965 and 15 million in 1968.

The sheer novelty of advertisements on television, and often of television itself, meant that the early commercials had a considerable impact upon viewers, producing some dramatic effects on sales. Retailers, who soon became aware of this, tended to show a marked preference for products which were to be promoted on television – a vital marketing consideration which was to influence the form of many a future campaign. Advertising agencies also pressed the claims of television from the outset, stressing the advantages offered by sound and movement, by reaching audiences in their own homes, and by the ability to repeat a message several times in one evening. Agency planners appreciated the sophisticated research methods which, by using meters linked to a sample of sets in conjunction with special diaries kept by viewers, soon made it possible to estimate the size and composition of the audience at any given time. In addition, television offered agencies the prospect of a higher rate of profit, since instead of being involved in production work as they were for each press insertion, adapting a basic advertisement to different sizes and mechanical requirements, they made one commercial and received 15 per cent commission every time it was screened.

From the outset therefore, television advertising was remarkably successful. It might have been more so had agencies been fully prepared for the challenge which faced them. Apart from a little cinema and radio advertising, however, their background lay almost exclusively in the realm of print. Consequently, early commercials often look and sound like adaptations of press advertisements, rather than attempting to exploit the creative potential of the new medium. Needing expertise in the television field, agencies imported American producers, whose background was often in sponsored programmes rather than commercials, and therefore of little value. Alternatively they engaged ageing British thespians whose contribution was even more doubtful. It was not really until the evolution of the specialist agency producer, with a proper understanding of production techniques and requirements, that the medium began to be exploited to anything like its full potential.

Radio

Another major change on the media scene has been the development in Britain of independent local radio stations. For many years the official attitude was strongly opposed to commercial broadcasting, though as we have seen, this was probably at variance with the views of a large section of the population which listened to programmes from continental stations during the 1930s. There were hopes of a change after the war, but when a Government White Paper on broadcasting was published in 1946, it not only ruled out commercials on the BBC but also stated, 'The Government, moreover, intend to take all steps within their power, and to use their influence with the authorities concerned, to prevent the direction of commercial broadcasts to this country from abroad.' It was nevertheless unable to stop the resumption in that year of transmissions from Radio Luxembourg. There had been a proposal that the British and French governments should use the station for broadcasts to Germany and Austria, but when they were unable to reach an agreement with the Luxembourg authorities, many British advertisers, who because of the newsprint shortage were unable to buy the press space they needed, happily availed themselves of the facilities.

The report of the Beveridge Committee in 1951 shows some relaxation of the hard line. Although the majority report recommended a continuation of the BBC monopoly and a continued ban on commercial advertising or sponsored programmes without the written consent of the appropriate minister, one member did advocate in a minority report that sponsored radio should be allowed, while Lord Beveridge himself was one of three members who recommended that the BBC should accept advertisements, though not sponsored programmes. The time was not yet ripe for such proposals, however, and the Government of the day accepted the majority report. A typical reaction was that of Lord Hailsham, who declared in the House of Lords, 'Commercial broadcasting is to be condemned because it distorts the purposes of broadcasting by reason of the fundamental purpose for which the vehicle is used – not broadcasting for its sake but its use as a medium in which advertisements can live.'

Four years later the newspaper publishers at last lifted their ban on publicity for commercial broadcasting, imposed twenty-two years previously. Always ridiculous, it would have been even more so had it continued while the inclusion of commercial television details was permitted. As a result of the relaxation, some papers printed Radio Luxembourg programme details alongside those of the BBC though by this time Luxembourg was itself badly hit by the spread of television. Particularly after 1955 its audience dwindled alarmingly, so much so that many advertisers gave up using radio. Realising that it could not win in such a situation, the station decided to avoid direct competition with television by appealing to teenagers, concentrating particularly on the period after peak viewing had finished, and feeding them a concentrated diet of 'pop' music not obtainable elsewhere. This move took advantage of the spread of cheap transistor radios, which meant that the audience could be reached even when not at home, and that the teenager could retreat to his or her own room to listen to pop music, while the parents downstairs settled for something more sedate. It also offered advertisers a means of reaching the teenage market at a time when its growing spending power and importance were just becoming apparent.

What finally seems to have compelled the acceptance of commercial broadcasting was the success of the pirate radio stations in the mid-1960s. The potentially large audiences for programmes of recorded music, which were relatively cheap to produce, tempted a number of companies to set up commercial radio stations, situated on disused forts or on ships anchored just outside territorial waters. Dispensing pop records with a levity and informality which came as a revelation to BBC listeners, they achieved such popularity with young people that the Government felt constrained to act against them. Border adjustments were made in September 1964 to bring the three forts housing transmitters within British jurisdiction, though no further action was taken immediately. Then in 1967 the Marine Broadcasting Offences Act made it an offence to supply or to buy advertising time on the pirate stations, which were thereby effectively killed off.

In the heyday of pirate radio there were ten stations operating: Radio Caroline (with two ships), Radio London, Radio 390, Radio City, Radio Scotland, Radio 270, Radio Essex and Radio England/Britain Radio. Radio Caroline in 1966 was claiming national coverage, and Caroline and London together estimated their audience as exceeding 13 millions. Although a fleeting phenomenon, the pirates were important in two respects. Firstly, they demonstrated a large public demand for a particular type of popular programme. And secondly, they proved that commercial stations could be operated profitably, because of the support they attracted from advertisers.

In 1971 the Government introduced the Sound Broadcasting Bill, which received the royal assent the following year. It provided for the setting up of sixty independent local radio stations to be under the control of the Independent Broadcasting Authority, an extended version of the Independent Television Authority. In the event only nineteen contracts were awarded initially, though the major conurbations covered meant that around two-thirds of Britain's population could receive independent radio. At the time of writing, Mrs Thatcher's Government has promised to press ahead with the remaining stations, and plans are well advanced to bring the number up to 44, covering 75 per cent of the population. The pioneers of prewar commercial radio and the pirates of the 1960s have been vindicated.

Other Media

Fashions in advertising change; and this is as true of media as it is of creative treatments. The poster, once regarded as a distinct art form and so much an essential part of any campaign, has suffered a decline since World War II. Viewed in the long term this was probably inevitable. In their Victorian heyday, posters were almost the only means of visual mass communication in colour, but that position has been eroded since the beginning of the twentieth century by improvements in printing technology, which brought colour advertising to the press, by the cinema, and more recently by the advent of colour television. Although the poster has now found a new niche, placed conveniently near supermarkets and shopping centres as a permanent reminder of the transient television commercial, it will certainly never regain its former popularity.

The enamelled sign, which also enjoyed its heyday in the years before 1914, has now all but disappeared. The rationing of steel during and after World War II, the loss of many sites due to enemy bombing and later to urban redevelopment, the erection of large-scale poster hoardings to mask bombed sites, the disappearance of the traditional user such as the small baker or ice-cream company, and the requirements of planning legislation – all these factors have contributed to the sign's fall from favour.

The fortunes of the cinema have also declined in recent times. The years immediately following the war were a boom period, with 1946 seeing 635 million admissions annually to 4,703 cinemas. Within a quarter of a century, this had been reduced, under the impact of television, to 163 million admissions and 1,482 cinemas. Initially, the resumption of BBC television transmissions affected audiences, and so tended to push down the rates which the cinema advertisement contractors were able to charge to advertisers. Then in the later 1950s, Board of Trade figures show admissions to have been significantly lower in those areas which could receive ITV programmes. As more independent TV

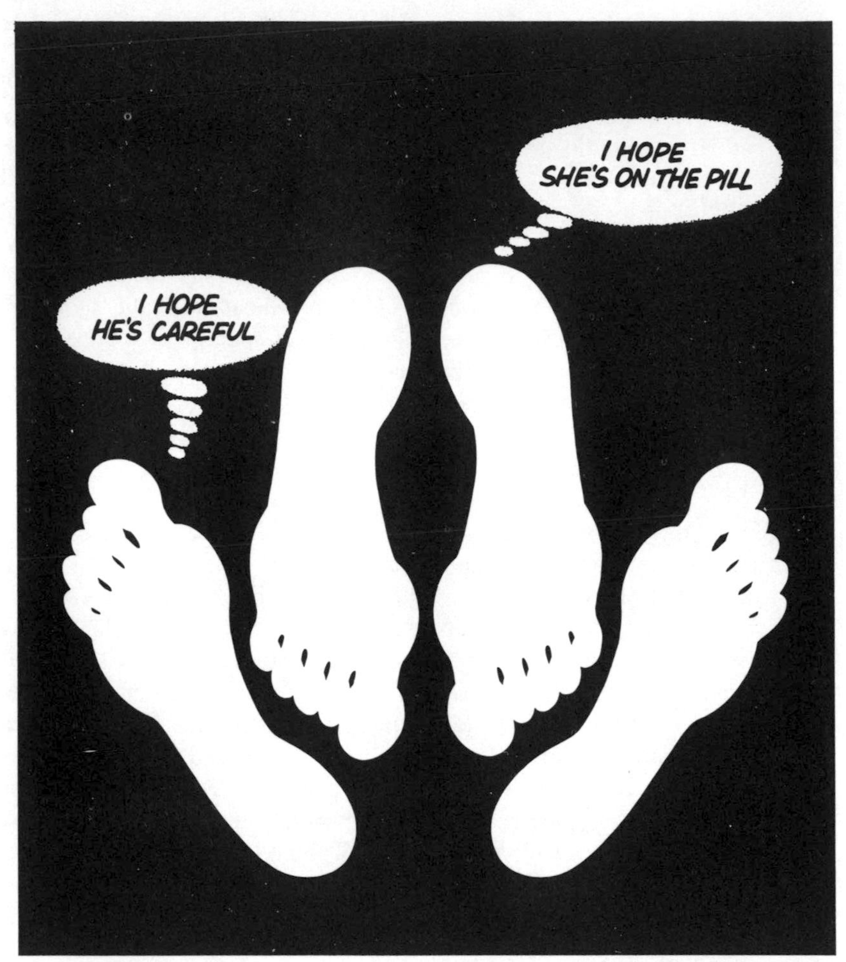

Some hope!

Did you know an unplanned baby is born in Britain every few minutes?

The trouble is, it's a great deal easier to start a baby than you think, especially if you take chances.

A man takes a chance if he just hopes the girl is on the pill or is 'safe.'

A girl takes a desperate chance if she just hopes he'll withdraw. (A man sometimes promises to withdraw and then doesn't. And even if he does withdraw, you can still get pregnant).

If you're a man at least ask the girl if she's on the pill and wear a contraceptive if she's not. You can buy them from chemists, barbers or slot machines.

If you're a girl you should never rely on a man. You can get advice and free contraceptives from doctors or Family Planning Clinics – whether you are married or not.

You'll find clinics listed in your telephone book.

The Health Education Council

78 New Oxford Street, London WC1A 1AH. 01-637 1881

These campaigns produced by Saatchi and Saatchi for the Health Education Council are excellent examples of the recent trend to use advertising for social purposes.
(By courtesy of the Health Education Council)

This is what happens when a fly lands on your food.

Flies can't eat solid food, so to soften it up they vomit on it.

Then they stamp the vomit in until it's a liquid, usually stamping in a few germs for good measure.

Then when it's good and runny they suck it all back again, probably dropping some excrement at the same time.

And then, when they've finished eating, it's your turn.

Cover food. Cover eating and drinking utensils. Cover dustbins.

The Health Education Council

stations were opened, therefore, they not only affected the cinema audience still further, but also siphoned off some of the advertising revenue.

Of late it appears that this slide has been halted and possibly even reversed. More imaginative film productions, the rebuilding of old-style massive auditoriums into complexes of several small cinemas with air conditioning and comfortable seating, and the change of emphasis in the function of a cinema from a place showing films to a centre of entertainment have all helped to make cinema-going more attractive. Even so, the cinema today accounts for rather less than one per cent of national advertising expenditure.

New media

The search for new methods of bringing advertising messages to the attention of the public has been pursued in recent years much as it has since the middle of the nineteenth century. The minicabs of the early 1960s were decorated with advertisements. London Transport offered buses specially painted to the advertiser's requirements. *Picture Post*, before its demise, experimented with three-dimensional advertisements, supplying a pair of special spectacles free with every copy. Advertisements have appeared on sports equipment and clothing, on T-shirts, and on transparent sandwich-boards carried by a topless model. They have been relayed to housewives in bingo halls, launderettes and supermarkets, and to businessmen in hotels. Advertising messages appear on sports grounds so as to be within range of television cameras. Some companies have invested in sponsorship. At the time of writing, an estimated £30 million is spent annually on sports, and a further £1.5 million on the arts; but the benefits to be derived from much of this expenditure are open to question. The future for sponsorship seems to lie not so much in its effectiveness as an advertising medium as in providing a means for companies to parade their social consciences in public.

The advertising agency

The advertising agency has undergone considerable changes in the last three decades. During and immediately after the war, as we have seen, the main problems confronting agency clients were related to the management of supply rather than the stimulation of demand, so that agencies were to a large extent concerned with filling spaces with something tasteful and amusing. Advertising which actually made the reader want to buy the product was often positively discouraged. By the mid-1950s the picture had changed as competition increased following the dismantling of wartime controls, and as commercial television became part of the advertiser's armoury. Agencies found themselves having to work in a completely new medium at the same time as they were facing the cold blast of business reality. Since advertising is very much a young man's province, this meant that many of the people working in agencies had been recruited since the war, and had not been confronted before with real competition.

It was at about this time that American agencies began to make their presence felt in London. Business conducted internationally requires international agency service, so when American companies came to Britain, their agencies came too. In 1937 only four American agencies had branches outside the United States. By 1960, the number had risen to thirty-six, with a total of 281 offices. In London they sometimes set up their own operations from scratch, but more often they bought out existing British agencies – a trend which has continued until at the time of writing only four of the top twenty agencies in Britain are still British owned.

The American invaders brought with them a new kind of expertise. While Britain's manufacturers had been struggling through the years of rationing to satisfy a restricted demand, and their agencies had busied themselves with advertising which has not actually intended to sell, techniques of marketing and promotion had been tested and refined in the United States. Companies and agencies were reorganised. A new marketing vocabulary emerged. And a new school of researchers, headed by Dichter, Cheskin and their followers, claimed to hold the key to human motivation.

The wider range of services offered by American agencies, together with their experience in working for more sophisticated clients, was bound to make them attractive to British companies faced with trying to repel inroads into the home market. The British agencies reacted in alarm, and began to offer a wide range of 'extras' to any company whose advertising they handled. Marketing, public relations, research, and other services were provided free of charge, paid for out of the agency's commission. As they did not have the expertise themselves, talent had to be imported, and agency corridors abounded with crew-cuts and American accents. British advertisers, to whom marketing was the new panacea in the way that advertising had been a century before, thankfully accepted what was offered, with the result that companies knowing nothing about marketing theory but a lot about their business had their futures dictated by people who knew plenty about marketing theory and nothing about the business. It was only when the first generation of home-produced marketing men began to occupy positions of responsibility in British companies that the balance was restored.

The heady days of the mid- and late 1950s were a boom time for agencies. Money flowed in as rationing disappeared, television spread over the country, and companies increased their spending levels to fight off competitors threatening their traditional markets. New departments were opened almost regardless of cost. With too few qualified and experienced staff to go round, vastly inflated salaries were paid to tempt people from one agency to another. It was a situation that could not last. By the mid-1960s agency fortunes were beginning to decline, hit by the general economic uncertainty which followed two General Elections in seventeen months, a credit squeeze, and the hated Selective Employment Tax. There were reports of unemployment in the agency world as staffs were reduced and mergers hastily arranged to save on overheads. Directors and senior executives announced to a sceptical trade press that they were opting for early retirement, or becoming consultants. Famous agencies of prewar days disappeared overnight.

Perhaps agencies might have ridden out their difficulties more successfully had they been in better financial shape, and to this extent we can trace the roots of the problem back to the years of restraint during and after the war. When newspaper advertisements were restricted in size, and alternative media in short supply, the amount of working capital needed to finance agency operations was relatively small. When the expansion came in the fifties, they therefore often found themselves undercapitalised and having to borrow heavily to finance clients' growing media expenditure. At the same time they were spending heavily, as we have seen, in providing extra services and paying larger salaries, and as a result became particularly vulnerable to such business hazards as the slow payer. American agencies, generally bigger and with more substantial finances behind them, tended to suffer far less than the British, and the prospect of selling out to an American concern became still more attractive.

Some agencies opted for a different line of defence, and turned themselves into public companies. In doing so they attracted a dangerous predator in the form of the asset-stripper, who stalked them on the Stock Exchange to gain control of the valuable leases they held on prestigious office buildings. John Bentley, a master in the art, gained control of Dorlands in 1971, that agency having already taken over Crawfords with their prime site in Holborn. Bensons discovered in the same year that their Kingsway offices were valued at £3 million and £4 million with vacant possession, so arranged a protective merger with Ogilvy and Mather.[1]

The pressures on agencies in recent years have not been those of economic circumstance alone. They have also been subjected to increasing competition from within the advertising business in the shape of media consultancies, offering advertisers a media-buying service only, and rebating part of the commission on the largely fictional understanding that the money returned would be used to buy creative work. In that way – at any rate in theory – the agency offering a full service was not subject to price competition. The no-rebating clause, it will be remembered, was originally introduced into the agency recognition agreement in order to protect the press against financially unstable agencies. Now it was the media who, by destroying one of the main defences of the service agency, were in effect questioning the whole structure of the advertising business.

From the agencies' point of view, worse was to come when in 1979 the

Newspaper Publishers Association and the Newspaper Society opted to change the basis of agency recognition. The move was largely forced upon them, since the extension of the Restrictive Trade Practices legislation in 1976 to cover services meant that the joint recognition agreement operated by the two organisations had to be registered with the Office of Fair Trading. It was decided after discussion with legal advisers and OFT officials that only two aspects of the existing agreement would be acceptable under the terms of the legislation: the financial vetting of applicants, and the obligation of recognised agencies to observe the British Code of Advertising Practice. A new agreement was therefore introduced, which omitted any reference to the payment of commission, the prohibition against rebating, and the limitation of recognition to certain types of agency. Since January 1979, the payment of commission has in theory been a matter for individual negotiation between each agency and newspaper, rather than between the agency and the publishers' organisations as before, and with the restriction on rebating gone, some advertisers have once more begun to choose their agency on the basis of price reductions. In addition, agencies are also facing direct competition from companies' advertising departments, which can now be accorded the treatment in terms of commission that was previously reserved for agencies alone.

One result of the troubles of recent years has been a large-scale shedding of staff by older agencies. According to figures published by the Institute of Practitioners in Advertising, the number of staff employed by their members fell from 20,000 in 1966 to 14,000 in 1974, with 1971 alone seeing a drop of 9% from 17,200 to 15,600. The situation seems to have stabilized, however; and the years 1975–1980 even saw a modest increase from 14,700 to 15,500.

Criticism and control

Since World War II, advertising has probably been subjected to a greater volume of criticism than at any time in its history. This is not to say that it has become less truthful – standards in this respect are higher now than they have ever been. What has happened is that a change has taken place in the climate of public and political opinion which has brought advertisements under much closer scrutiny. Increased emphasis has been placed in general terms upon consumer protection. Consumers themselves have probably become more aware of advertising now that it is brought directly into their homes by the peculiarly intrusive medium of television. And a wide variety of writers have examined the ethics of 'persuasion', the possibilities of mass manipulation, and the economics of the advertising-inspired acquisitive society.

The Labour Party has tended to become particularly critical of the activities of advertisers. In 1959 a public meeting called by Francis Noel-Baker, M.P., set up the Advertising Inquiry Committee, an independent body which was to watch out for 'all kinds of socially harmful advertisement'. Two years later the party set up an independent commission under the chairmanship of Lord Reith, which recommended the establishment of a National Consumer Board financed by a levy on advertising. In 1972, a Green Paper on Advertising was published, in which advertising was condemned for creating an imbalance in the relationship between consumer and producer – a state of affairs which it was proposed to rectify by the creation of a National Consumers Authority:

> This Authority should be independent. It should have an income of millions rather than thousands, and thus be enabled to test claims on behalf of consumers, to investigate complaints and to publish its work, (and that of others) effectively. The establishment of a statutory code to govern advertising practice is suggested. The Authority would advise on its provisions, enforcement and needed revisions.

The troubles besetting the newspaper industry were attributed to 'excessive reliance on advertising revenue', which it was felt might compromise the freedom of the press, together with 'the habit of advertisers of concentrating on papers already successful'. In addition, advertising was castigated for '. . . its tendency to over-encourage gross materialism and dissatisfaction and its tendency to irresponsibility'. Since many of the problems were seen as arising from 'an excess of advertising above a necessary and reasonable level', it was proposed to disallow 50 per cent of all advertising expenditure as a deductable expense for tax purposes. As well as financing the National Consumers Authority, it was felt that this would lead to competition in terms of price reductions on products rather than through advertising. The taxation of advertising was subsequently adopted as official party policy.

The teaching profession has at times been extremely critical of the influence of advertising on children. The Annual Conference of the National Association of Schoolmasters in 1962 heard Mr Terry Casey state their case in the following terms:

> Perhaps the most pervasive anti-educational influence is that of modern advertising, for that *exists* to circumvent the reasoning faculty and weaken judgment. Some of it is puerile, but it can be subtle. Of the former kind are the many variants of the *ex parte* claim that 'Bloggs makes the best – whatever it is. This must be so because Bloggs says it is so'. Millions of young minds, which we seek to train to think, are constantly bombarded with this sort of nonsense. Not content with bad logic, resort is had to bad manners. Children themselves are recruited as advertising agents, and are urged to make importunate demands upon their parents to buy this or that product. 'Don't forget my fruit gums, Mum!' is not even prefaced with the little word 'please'.
>
> Under the rough treatment of the 'blurb' writers, adjectives have lost their vitality and almost their validity because of the excessive use of superlatives. In school we try to enrich vocabularies, but many children are reduced to the verbal poverty of using the prepositional prefix 'super' as an all-purpose adjective denoting approbation, thanks to the baleful influence of the 'Ads'. Psychology, the science which we thought was to be the handmaiden of education, has been prostituted to serve the ends of salesmanship, the panjandrum of the inflated economy. If

advertising really is necessary to keep the wheels of industry and commerce turning, is it too much to ask that it be presented in ways which do not offend good taste nor affront good sense?[2]

One result of the generally more critical attitude towards advertising has been an increase in the amount of legislation affecting the content of advertisements, both directly and indirectly. Apart from the widely known Trade Descriptions Act, there are over 60 statutes and statutory instruments currently in force which relate to advertising, the most important of them being listed in Appendix L of the British Code of Advertising Practice, which is reproduced in Appendix B of the present work. For a detailed examination of their scope and significance the reader is referred to Dr Richard Lawson's definitive *Advertising Law*. Advertising on television is particularly tightly controlled, the Independent Broadcasting Authority having a statutory responsibility for programme content which includes advertising. This it discharges in respect of commercials by ensuring that they comply with its own Code of Practice, checking them before tranmission not only for points of presentation but also to make certain that all claims are capable of substantiation. Radio commercials, for which the I.B.A. is again responsible, are also subject to prior approval, but since the medium is used mainly for local campaigns, vetting in most instances is left to individual stations.

Mounting criticism has also forced the advertising business to tighten its own internal controls. Medical advertising in particular has come under increasingly close scrutiny, with the Proprietary Association of Great Britain revising its Code on a number of occasions, and the British Code of Standards in Relation to the Advertising of Medicines and Treatments, published under the auspices of the Advertising Association in 1948, subsequently being incorporated into the British Code of Advertising Practice. Voluntary action in this traditionally difficult area seems to have been successful. The Proprietary Association today works closely with the Department of Health, and regulations made under the Medicines Act of 1968 leave the detailed control of advertising very largely in the hands of the self-regulatory bodies. Even the Price Commission was impressed with the job which had been done:

Self regulation of advertising by the industry has been initiated by the Proprietary Association of Great Britain (PAGB). This has been responsible for stopping the early advertising abuses which even now colour the image of the industry. The first Code of Practice was introduced in 1936 and this has been systematically updated since then to improve advertising standards and to take into account the development of new advertising media such as commercial television and radio. In addition to the controls imposed by the PAGB the advertising industry itself has imposed its own system of control through the Advertising Standards Authority.

The number of complaints about proprietary medicines advertising is about 0.2 per cent of all complaints and the number upheld is less than 0.1 per cent. The conclusion is therefore that the system of control is effective.

The advertising business has also made considerable efforts to improve standards on a more general level, though in responding to public pressure it may have moved too little and too late. A notable step forward was taken in 1961 when the Advertising Association Conference saw the unveiling of the British Code of Advertising Practice, providing for the first time a set of formal standards to be observed and applied by all sides of the business. This was not enough to still the critical voices, objections being made to the framing of the Code on the grounds that it did not go far enough, and to the standing committee responsible for its enforcement because it represented advertising interests rather than those of the consumer. The following year therefore saw the setting up of a new body, the independent Advertising Standards Authority, which had as its object 'The promotion and enforcement throughout the United Kingdom of the highest standards of advertising in all media, so as to ensure in co-operation with all those concerned that no advertising contravenes or offends against these standards.' The chairman of the Authority was named as Professor Sir Arnold Plant of the London School of Economics, whose impartiality was beyond doubt; among its ten members was Vic Feather of the TUC. The sceptics still remained unconvinced, however, arguing that the Authority was not strong enough, was biased in favour of advertising, and that its working was comparable to that of the police investigating complaints against themselves.

By 1974 it was becoming abundantly clear that unless justice were seen to be effectively enforced, the Labour Government would introduce a statutory code of practice together with suitable machinery to ensure its observance. Faced with this threat, the industry made considerable revisions to its own system. The Advertising Standards Authority's permanent secretariat was strengthened. A revised edition of the Code of Practice was produced, with copies going to every Citizen's Advice Bureau in the country. Massive advertising campaigns were mounted, telling the public about the Authority and its work, and urging them to complain if they saw an advertisement that was not legal, decent, honest and truthful. Regular bulletins were introduced giving details of complaints received and the action taken. A monitoring system was begun to keep a check on particular categories of advertisement where problems were likely to occur. And the whole machinery of control was now financed by a levy on display advertising of 0.1 per cent to be collected by a new body known as the Advertising Standards Board of Finance (ASBOF). Meanwhile the Authority had also absorbed the work of the Advertisement Investigation Department of the Advertising Association, which had given so many years of faithful service.

The Council of the Advertising Standards Authority now consists of twelve members appointed by the Chairman, all of whom serve as individuals and not as representatives of any business or sectional interest. Eight are drawn from various areas of public life, and the others from the advertising industry to provide expert advice. The ASA is really the public face of advertising control. Another body, the Code of Advertising Practice Committee, co-ordinates activities within the advertising industry itself. Consisting of members of the twenty organisations subscribing to the Code (see Appendix A) it is responsible

Are you legal, decent, honest and truthful?

Advertisers have to be.

Enquiries to: The Advertising Standards Authority,
2-16 Torrington Place, London WCIE 7HN
Telephone: 01-580 5555

(By courtesy of the Advertising Standards Authority)

for ensuring that people working in all branches of advertising are aware of and understand the provisions of the Code, and are prepared to enforce them. It can specify certain classes of advertisement for pre-clearance, currently vetting those for cigarettes, pregnancy testing and counselling, abortion, vasectomy, and sterilisation. It also deals with disputes on copy matters arising between advertisers, and if required will provide pre-publication advice on the admissibility of advertising claims.

The new method of working has undoubtedly been successful in ensuring stricter observance of the Code of Advertising Practice. The Authority's Annual Report for the year 1976–7 gives the following breakdown of complaints received during a sample period:

> The number of complaints which came within the ASA's remit over a nine week period were 1,592, against a background of something of the order of 4½ million advertisements published each week. Of that number, 183 were complaints not about advertisements but about a failure to deliver goods ordered by mail. (Because such goods are bought as a direct result of an advertisement, the ASA has a special responsibility for bringing such complaints to a satisfactory conclusion). Of the remaining complaints, 295 were found to be justified. This represents 18.5% of all complaints received in the period, but only 0.006% of the estimated total number of print advertisements published during the nine weeks concerned. The complaints which were upheld ranged from technical breaches of the Code and genuine over-sights to a very few intentionally misleading claims. A substantial proportion were concerned with questions of taste and decency: an area where self-regulation need fear no competition from the law.

In spite of this impressive record, there still remain some awkward loopholes. Enforcement of the Code is only effective if the media carrying the offending advertisement belong to one of the organisations which have agreed to uphold its provisions. In the case of an advertiser using 'rogue' media, or sending his material through the post, the Authority is powerless. In future it will surely be this area which will attract the attention of proponents of statutory control.

In addition to the part played by the Authority in advertising control, it should be remembered that considerable work is done behind the scenes by individual companies and organisations within the business. The Newspaper Society, by maintaining its own Advertisement Investigation Department, running training courses and seminars, and publishing essential information in handy reference form, keeps the regional press up to date and on its guard. Publishers' organisations operate guarantee schemes to protect readers against possible loss when sending off money in 'direct response' to mail order advertisements. The Incorporated Society of British Advertisers continues to supply its members with a confidential bulletin giving details of current sharp and illegal practices. Agency standards are upheld by the Institute of Practioners in Advertising, which in 1957, for example, banned the use by its members of subliminal advertising – messages flashed at such speed that they are received by the brain without the recipient's conscious knowledge. Students taking the industry's professional examination – the Diploma of the Communication Advertising and Marketing Education Foundation – now also face compulsory questions on legal and voluntary controls. It remains to be seen whether all these efforts will be sufficient to head off the threat of tighter legal control, including compulsory pre-vetting of advertisements, as is the case on television. The British press has always been wary of any attempt to censor its columns, and there remains the fear that machinery established for the ostensible purpose of checking advertising could very easily be converted to control the editorial sections. Perhaps a few misleading advertisements are a small price to pay for democracy.

In addition to pressure for higher standards of advertising, the industry has also had to face calls for an end to the advertising of particular products. The case in which feelings have run highest has been that of cigarettes, following the publication of evidence linking smoking with lung cancer. At the outset the industry fiercely resisted any kind of curb. The public, it was argued, should be permitted to smoke themselves to death if they so desired. In any case, advertising did not encourage people to smoke but only to switch brands. A typical reaction was that of the poster industry's Joint Censorship Committee, which in 1962 banned a Ministry of Health poster with the wording 'Cigarettes cause lung cancer' on the grounds that this was not the same as saying 'Cigarette smoking is a cause of lung cancer' – a decision described by Lord Hailsham as 'absolutely indefensible and indeed irresponsible, illogical quibbling'.

Gradually the industry was forced to give way. In 1962 the Independent Television Authority and the tobacco manufacturers agreed on a code of practice which put an end to the use of romantic situations, the over-emphasis on the pleasure to be derived from smoking, and the use of appealing personalities or settings. The screening of cigarette commercials was also limited to times when children were least likely to be watching. Three years later cigarettes disappeared completely from the commercial break, despite vehement protests from the Advertising Association, the Institute of Practitioners in Advertising, and the Incorporated Society of British Advertisers. Meanwhile, a number of newspapers and magazines were announcing that they would not accept any further cigarette advertising, among them the *Radio Times* and *Listener*, whose decision announced in 1969 was estimated to have cost them £500,000 in lost revenue within a year. The cigarette companies, for their part, actually increased their expenditure in the years after the television ban, and sought to circumvent it by such means as sponsorship.

At the time of writing, the appeals which can be made in cigarette advertising are set out in Appendix H of the *British Code of Advertising Practice*, which prohibits virtually every type of claim traditionally employed. Each advertisement also has to carry a warning that smoking can damage the health. Calls for a complete ban on cigarette advertising still persist, however, and there seems little doubt that this will eventually come, ending what must surely rank as one of the most contentious episodes in British advertising.

Epilogue

OUR STORY HAS now reached the present day, with society facing a period of considerable change. The action of the main oil-producing nations in cutting back production and raising prices has brought severe economic problems in its wake. Industrial output is declining, and the rate of inflation remains obstinately high. The setbacks and changes of direction in recent years have caused

HERE'S HOW YOU CAN HELP STOP THE RIPPER KILLING AGAIN.

Let's get one or two things straight about the Yorkshire Ripper.

There is nothing heroic about his actions.

He is, in fact, a vicious maniac who has brutally murdered twelve women (some prostitutes, some not) who happened to be in the wrong place at the wrong time.

And his method of killing is so sick that it has turned the stomachs of even the most hardened police officers.

He must be stopped. And you can help.

I have already written concerning the recent Ripper murders. I told him and I am telling you to warn them I'll strike again and soon when heat cools off.

LOOK CLOSELY AT THE HANDWRITING.

It's the writing of a sadistic killer.

And if you think you recognise it from a note, letter, envelope, signature, cheque, anything, report it to your local police.

LISTEN TO THE KILLER'S VOICE.

By phoning **LEEDS (STD 0532) 464111** you can hear probably the most important clue to the killer's identity. His voice.

It won't be a pleasant experience, but it could lead to the end of these brutal murders.

If you think you recognise the voice, tell the police.

THINK ABOUT THE PEOPLE AROUND YOU.

Their voices (North Eastern accent?)

Their handwriting (is it like the sample?)

Their travels to and from the North East.

To and from the Bradford, Leeds, Preston, Huddersfield, Manchester or Halifax areas. Or northwards from anywhere south of any of these areas.

Their attitudes towards women, especially prostitutes.

If it adds up to reasonable grounds for suspicion, however slight, report it to the police.

DO THESE DATES AND PLACES MEAN ANYTHING TO YOU?

Think very carefully about these dates and places.

What were you doing? What do you remember? Anything odd or out of place. The slightest detail could help.

30-31 Oct. 1975: Leeds	1-2 Oct. 1977: Manchester
20-21 Nov. 1975: Preston	21-22 Jan. 1978: Bradford
20-21 Jan. 1976: Leeds	31-1 Jan/Feb 1978: Huddersfield
5-6 Feb. 1977: Leeds	16-17 May 1978: Manchester
23-24 April 1977: Bradford	4-5 April 1979: Halifax
26-27 June 1977: Leeds	1-2 Sept 1979: Bradford

A WORD OF WARNING.

It is now believed that the Ripper draws no distinction between ordinary women and prostitutes.

So, please, if you're a woman, think twice about going out alone at night. Especially in the type of areas the Ripper favours.

£30,000 REWARD.

Money is the last reason for putting away this monster. But if it helps you think hard and helps us stop the killing, it's yours for information leading to the arrest of the murderer.

WEST YORKSHIRE METROPOLITAN POLICE

Help us put away the Ripper.

A striking example of the social use of advertising.
(By courtesy of Graham Poulter & Associates)

economists and marketing men to talk of 'discontinuity' in place of the cheerful predictions of accelerating rates of growth. Reserves of important raw materials are limited, which in turn has raised the question of whether commercial concerns can continue to be allowed the freedom to manufacture whatever they can sell at a profit, regardless of the wider social implications. Researchers and forecasters, taking stock of the situation, must also try to estimate the likely effects of such influences as increased leisure time, improved contraception methods, immigration, and the silicon chip.

Business, whether it be state or private enterprise, will need to respond to these changes, and advertising will surely have a major part to play in conveying information and regulating demand. As conditions become more difficult, however, so advertisers will become more demanding about the way their money is spent. Heavier emphasis on research seems likely, to define the target audience for a campaign as accurately as possible and to ensure that an advertisement is communicating efficiently and effectively. But while research can provide the ammunition and direct the aim, it cannot create. The writing and designing of advertisements in the future will continue to demand a peculiar blend of skill, flair, and imagination. And in the twenty-first century, as in the past, the most important factor in advertising success will be the truly original creative idea.

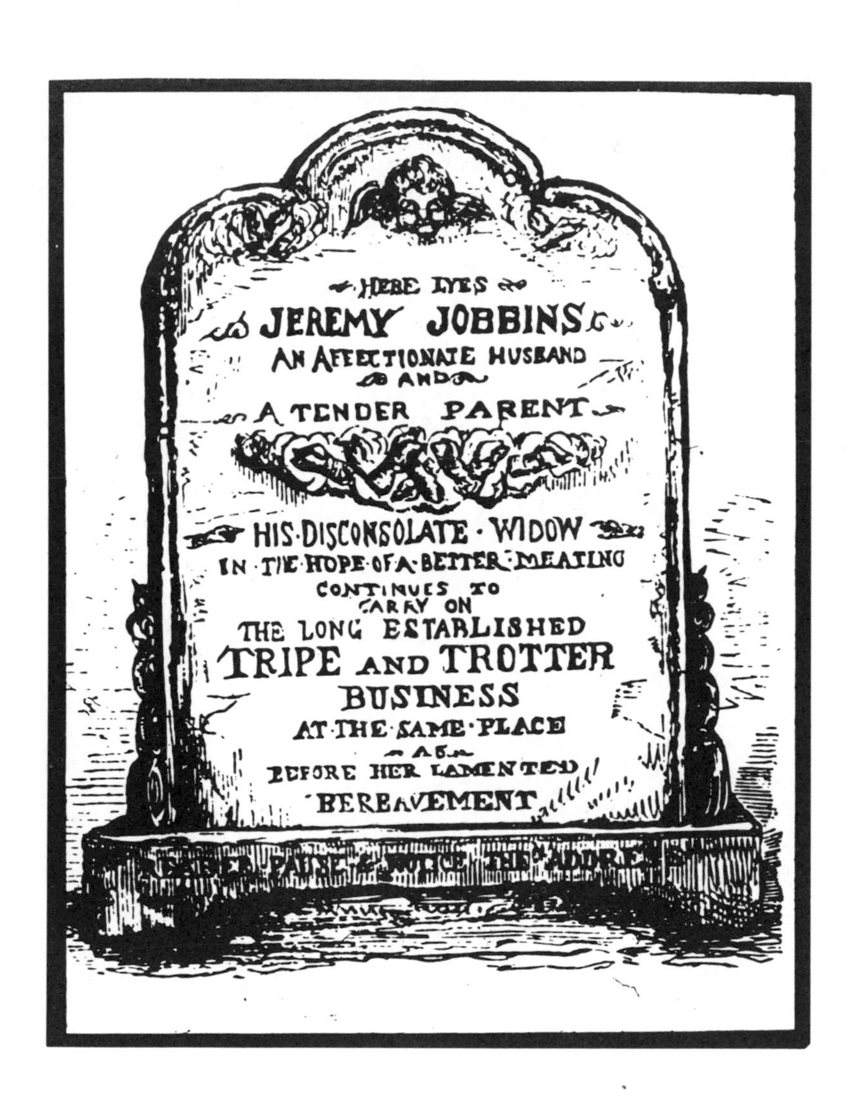
HERE LYES
JEREMY JOBBINS
AN AFFECTIONATE HUSBAND
AND
A TENDER PARENT
HIS·DISCONSOLATE·WIDOW
IN·THE·HOPE·OF·A·BETTER·MEATING
CONTINUES TO
CARRY ON
THE LONG ESTABLISHED
TRIPE AND TROTTER
BUSINESS
AT·THE·SAME·PLACE
AS
BEFORE HER LAMENTED
BEREAVEMENT

Appendix A

Organisations whose representatives constitute the Code of Advertising Practice Committee, and who support the *Code of Advertising Practice.*

Advertising Association
Association of Independent Radio Contractors
Association of Mail Order Publishers
British Direct Marketing Association
British Poster Advertising Association
British Sign Association
Bus Advertising Council
Direct Mail Producers Association
Incorporated Society of British Advertisers
Independent Television Companies Association
Institute of Practitioners in Advertising
Institute of Sales Promotion
Newspaper Publishers Association
Newspaper Society
Periodical Publishers Association
Proprietary Association of Great Britain
Scottish Daily Newspaper Society
Scottish Newspaper Proprietors Association
Screen Advertising Association
Solus Outdoor Advertising Association

Appendix B

Appendix L of the British Code of Advertising Practice

Statutes and statutory instruments with special relevance to advertising and related trading practices

In addition to statutory provisions there are certain common law rights which can also have a relevance to advertising and retail trade practices. Examples of these are libel, slander of goods and slander of title.

The legal rules governing advertising, both statutory and common law, can be extremely complicated and professional advice should be sought when in doubt.

Accommodation Agencies Act 1953	Forbids advertisements for letting of houses and flats not authorised by the owner or his agent.
Administration of Justice Act 1970.	Inter alia penalises the harassment of debtors.
Administration of Justice Act 1977	Facilitates the referral of county court proceedings to arbitration. This is of importance in connection with the changes in procedure introduced by the County Courts (New Procedure) Rules 1971 which facilitate and make cheaper the pursuit of consumer and other minor claims in County Courts.
Adoption Act 1976 (s.58)	Restricts advertisements concerned with the adoption of children.
Advertisements (Hire-Purchase) Act 1967	Regulates advertisements giving hire-purchase terms.
Betting, Gaming and Lotteries Act 1963 (ss.10 and 22)	Controls advertisement of betting shops, prohibits sending of betting circulars to minors.
Building Societies Act 1962 (ss.14,51, 52, 57)	Empowers Registrar to make regulations controlling advertising by building societies.

Business Advertisements (Disclosure) Order 1977	Prohibits disguised business sales.
Cancer Act 1939 (s.4)	Forbids the advertising of any offer to treat for, prescribe for or advise on cancer.
Children Act 1958 (s.37)	Prohibits anonymous advertisements offering to undertake care of children.
Civil Aviation (Licensing) Act 1960 (s.7)	Prohibits with certain exceptions (see below) the use of aircraft and balloons for displaying advertisements.
Civil Aviation (Aerial Advertising) Regulations 1971	Permits aircraft and balloons to display an inscription identifying its owner, charterer or manufacturer.
Coinage Offences Act 1936	Prohibits the reproduction of coins of the realm (*Note:* The Royal Mint should be consulted on representation of coins in advertisements).
Companies Act 1948 (ss. 50, 108)	Requires advertisement of any prospectus inviting the public to invest money in companies and other matters concerning companies' names, etc.
Consumer Credit Act 1974	Provides for system of licensing and control for suppliers of credit or suppliers of goods on hire or hire purchase. Inter alia, prohibits sending of circulars to minors offering loan facilities. Regulations to be made under the Act will govern form and content of credit advertisements.
Consumer Safety Act 1978	Empowers Secretary of State for Prices and Consumer Protection to make regulations to ensure the safety of goods and to require appropriate information to be given to the consumer.
Consumer Transactions (Restrictions on Statements) Order 1976	Prohibits advertisements which purport to apply terms made void by the Unfair Contract Terms Act 1977.
Copyright Act 1956	Governs copyright in all matters, including advertising material in all media.
Criminal Justice Act 1925 (s. 38)	With the Forgery Act 1913 (s. 9) prohibits the reproduction of bank notes in advertisements (the conditions upon which suitably distorted or obscured representations of bank notes are permissible may be obtained from the Bank of England).
Powers of Criminal Courts Act 1973	Provides, inter alia, that those convicted of offences against certain consumer protection statutes (e.g. Trade Descriptions Act 1968) may be ordered to pay compensation to the consumers adversely affected as a result of the commission of the offence.

Customs and Excise Act 1952 (ss. 162 and 164) as amended by Finance Acts 1964 (s. 2) and 1967 (s.5)	Prohibits misdescription in advertisements of beer and spirits.
Defamation Act 1952	Governs law of libel.
Design Copyright Act 1968	Provides copyright protection for the design of certain articles.
Employment Agencies Act 1973	Establishes a system of licensing of employment agencies, and enables the Government to make regulations for proper conduct, including regulations to control advertising by agencies.
Energy Act 1976 (s. 15)	Requires advertisements for new cars which make mention of fuel consumption to specify results of official fuel consumption tests.
Fair Employment (Northern Ireland) Act 1976	Prohibits advertisements published in Northern Ireland indicating an intention to discriminate on the grounds of religious belief.
Fair Trading Act 1973	Provides for the appointment of a Director-General of Fair Trading and staff, to keep a close and continuous watch over the effect upon consumers' interests of trading practices and commercial activities of all kinds, and to recommend Government action where necessary. Where the Director-General considers that a particular trade practice misleads or is otherwise to the disadvantage of consumers, he may propose that an order be made to regulate or prohibit the practice. If the proposal commends itself to the Consumer Protection Advisory Committee, the Secretary of State of the Department of Trade and Industry has power to make regulations accordingly. Also regulates multi-level marketing or pyramid schemes.
Finance Act 1965 (s.15)	Restricts cost of advertising gifts.
Food and Drugs Act 1955 (as subsequently amended)	Contains certain requirements as to advertising and labelling of food: also power to make regulations such as Labelling of Food Orders which set out specific requirements for advertising and labelling, n.b. in particular the Labelling of Food Regulations 1970 and the Labelling of Food (Amendment) Regulations 1972.
Gaming Act 1968 (s. 42)	Restricts advertisements for the provision of gaming facilities.
Geneva Convention Act 1957 (s. 6)	Forbids unauthorised use of Red Cross or Red Crescent by, inter alia, advertisers.
Hearing Aid Council Act 1968	Regulations made hereunder place restrictions upon advertising by hearing aid dispensers.
Indecent Advertisements Act 1889	Provides penalties for indecent advertisements.

Independent Broadcasting Authority Act 1973	Provides for the control of advertising on commercial television and radio.
Insurance Companies Act 1974	Provides for additional control by Government of the operation of insurance companies, so as to avoid harm to the consumer as a result of incompetence or fraud. Contains powers to make orders for the regulation of advertising.
Legal Aid Act 1974	Makes improved provision for free or low-cost advice and assistance to, inter alia, consumers pursuing their legal rights against traders.
London Cab Act 1968, as amended by London Cab Act 1973	Prohibits the use of the words *taxi* or *cab* in advertising for private hire cars.
Lotteries and Amusements Act 1976	Prohibits commercial lotteries (except gaming) and controls prize competitions.
Mail Order Transactions (Information) Order 1976	Requires mail order advertisements to state name and address of seller.
Marine, etc. Broadcasting (Offences) Act 1967	Prohibits off-shore radio stations and advertisements from and for them.
Medicines Act 1968 and regulations made thereunder	Institutes a system under which advertisements for medicines must conform to the terms of a licence issued by the Medicines Commission in respect of each product concerned. Provides penalties for misleading advertisements for medicines.
Misrepresentation Act 1967	Provides remedies for persons who have been misled into contracts by reliance upon inaccurate statements (e.g. in advertisements) by other parties to the contract (e.g. by advertisers).
Control of Pollution Act 1974	Prohibits use of loudspeakers in the street for advertising purposes.
Obscene Publications Act 1959	Prohibits publication of obscene matter.
Obscene Publications Act 1964	Prohibits possession of obscene articles for publication for gain.
Opticians Act 1958	Sets up body responsible for opticians and rule making, which includes restrictions on advertising.
Patents, etc. (International Conventions) Act 1938	Defines application of trade marks as trade descriptions.

Pharmacy and Poisons Act 1933	Requires proper naming of poisons.
Post Office Act 1953 (ss. 61, 62, 63) and Fictitious Stamp Regulations 1937	Forbids the reproduction in any advertisement of any postage or insurance stamp except under conditions laid down by the Postmaster-General *Note:* Postal Headquarters should be consulted as to the propriety of any particular proposal to use stamps in advertisements.
Prevention of Fraud (Investments) Act 1958 (as amended)	Governs statements made in advertisements inducing persons to invest money.
Prices Act 1974 and regulations made thereunder	Empowers Secretary of State to make regulations requiring prices of particular goods to be clearly marked and to require retailers to display information about the range of prices at which good are commonly sold.
Professions Supplementary to Medicine Act 1960	Provides for establishment of disciplinary committees for the regulation of professional matters including advertising of specified professions supplementary to medicine.
Protection of Depositors Act 1963	Governs advertising of those seeking deposits of money.
Race Relations Act 1976	Prohibits advertisements indicating an intention to discriminate on racial grounds.
Representation of the People Act 1949 (ss. 63, 94, 95)	Restricts expenditure on advertising at elections and requires name of printer on all election material.
Road Traffic Act 1960	Imposes restrictions on advertising of excursions made by public service vehicles.
Sale of Goods Act 1893	Important, especially in relation to mail order advertisements, in connection with the terms and conditions which may be implied in relation to any resulting sale.
Sex Discrimination Act 1975	Prohibits advertisements indicating an intention to discriminate on grounds of sex.
Sunday Observance Act 1780	Affects advertisements for Sunday entertainments.
Supply of Goods (Implied Terms) Act 1973	Guarantees consumers rights under the Sale of Goods Act, 1893, and makes them inalienable, effectively ending the usefulness of the bogus 'guarantee'.
Textile Products (Indications of Fibre Content) Regulations 1973	Lays down rules for describing the fibre content of textiles.

Theft Act 1968 (s. 23)	Controls content of advertisements seeking return of stolen goods.
Town and Country Amenities Act 1974	Provides for control of advertisements in conservation areas and areas of special control.
Town and Country Planning Act 1962 and orders made thereunder. Control of Advertisements Regulations 1969	Controls outdoor advertising and empowers Minister to make specific regulations and orders.
Trade Descriptions Act 1968	Prohibits, inter alia, misleading statements about goods and services made in advertisements.
Trade Descriptions Act 1972	Requires indication of origin of certain imported goods.
Trade Marks Act 1938	Governs law relating to trade marks.
Trading Stamps Act 1964	Lays down conditions for trading stamp operations.
Unsolicited Goods and Services Acts 1971 and 1975 and regulations made thereunder	Makes provisions concerning the rights and duties of recipients of unsolicited goods, amends the law with respect to charges for entries in directories and prohibits the unsolicited distribution of advertisements dealing with certain publications on matters of human sexual technique.
Venereal Diseases Act 1917	Controls advertising concerning the treatment of venereal disease.
Weights and Measures Act 1963 (and regulations made thereunder) as amended by the Weights and Measures etc. Act 1976	Lays down requirements for weights and measures on labels and packs and gives powers to make specific regulations.

Appendix C

Table of Legal Cases

Alpar v *Tatler and Bystander, Advertiser's Weekly* (4 Nov. 1937), (p. 167).
Lord Byron v *Johnston* [1816] 2 Mer. 29, (p. 130).
Cadbury v *Emil Draps and Co. and A. W. Golding, Advertiser's Weekly* (21 Jan 1927), (p. 168).
Carlill v *Carbolic Smoke Ball Co.* [1892] 2 QB 256; 1893 1 QB 256, (pp. 134–6).
Clark v *Freeman* [1848] 11 Beav. 12, (pp. 130–1).
Croft v *Day* [1844] 7 Beav. 7, (pp. 133–4).
Dockrell v *Dougall* [1899] TLR 333, (p. 130).
Evans v *Harlow* [1844] 1 QB 636, (p. 129).
Harman v *Delany* [1731] 2 Str. 898, (p. 129).
Holloway v *Holloway* [1850] 13 Beav. 13, (p. 134).
Hubbuck v *Wilkinson, Heywood and Clarke* [1899] 1 QB 86, (pp. 129–30).
Latimer v *Western Morning News* [1871] 25 LT 44, (p. 129).
Plumb v *Jeyes Sanitary Compound Co. Ltd., The Times* (11 April 1937), (p. 167).
Reddaway v *Banham* [1896) AC 199, (p. 134).
Routh v *Webster* [1847] 10 Beav. 10, (p. 132).
Russell v *Webster* [1874] 23 WR 59, (p. 129).
Tolley v *J. S. Fry and Sons Ltd.* [1931] AC 333, (pp. 165–7).
Western Counties Manure Co. v *The Lawes Chemical Manure Co.* [1875] 9 EX.218, (p. 174).
Wood v *Letrick Ltd., The Times* (12 and 13 Jan. 1932), (pp. 167–8).
Young v *Macrae* [1866] 33 LJQB 6; 3 B & S 264, (p. 129).

References

(Published in London unless otherwise stated)

2. The Beginnings

1. Quoted by J. P. Wood, *The Story of Advertising*, (New York, 1958) p.18.
2. F. Dahl, quoted by Cranfield, *The Press and Society*, (1978) p.6.
3. Quoted by Frank Presbrey, *History of Advertising*, (New York, 1928) p.42.
4. Daniel Defoe, *A Journal of the Plague Year*, (1969) pp.30–31.
5. Quoted by B. B. Elliott, *A History of English Advertising*, (1962) p.14.
6. Quoted by Elliott, op. cit. p.24.

The advertisements included in this chapter are drawn from the works by Cranfield and Elliott.

3. The Industrial Revolution

1. A. Aspinall,'The Circulation of Newspapers in the Early Nineteenth Century', *Review of English Studies*, (Jan. 1946).
2. R. B. Walker, 'Advertising in London Newspapers 1650–1750', *Business History*, XV, 2 (1973).
3. Ibid.
4. *Household Words*, 22 March 1851.
5. The following section draws heavily on Bruttini, 'Advertising and the Industrial Revolution', *Economic Notes* vol. 4 nos. 2–3, (1975).
6. G. N. Watson, 'Some Eighteenth Century Trading Accounts,' in F. N. L. Poynter (ed.), *The Evolution of British Pharmacy*, (1965).
7. Walker, op. cit.

4. Advertising Takes Shape, 1800–1855.

1. The following figures are taken from the records of the Charles Barker agency.
2. *Parliamentary Debates*, xxxi, (7 June 1815) col.663.
3. Letter to Joseph Smith, PRO 30/8/176 (9 Jan. 1792). I am indebted to Mr D. A. Simmonds, company secretary of Schweppes, for this reference.
4. Full details of this survey are contained in the writer's unpublished thesis, *The Development of Commercial Advertising 1800–1914*, (University of London Ph.D. 1979).

5. 'Anecdotes of Coleridge and of London Newspapers', *Gentleman's Magazine*, new series x (July, 1838).
6. F. H. Howitt, *The Country Printer's Job Price Book*, (1849) p.9.
7. 'Anecdotes of Public Newspapers', *Gentleman's Magazine*, new series x, (Sept. 1838).
8. John Corry, *Quack Doctors Dissected*, (Gloucester, undated) p.5.
9. The following figures are taken from A. P. Wadsworth, 'Newspaper Circulations 1800–1954', *Proceedings of the Manchester Statistical Society*, (9 March 1955).
10. T. Catling, *My Life's Pilgrimage*, (1910) p.17.
11. J. Crawfurd, *The Newspaper Stamp and the Newspaper Postage Compared*, (1836) pp. 21–22.
12. 'The Provincial Newspaper Press', *Westminster Review* xxiii, (Oct. 1829).
13. (Charles Knight), *The Newspaper Stamp and the Duty on Paper*, by the Author of the Results of Machinery, (1836) p.41.
14. 'Anecdotes of Coleridge and of London Newspapers', *Gentleman's Magazine*, new series x, (July, 1838).
15. 'Notes on the Newspaper Stamp', *Fraser's Magazine*, xliv, (1851).
16. (J. F. Wilson), *A Few Personal Recollections by An Old Printer*, (1898) p.11.
17. 'The Provincial Newspaper Press', *Westminster Review*, xxiii, (Oct. 1829).
18. An Advertiser, *A Guide to Advertisers*, (1851) p.9
19. 'Advertisements', *Quarterly Review*, cxciii 1855 p. 225.
20. W. H. Pyne. *Costume of Great Britain*, (1808) quoted in *The Poster* (Feb. 1899).
21. G. S. Harris, patent application no. 5024 of 21 Oct. 1824.

5. **The Great Expansion,** 1855–1914.

1. Virginia S. Berridge, *Popular Journalism and Working Class Attitudes 1834–1886*, (University of London Ph.D thesis, 1976).
2. D. S. Dunbar, 'Estimates of Total Advertising Expenditure in the U.K. before 1948', *Journal of Advertising History*, (Dec. 1977).
3. B. W. E. Alford, *W. D. & H. O. Wills*, (1973) p. 127.
4. C. Moran, *The Business of Advertising*, (1905) pp. 64–5.
5. Quoted by Ervine Metzl, *The Poster–Its History and Its Art*, (New York, 1963) p.56.
6. Quoted by D. Hudson, *James Pryde* (1949).
7. Dudley Hardy, 'The Art of the Hoarding', *New Review*, (July, 1894).
8. Reliable Advertising and Addressing Agency, *Prospectus*, (1908).
9. Post Office Records, PO/3081/79.
10. S. D. Chapman, *Jesse Boot of Boots the Chemist*, (1974) pp.76–7.
11. S. H. Benson in *Printer's Ink*, (5 May, 1909).
12. Paul Derrick, 'The Advertising Agent as a Factor in Modern Business', *Magazine of Commerce*, (March, 1907).
13. Herts County Record Office, *Herts and Essex Observer* C9/1.
14. Wareham Smith, 'Advertising' in *Harmsworth Self-Educator*, vol. (1907) viii, pp.6857–62.
15. Eric Field, *Advertising–The Forgotten Years*, (1959) p.11 *et seq.*
16. Henry Sell, *Dictionary of the World's Press*, (1883–4) pp.29–30.
17. Walter Judd, *Financial Advertising*, (?1912) p.9.
18. A. L. Teele, *Ideal Advertising* (1892) pp.11–12.

6. **Criticism and Control in the Nineteenth Century**

1. An account of this scheme is given by E. S. Turner, *The Shocking History of Advertising*, (Harmondsworth, 1965) pp.93–5.

2. Newspaper Society *Circular*, (Dec. 1898).
3. *The Times* (17 Aug. 1901).
4. Public Record Office Transport Records, Rail/113/37.
5. Post Office Records, PO/8729/1895.
6. Ibid., PO/13410/1917.
7. Ibid.
8. *The Times* (11 Oct. 1910).
9. Ibid. (11 Jan. 1913).

7. The First World War

1. The original letter is in the library of the Institute of Practitioners in Advertising.

8. The Interwar Period

1. D. S. Dunbar, 'Estimates of Total Advertising Expenditure in the UK before 1948', *Journal of Advertising History*, (Dec. 1977).
2. *Advertiser's Weekly*, (24 Oct. 1924).
3. Ibid, (14 April 1938).
4. Ibid, (9 June 1938).
5. Ibid, (9 Sept. 1935).
6. Ibid, (31 Oct. 1935).
7. Ibid, (20 Feb. 1936).
8. Ibid, (5 Oct. 1935).
9. Quoted in *Advertiser's Weekly*, (1 August 1935).
10. Ibid, (12 Nov. 1936).
11. Cadbury *v* Emil Draps and Co. and A. W. Golding, *Advertiser's Weekly*, (21 Jan. 1927).

9. The Second World War

1. George Begley, *Keep Mum*, (1975) pp.14–15.
2. Based on figures produced by the *Statistical Review of Advertising.* Although these differ from those given by Dunbar in the *Journal of Advertising History*, the fluctuations are roughly comparable in instances where comparison is possible. Dunbar, however, only gives a figure for one year of the war (1943).

10. The Latest Phase

1. Piggott, *OBM 125 Years*, (1975) p.71.
2. *New Schoolmaster*, (May 1962) p.66.

Bibliography

Manuscript and other Original Records

Charles Barker and Co. Correspondence and Record Books (1826–47).
Herts and Essex Observer Records, at the Herts. County Record Office.
Post Office Records, St. Martins le Grand.
Public Record Office, Transport Records.
Scapa Society Papers, at County Hall, London.
White's Advertising Agency Account Book.
The Archives of *The Times*, New Printing House Square.

Original sources – Periodicals

Articles of particular interest are listed separately under each title.

Advertisers Guardian (ed. Louis Collins, Thomas Dixon).
Advertisers Protection Society, *Circular.*
Advertiser's Weekly.
Advertising.
Advertising World.
The Circulation Manager.
'The Advertisers Protection Society and Circulations', (Feb. 1913).
'The Problems of the Provincial Weekly Press', (May 1913).
'Pears' Pictures', (Aug. 1913).
'Why an Association of Advertising Agents is Impossible at Present', (Feb. 1914).
Edinburgh Review.
'The Periodical Press', lxxvi (May 1823).

'Mr Robert Montgomery's Poems and the Modern Practice of Puffing', (Macaulay), ci (April 1830).
'The Advertising System', clv (Feb. 1843).
'The Newspaper Press', ccviii (Oct. 1855).

Fortnightly Review.
'The Craft of the Advertiser', (W. Teignmouth Shore), (Feb. 1907).

Fraser's Magazine.
'Notes on the Newspaper Stamp', xliv (1851).
'The Grand Force', lxxxix (1869).

Gentleman's Magazine.
'Anecdotes of Coleridge and of London Newspapers', (Daniel Stuart), (July 1838).
'Anecdotes of Public Newspapers – The British Press and Globe', (George Lane), (Sept. 1838).

Household Words.
'The King of the Billstickers', (Charles Dickens), (22 March 1851).

Journal of the Royal Society of Arts.
'Advertising' (Edmund Street) lxi (24 Jan. 1913).

The Leisure Hour.
'Old Modes of Advertising', (Feb. 1860).

The London Magazine.
'The Art of Advertising Made Easy', (P.A.Z.), (Feb. 1825).

The Magazine of Commerce.
'The Advertising Agent as a Factor in Modern Business', (Paul Derrick), (Mar. 1907).
'Wanted – An Institute of Advertising', (Howard Bridgewater), (Mar. 1908).

National Review.
'The Age of Disfigurement', (Richardson Evans), (Oct. 1890).

New Review.
'The Art of the Hoarding', (Cheret, Hardy, and Beardsley), (July. 1894).

Newspaper Press Directory.

Nineteenth Century.
'The March of the Advertiser', (H. J. Palmer), (Jan. 1897).

Penny Magazine.
'On Printing Posting-bills', (22 Jan. 1842).

The Poster.

Progressive Advertising and Outdoor Publicity.

Printer's Ink. (British edition).

Profitable Advertising.

Provincial Newspaper Society *Circular.* (The Society dropped 'Provincial' from its title in 1889).

Quarterly Review.
'Advertisements', cxciii (June 1855).

Sell's Dictionary of the World's Press.
Sala's Journal.
'Hoardings and Hysterics' (G. A. Sala) (3 Dec. 1882).
Tait's Edinburgh Magazine.
'London Sights III – The Streets', i (1834).
'The Unstamped Press in London', i (1834).
Westminster Review.
'The Newspaper Press', xix (Jan. 1829).
'The Provincial Newspaper Press', xxii (Oct. 1829).
World's Press News.

Other original sources

(Published in London unless otherwise stated)

'An Adept with 35 Years' Experience', (Donald Nicoll), *Publicity – An Essay with Ancient and Modern Instances*, (1875).
'An Advertiser', *A Guide to Advertisers*, (1851).
S. H. Benson, *Wisdom in Advertising*, (1901).
Howard Bridgewater, *Advertising*, (1910).
Thomas Catling, *My Life's Pilgrimage*, (1910).
William Cobbett, *Prospectus of a New Daily Paper to be Entitled The Porcupine*, (1800).
John Corry, *Quack Doctors Dissected*, (Gloucester, undated).
Sir William Crawford, *How to Succeed in Advertising*, (1931).
John Crawfurd, *A Financial and Historical View of the Taxes*, (1834).
John Crawfurd, *The Newspaper Stamp and the Newspaper Postage Compared*, (1836).
'Cryptus', The Royal Road, (1906).
Deacon's Advertising Agency, *Newspaper Handbook and Advertiser's Guide*, (5th and 12th editions undated).
Paul E. Derrick, *How to Reduce Selling Costs*, (3rd edition, 1920).
G.R.E., *The Penny Newspaper*, (1883).
Richardson Evans, *An Account of the Scapa Society*, (1926).
Eric Field, *Advertising – The Forgotten Years*, (1959).
Cyril C. Freer, *The Inner Side of Advertising*, (1921).
G. W. Goodall, *Advertising: A Study of Modern Business Power*, (1914).
H.A.B., *About Newspapers*, (Edinburgh, 1880).
Charles Hiatt, *Picture Posters*, (1896).
Sir Charles Higham, *Advertising*, (1931).
House of Commons Accounts and Papers
'Return of the Numbers of Advertisements and the Amount of Duty Paid 1826–40', xxx, 1849 (506).

'Return of the Numbers of Advertisements and the Amount of Duty Paid 1841–48', xxx, 1849 (160).
'Report and Minutes of the Select Committee on Newspaper Stamps', x, 1851 (436).

House of Commons Reports of Commissioners
'Inquiry into the Revenue Arising in Ireland &c', x, 1826 (436).

Walter Judd, *Financial Advertising*, (1912).

Charles Knight (ed.), *London*, (1843).

(Charles Knight), *The Newspaper Stamp and the Duty on Paper*, by the Author of *The Results of Machinery*.

The Labour Party, *Report of a Commission of Enquiry into Advertising*, (1966).

The Labour Party, *Advertising*, (Opposition Green Paper, 1972).

William Le Queux, *Scribes and Pharisees*, (novel), (1896).

E. L. Maxwell, *Modern Advertising*, (1904).

Henry Mayhew, *London Labour and the London Poor*, (New York edn., 1968).

J. R. McCulloch, *Dictionary of Commerce*, (1834 and 1852 edns.).

Moody's Advertising Agency, *The Advertiser's Guide to Publicity*, (Birmingham, 1887).

Clarence Moran, *The Business of Advertising*, (1905).

The National Board for Prices and Incomes, *Costs and Revenues of Independent Television Companies*, (Report no. 156, 1970).

L'Office-Correspondance, *Tarif*, (Paris, 1831).

'One Who Thinks Aloud', *The Language of the Walls*, (Manchester, 1855).

The Periodical Press of Great Britain and Ireland, (1824).

(Prince Pückler-Muskau), *A Regency Visitor. The English Tour of Prince Pückler-Muskau described in his Letters*, (ed. E. M. Butler, 1957).

R.K.D., *A Letter to Viscount Lord Althorp on the Proposed Reduction in the Newspaper Stamp and Advertisement Duties*, (1831).

The Reliable Advertising and Addressing Agency, *Prospectus*, (1908).

The Royal Blue Book, (1829).

Thomas Russell, *The Curious Side of Advertising*, (series of articles in the *Evening News*, Nov. 1910).

Thomas Russell, *Commercial Advertising*, (six lectures given at the London School of Economics 1919, 2nd. edn., 1925).

Henry Sampson, *A History of Advertising*, (1874).

James Savage, *An Account of the London Daily Newspapers*, (1811).

Clement K. Shorter, 'The Romance of the House of Pears', reprinted from *The Sphere* with additions in *Pears Cyclopaedia*, (20th edn., 1916).

R. Simmat, *The Principles and Practice of Advertising*, (1935).

G. Smeeton, *Doings in London*, (?1840).

Adolph Smith and James Thomson, *Street Life in London*, (1877).

Thomas Smith, *Successful Advertising*, selected edns. (7th 1885; 9th 1887; 21st 1899).

Thomas Smith, *21 Years in Fleet Street*, (1899).
Wareham Smith, 'Advertising' in *Harmsworth Self-Educator*, vol. viii, (1907) pp.6857–62.
Wareham Smith, *Spilt Ink*, (1932).
William Smith, *Advertise, How? When? Where?* (1863).
J. D. Symon, *The Press and its Story*, (1914).
F. W. Taylor, *The Economics of Advertising*, (1934).
A. L. Teele, *Ideal Advertising*, (1892).
G. M. Westmacott, *Letter on the Stamp Duties*, (1836).
H. Whorlow, *The Provincial Newspaper Society – A Jubilee Retrospect*, (1886).
(J. F. Wilson), *A Few Personal Recollections by An Old Printer*, (1898).

University Theses

J. D. Andrew, The Derbyshire Newspaper Press, 1720–1825, (Reading M.A., 1954).
Ivor Asquith, James Perry and the Morning Chronicle, 1790–1821, (London Ph.D., 1973).
V. S. Berridge, Popular Journalism and Working Class Attitudes, 1854–86, (London Ph.D. 1976).
D. F. Gallop, Chapters in the History of the Provincial Newspaper Press, (Reading M.A., 1952).
T. R. Nevett, The Development of Commercial Advertising in Britain 1800–1914, (London Ph.D., 1979).

Secondary sources – Articles

A. Aspinall, 'Statistical Accounts of the London Newspapers in the Eighteenth Century', *English Historical Review*, lxiii, (1948).
A. Aspinall, 'Statistical Accounts of the London Newspapers 1800–1836', *English Historical Review*, lxv, (1950).
A. Aspinall, 'The Circulation of Newspapers in the Early Nineteenth Century', *Review of English Studies*, (Jan. 1946).
Ivon Asquith, 'Advertising and the Press in the Late Eighteenth and Early Nineteenth Centuries', *Historical Journal*, xviii, (1975).
Asa Briggs, 'Press and Public in Early Nineteenth Century Birmingham', *Dugdale Society Occasional Papers*, No. 8, (1948).
A. Bruttini, 'Advertising and the Industrial Revolution', *Economic Notes*, vol. 4 no. 2–3, (1975).
D. S. Dunbar, 'Estimates of Total Advertising Expenditures in the UK before 1948', *Journal of Advertising History*, (Dec. 1977).
Harry Henry, 'Some Observations on the Effects of Newsprint Rationing (1939–1959) on the Advertising Media', *Journal of Advertising History*, (Dec. 1977).

Ellic Howe, 'Newspaper Printing in the Nineteenth Century', *Alphabet and Image*, No.4, (1947).
Edward S. Lauterbach, 'Victorian Advertising and Magazine Stripping', *Victorian Studies*, (Bloomington, Indiana, June 1967).
John P. May, 'Advertising Pre-testing Research – An Historical Perspective', *Quarterly Review of Marketing*, vol. 4 no. 2 (1978).
A. E. Musson, 'Newspaper Printing in the Industrial Revolution', *Economic History Review*, 2nd. series, x, (1957–8).
T. R. Nevett, 'London's Early Advertising Agents', *Journal of Advertising History*, (Dec. 1977).
H. J. Perkin, 'The Origins of the Popular Press', *History Today*, (July 1957).
Lawrence Stone, 'Literacy and Education in England, 1640–1900', *Past and Present*, 42, (Feb. 1969).
James R. Sutherland, 'The Circulation of Newspapers and Literary Periodicals, 1700–30', *The Library*, (4th series), 15, (1934–5).
James Thorpe, 'The Posters of the Beggarstaff Brothers', *Alphabet and Image*, no.4, (1947).
A. P. Wadsworth, 'Newspaper Circulations 1800–1954', *Proceedings of the Manchester Statistical Society*, (9 March 1954).
R. B. Walker, 'Advertising in London Newspapers 1650–1750', *Business History*, xv, 2, (1973).
C. H. Ward-Jackson, 'The Great Persuader' (Thomas Barratt), *Blackwood's Magazine*, (March 1975).
R. K. Webb, 'Working Class Readers in Early Victorian England', *English Historical Review*, lxv, (1950).

Secondary sources – Books

David Alexander, *Retailing in England during the Industrial Revolution*, (1970).
B. W. E. Alford, *W. D. & H. O. Wills*, (1973).
R. D. Altick, *The English Common Reader*, (Chicago, 1957).
A. Aspinall, *Politics and the Press*, (1949).
D. Ayerst, *Guardian, Biography of a Newspaper*, (1971).
C. Beglec and A. Morley, *Street Jewellery – A History of Enamel Signs*, (1978).
George Begley, *Keep Mum! Advertising goes to War*, (1975).
W. Turner Berry, 'Printing and the Allied Trades 1850–1900', in *History of Technology*, (ed. C. Singer, 1954).
John Braun, *Advertisements in Court*, (1965).
S. D. Chapman, *Jesse Boot of Boots the Chemist*, (1974).
T. A. B. Corley, *Quaker Enterprise in Biscuits*, (1972).
G. A. Cranfield, *The Press and Society*, (1978).
Bernard Darwin, *The Dickens Advertiser*, (1930).

D. S. Dunbar, *Almost Gentlemen: the growth and development of the advertising agent 1875–1975*, privately printed by the J. Walter Thompson Co., (1976).
B. B. Elliott, *A History of English Advertising*, (1962).
Paul Ferris, *The House of Northcliffe*, (1971).
John William Ferry, *A History of the Department Store*, (New York, 1960).
Ann Francis, *A Guinea a Box*, (1968).
Marcel Galliot, *La Publicité à Travers Les Âges*, (Paris, 1954).
Gatley on Libel and Slander, 7th edn., eds. McEwen and Lewis, (1974).
Peter Golding, *The Mass Media*, (1974).
R. Grenville-Smith and A. Barrie, *Aspro – How a Family Business Grew Up*, (1976).
P. Hadley (ed.), *A History of Bovril Advertising*, (1970).
Bevis Hillier, *Posters*, (1974).
Diana and Geoffrey Hindley, *Advertising in Victorian England 1837–1901*, (1972).
Patricia Hollis, *The Pauper Press*, (Oxford, 1970).
Ellic Howe, *Newspaper Printing in the Nineteenth Century*, (1943).
James B. Jeffereys, *Retail Trading in Great Britain 1850–1950*, (1954).
Thomas Artemus Jones, *The Law of Advertisements*, (1906).
Philip Kleinman, *Advertising Inside Out*, (1977).
David S. Landes, *The Unbound Prometheus*, (Cambridge, 1968).
J. Larwood and J. C. Hotten, *A History of Signboards*, (1866).
Richard Lawson, *Advertising Law*, (Plymouth, 1978).
Alan J. Lee, *The Origins of the Popular Press in England 1855–1914*, (1976).
Ramsay Macmullen, *Roman Social Relations 50 B.C. to A.D. 284*, (New Haven, 1974).
P. Mathias, *Retailing Revolution*, (1967).
Ervine Metzl, *The Poster – Its History and Its Art*, (New York, 1963).
G. H. Saxon Mills, *There is a Tide*, (1954).
Stanley Morison, *The English Newspaper*, (Cambridge, 1932).
Musée de l'Affiche, *Catalogue: Trois Siècles de l'Affiche*, (Paris, 1978).
J. Pearson and G. Turner, *The Persuasion Industry*, (1965).
Stanley Piggott, *OBM 125 Years*, (1975).
R. Pound and G. Harmsworth, *Northcliffe*, (1959).
N. J. G. Pounds, *An Economic History of Medieval Europe*, (1974).
Frank Presbrey, *The History and Development of Advertising*, (New York, 1929).
Maurice Rickards, *Banned Posters*, (1969).
Maurice Rickards, *The Rise and Fall of the Poster*, (Newton Abbott, 1971).
Peter Roberts, *Any Colour so long as its Black*, (Newton Abbott, 1976).
Attilio Rossi, *Poster*, (Feltham, 1969).
Herbert Schindler, *Monografie des Plakats – Entwicklung, Stil, Design*, (Munich, 1972).
Philippe Schuwer, *History of Advertising*, (1966).

Cyril Sheldon, *A History of Poster Advertising*, (1937).
S. H. Steinberg, *Five Hundred Years of Printing*, (1959).
Dick Sutphen, *The Mad Old Ads*, (1968).
Helen Tanzer, *The Common People of Pompeii*, (Baltimore, 1939).
Walter Taplin, *The Origin of Television Advertising in the United Kingdom*, (1961).
The History of The Times.
E. S. Turner, *The Shocking History of Advertising*, (Harmondsworth, 1965).
Twenty One Years of Independent Television, (1976).
Michael Twyman, *Printing 1770–1970*, (1970).
Fritz Thyssen Stiftung, *Das Fruhe Plakat in Europa und den USA*, vol. i, (Berlin, 1973).
A. L. Waugh, *The Lipton Story*, (1951).
R. K. Webb, *The British Working Class Reader*, (1955).
Cynthia L. White, *Women's Magazines 1693–1968*, (1970).
Alan Whitworth, *Fifty Years Service to Advertisers – The Story of the Incorporated Society of British Advertisers*, (1950).
Joel H. Wiener, *The War of the Unstamped*, (New York, 1969).
Francis Williams, *Dangerous Estate*, (1957).
C. H. Wilson, *History of Unilever*, (1956).
Winfield and Jolowicz on Tort, 10th edn., ed. W. H. V. Rogers, (1975).
James P. Wood, *The Story of Advertising*, (New York, 1958).
Robert Wood, *Victorian Delights*, (1967).

Index